Indian National Army

Indian National Army

Edited by:

Purabi Roy

Saradindu Mukherji

INDIAN COUNCIL OF HISTORICAL RESEARCH
NEW DELHI

AGAM KALA PRAKASHAN
DELHI

First Published 2021

ISBN: 978-81-942937-2-9

Published by:
Indian Council of Historical Research
35 Firozshah Road, New Delhi
in association with

Smt. Lila Devi
For **Agam Kala Prakashan**
34, Central Market, Ashok Vihar
Delhi - 110 052
Tel.: 91-11-27212195, 43513480
Fax: 91-11-27212195
Email: agamkala101@gmail.com, agambook@yahoo.com
www.agamkala.com

Composed by:
Sushil Kumar
Delhi - 110 052
Mobile: 9891395309

Printed in India

CONTENTS

FOREWORD

I have great pleasure in placing before the reading public the Proceedings of an ICHR's National Seminar under the title of Indian National Army, especially when the entire nation is celebrating 75 years of India's Independence passionately, under AZADI KA AMRIT MAHOTSAV. The present Volume is a great revelation for a part of obliterated history which remained untouched and unchallenged for last 75 years. I consider that this is an unparallel contribution and scholarly presentation from civilians and military desks. The collection of articles reveals an indispensible scrutiny of archival information, narratives and personal experiences and memoirs are unique of their content. As Major General A. C. Chatterji, a close associate of Netaji remarks that he has not been able to divulge fully some facts regarding the struggle, which it may be possible to disclose later. I feel this publication is of that kind which is going to bring new facts and narratives based upon the sources recently sought.

I am grateful to the editors – Prof. Purabi Roy and Dr. Saradindu Mukharji for taking up the task of editing the volume meticulously. At the same time, I appreciate the efforts of Dr. Md. Naushad Ali for assisting the editors in proof-checking and other formalities. I also wish to thanks sincerely to all the contributors of the Volume.

I compliment the officials and staff of the ICHR for extending their services in bringing out this publication with care and attention. My Thanks are also due to Dr. Rajesh Kumar, Director (Journal,

Publication & Library), Dr. Omjee Upadhyay, Director (Research & Administration), Dr. Saurabh Kumar Mishra, Dy. Director (Journal) and Shri Nardev Sharma for the sincere efforts they put in during the process of this publication. Last, but not the least, I thank Smt. Lila Devi and Shri Ashok Kumar Pandey of the Agam Kala Prakashan to give their personal attention to help in bringing out the publication in a neat and presentable format.

Kumar Ratnam
Member Secretary, ICHR

Editors' Note

Purabi Roy & Saradindu Mukherji

The present volume is a great revelation for a part of obliterated history which remained untouched and unchallenged for seventy five years. A three day National seminar on Indian National Army is one of the major events organized by Indian Council of Historical Research where the opening remark by Prof. V. Sudershan Rao, chairman ICHR, read: "This day is a great day in the History of ICHR for remembering and offering respects to Subhas Chandra Bose and the Indian National Army."

This is an unparallel contribution and scholarly presentation from civilians and military desks. One should be aware of the facts that the rapid pace and complexity of a changing world will require both military and civilian authorities to closely collaborate inorder to understand each other's needs. This daunting challenge is the touchstone for strengthening civil-military relations.

The collection of articles reveals an indispensable scrutiny of archival information, narratives and personal experiences and memoiers are unique of their content. They are from fascinating sources and astounding revelations of the civilians and armed forces.

The main objective of the present volume is to bring out aspects of formation, constitution and contribution of INA towards Indian independence as well as engaged in assessing the thought provoking impact and legacy of INA.

The second world war theatre in South East Asia would have remained incomplete without the impetus of revolutionary Rash Behari Bose the founder of Indian Independence League. With his initiative and leadership the Indians residing in South East Asia raised voice against the British rule. It was Rash Behari Bose who induced Subhas Chandra Bose to come over to South East Asia from Europe, took the command of the Indian National Army INA.

Sumit Mukherjee took a challenge and successfully made a comparative study of great personalities: Rash Behari as a revolutionary and Subhas Cnandra as an activist as well as strategist. One was responsible of uniting the revolutionaries in South East Asia, the other was visionary with uncompromising courage and action organized the revolutionary army. Keeping the two figures in view the author attempted a parallel investigative analysis can go without comment. Mukherjee's comparative study of two personalties fought for the same cause with their individual talented approach is unique in every respect.

Md. Naushad Ali's article reminds the clarion call of both the "Bose"- where IIL, Indian legion and the propaganda machinery- "Azad Hind Radio" made a constant contact with the Indians abroad. The author has served the purpose in order to make force in the freedom struggle.

Military historian Kaushik Roy's sagacious comment on Indian Colonial Army and Indian National Army INA with historical as well as Geo-Political analysis is really admirable. INA under S.C. Bose had greater impact on the world global Politico- Military landscape, which Bose reorganized and revitalized. The reader may find that the author has raised many pertinent querries are yet to be solved. On the other side Major General G. D. Bakshi's Military evaluation of the structure, motivation and combat performance of the INA, which is one of the best secrets of war has been narrated by a professional. Major General's personal account of combat performance is an additional gain for a reader.

The World War II theatre in South east Asia where Japan a nation expanding its Military power for the reconstruction of Asia on the one hand and on the otherhand extended her full support to the Indian revolutionaries. In this background Colnel Gautam Das made a detail study of Japan's expansion into the Asian mainlands and thereafter began a future period of military expansionism under the pretext of creating greater East Asia Co-Prosperity sphere. And, finally the Japanese attack on Burma, reaching the maximum expansion of Japanese military conquest in Asia. With this historical background Major General Chakravorty introduces Subhas Chandra Bose in South East Asia and his negotiation with Japan. The IIL was an effective and cohesive force. Its sister organization the INA was an inseparable arm. These two gave meaning, hope and sustenance to overseas Indians. The zeal to free India from the British yoke was an ideal that had unified Indians abroad. Major General rightly agreed that the nation owes its independence to Bose and the INA and further pointed out that the British were not going to leave India unless they were threatened by own military .Thus the author observes that Bose strained every sinew in persuading the Japanese and raising the INA.

While opening the Rani Jhansi Training Camp for womens' section of INA, October 24, 1943, Netaji addressed:..." Sisters! this is an important landmark in the progress of our movement in East Asia. We are engaged in the great task of regenerating our nation. And it is only in the fineness of thing that there should be a stir of new life among our women folk".

It was through his mother that Bose entered into the spirit of the Indian Cultural traditions. Thus his mother, a devotee of "Shakti" was his preceptor who made him a devotee at the shrine of revolution. The period in which Bose was born was saturated and enriched by two streams: Religio-Cultural and Political. Swami Vivekananda merged them into one that is "Shakti" which Bose effected by imbueing with Religion and Nationalism. Shakti is his Bharat Mata whom he worshipped chanting

Bankim chandra's 'Bande Mataram.' Monmayee Basu with her firm conviction has established the fact that Netaji, in his revolutionary way, has ensured that women fought on a completely equal footing and went to the extent of creating a full all-women regiment that would fight for the liberation of the motherland. She emphasizes that an unimaginable unmatched action, the first of its kind. Netaji, therefore visualized women to be the great repositories of energy, strength and courage. Similarly Roshan khanijo depicted Netaji giving more emphasis as a social reformer. She believes that the Rani of Jhansi Brigade who trained as revolutionary inorder to combat in the battlefield which will make their future to dedicate the society where they would able to combat the bigger war for womens' right to equality and social justice.

Historicity, one of the best methods adopted by Abhijit Chowdhury, who presented through the lens of two brief narratives about Bose and the INA on the Eastern Frontier of Colonial India during World War II. The first memoir narrets one late officer's experiences during the war and aftermath. The other is from the memoires of Nagas from a village located in the Kohima sector. Fortunately the details of this unheard Naga memoires is one of the presentations by panelist Vekho Swuro. He narrets in detail how in 1944 Netaji with INA along with Japanese troops came to the naga hills using the shortest route from Burma (Myanmar). Both the narrations claim historical authenticity and genuineness which automatically will attract the readers. This new approach, both with the valuable experiences are very much living as well as interesting

Prof. Vashistha's INA and Rajputana gives the glimpse of the process of political awakening among the students and prajamandal leaders of nineteen Princely States of Rajputana. It elucidates the sacrifices of INA recruits of these states in the battle of Arakan and Imphal. The article is based on the primary source of the archival records and documents of Rajasthan State Archives, Bikaner.

Moirang served as the first and last Head Quarter of INA heroes and Indo-Japanese forces. The article is the contribution of joint authors Jugindro Singh and Madhu Singh. Their detail account rightly justified that Moirang the birthplace of Thangjing Culture and cradle of civilization came into the limelight of the freedom struggle of India. The authors feel that more research required to unanswered queries.

Just when you have convinced yourself that you have long ago imbibed the last- word on the secret side of World War II along comes Tapan Chattopadhyay and his remarkable study with full of fascinating sources. He has trawled through all the documentation and has given a revited history of the INA's secret service operation by Netaji in World War II. Deeply researched with full of fresh revelations written with authority and verve. Finally it is highly professional

Subhas Chandra Bose is India's International statesman and an astute student of international politics. His understanding of internationalism emanated from his burning nationalism. Saradindu Mukherji rightly pointed out that a leader of an enslaved nation could think, plan and act in so dynamic manner and on such a vast international scale was possible because of his determination, intelligence, experience and diplomatic skill. The author underlines that Bose's foreign policy was not only pragmatic but also ethically sound by analyzing his passionate sincerety and his masterly discourse in promoting India's freedom in the most difficult international situation during the World War II is remarkable, where as Nirmala Joshi argues Bose's basic concern and interest was to promote the cause of India's freedom , which was the main plunk of his foreign policy. In the words of Bose:" Foreign policy is a realistic affair to be determined largely from the point of view of nation's self interest. Take Soviet Russia, for instance - with all her communism in her internal politics she never allows sentiments and pious platitudes do not make foreign policy." Joshi ensures that in his approach of understanding Bose paid a special attention to Soviet foreign policy along with its calculative and appropriate diplomatic moves. And finally, Raj Kumar Sharma made an attempt to compare in the foreign policy matters how realist was Bose.

Media expert Sandhya Jain's detail search for Netaji's various activities, his mission and finally his disappearance leaves behind a very impressive and a full lenth picture of his struggle for freedom. Finally, what really happened to Netaji remains with challenge but unanswered.

Kingshuk Nag, resident editor (Retd) Times of India, Hyderabad asserts although the congress party is credited for India's freedom, it was Netaji and the INA who gave the last shove to the British Raj. Challenging various aspects with proper analysis the author proposed an appropriate title: "INA - forced the British out of India".

To conclude with the final call of Abhijit Bhattacharyya... Bose the eternal legend of "JAI-HIND" we pay homage to the memory of those INA, who laid down their lives for the freedom of our country.

JAI_ HIND

Introduction

Purabi Roy

Japan's victory over Russia in the 1904-1905 Russo –Japanese war was the first harbinger of Asian resurgence. A new era started and brought about Anglo- Japanese friendship. That victory was hailed with great joy not only by the Japanese but also by the Indians. Indian people looked upon the awakening of Japan with admiration. Japan's 1905 victory strongly influenced the freedom movement of India, which got a new impetus thereafter. The Indian revolutionary Rash Behari Bose set his eyes on Japan, a nation in the Far East that had secured a victory and was expanding its military power for the reconstruction of Asia. Any Indian participating in the struggle for liberating India was bound to be friendly with that country which would support his cause. Japan welcomed the willing revolutionaries and gave shelter to them. As a result Japan not only gave shelter to Rash Behari Bose but also to other Indian revolutionaries and extended her support to their activities.

In 1915, Rash Behari Bose escaped to Japan and established contact with the Black Dragon Society of Mitsuru Toyama. With Toyama's help, Bose could meet the important personalities of Gadar Party (which was formed by the Indians in San Francisco in 1912) living in Japan. Amongst them Bhagwan Singh became a close associate of

Rash Behari Bose. Bhagwan Singh was also close to Abani Mukherjee, another revolutionary, who later became one of the eminent figure of Commintern Third International, and spent a lot of time with him. A.H. Mohammad Barkatullah a muslim Independence activist, who went from India in 1909 as a teacher of Urdu at the Tokyo University of Foreign Studies and Sabharwal was another young Indian revolutionary were two other persons with whom Bhagwan Singh had regular contact. In September 1915 Heramba Lal Gupta was sent to Japan by the Berlin Committee of Indians in Germany. These revolutionaries were with the only one vision as to how to liberate India.

To liberate India, Rash Behari Bose was in exile in Japan for twenty five years, and the question of India's Independence always ignited his deep patriotism, which did not want the least. He visited all the South Asian countries and convinced the Indians there that freedom could be obtained only if those living overseas could organize: train, arm themselves and fight for Independence. With Japan's victory over the British Indian territory in South East Asia, Japanese intelligence came in touch with Pritam Singh, an ex-soldier of the Indian army. Through him, the Japanese wanted to make a dent into the Indian Army stationed in asia and win them over.

During the Malaya campaign in February 1942, Captain Mohan Singh surrendered to the Japanese Army and gave the idea of forming units out of the Indian Prisoners-of- war to fight the Britishers. Needless to say, Japan readily agreed to his proposal. Thus, on the military side Pritam Singh and Mohan Singh laid the foundation of the Indian National Army (INA) while on the political side Rash Behari Bose through the Indian Independence League tied together all Indians with the political motivation of liberating India with the Japanese help. Let us spare a thought for Swami Satyananda Puri, Captain Akram Khan, Mr. Inder Singh, the organizers and the masterminds behind the movement. Indian Independence League (IIL) was an effective and cohesive force. Its sister organization, the INA, was an inseparable arm. These two gave meaning and sustenance to the Indians during that period, and showed that an overseas Indian was no less patriotic than his counterpart in India. The League was a catalyst, a hurricane, which blew continuously and carried with it the force of will and strength of character. It gave meaning and hope to the overseas Indians. Wherever he was, his land of origin was dear to him. In March 1942, in a conference at Tokyo, the delegates present there decided to form an Indian Independence League to organize an Indian Independence Movement in East Asia. It was resolved that "Independence – complete and free from foreign domination, interference and control of whatever nature – shall be the object of movement." The conference further resolved that "military action against India will be taken only by the Indian National Army under the command of Indians."

The next conference was held at Bangkok beginning from June 15, 1942. The conference was attended by Indian delegates from Japan, Manchukuo, Burma, Hongkong, Borneo, Java, Malaya and Thailand. Rash Behari Bose was elected as the President of IIL and Singapore was made its headquarter. The IIL adopted a resolution requesting Subhas Chandra Bose to come to East Asia and transmitted the same to Germany through the help of Japan. This will be "A new voice in Asia." It is pertinent to note that neither Rash Behari Bose nor Captain Mohan Singh had the charisma which was needed to motivate the newly raised organisation and the same collapsed by December 1942. Captain Mohan Singh was arrested and the Prisoners of War returned to their Camps.

After completing the task of reorganising the Indian Independence League, launching preparations to revolutionise the army, and after conducting a successful campaign to mobilise the support of the Indian communities throughout Southeast Asia–a phase which lasted from July to October 1943, Netaji turned towards formation of the Provisional Government of Azad Hind (Free India). This had to be done before the Army could be sent for action in the battlefield.

This government was officially proclaimed in Singapore at a mass rally on October 21, 1943 where Netaji was unanimously elected as the Head of the State and the Supreme Commander of the Indian National Army. The Provisional Government of Free India had five Ministers with Netaji as the Head of the State, Prime Minister and Minister for War and advisers representing the Indian communities in East Asia. The first momentous decision which the new government took was its declaration of war on Britain and the United States, and it was decided in the night of 22-23 October 1943. Recognition of the Provisional Government came quickly from nine countries–the Axis Powers and their allies.The Japanese Army promised all-out support for the Provisional Government. The reorganized Indian National Army, where the women members of the IIL were organized under the name, "Rani of Jhansi Regiment". The children were mobilized into a *Balsena*. A new special service group called the "Bahadur Group" was formed with duties of espionage, sabotage and infiltration into India territories. Army has two tasks– (a) to fight for freedom, and (b) to stand as the defence force of Free India.

"One of Bose's aims in going to Tokyo was to ask the Japanese Government to turn over to Provisional Government (PG), the captured Andaman & Nicobar Islands in the Indian Ocean. They were symbolic as a place of exile for Indian prisoners of the British. Furthermore, in order to be a genuine government in international law, the PG needed territory. In addition, the Andamans and Nicobar would presage the liberation of all India, Bose said to Tojo. Tojo demurred, saying that the Islands were of strategic importance to the Navy, which would never agree. But Tojo consented to announce that the islands would be ceded to the PG in the near future. Tojo kept his word and made the announcement of the transfer in November 1943. In fact the actual transfer was never made and the ultimate jurisdiction remained with the Japanese Navy though Bose sent a Chief Commissioner. The Navy, however, refused to have an INA contingent on the islands."(Joyce Lebra's article on "Netaji and the Japanese", presented at the seminar *Netaji and the India's Freedom*, published in the Proceedings of the International Netaji Seminar 1973,edited by Sisir Kumar Bose, Executive Director, Netaji Research Bureau, Calcutta.)

October 21, 1943 was a great day not only in the life of Netaji and the Indians in the South-East Asia, but in the entire history of India's Independence Movement. The auditorium of Cathey Building in Singapore where the Delegates from Thailand, Hongkong, Java, Sumatra, Indo-China and Malaya assembled at a conference convened by the IIL, Netaji announced the formation of the Provisional Government of Free India, *Arzi Hukumate Azad Hind* or Azad Hind Government. He announced the personnel of the Azad Hind Cabinet and read out the Proclamation of Independence on behalf of the Azad Hind Cabinet.

Netaji mentioned, "In setting up this Provisional Government we are, on the one hand, meeting the exigencies of the Indian situation and are, on the other, following the footsteps of history. In recent times the Irish people set up their Provisional Government in 1916. The Czechs did the same during the last World War. And, after the last World War the Turks under the leadership of Mustapha Kemal Pasha, set up their Provisional Government in Anatolia."

"It is a government which aimed neither at territorial expansion nor at the supremacy of one over another, but at the assertion and acquisition of a nation's moral right to live as a free people." "It guarantees religious liberty, as well as equal right and equal opportunities to all its citizens." The birth of the Azad Hind Government was a triumph of the forces of spiritualism over militarism and its proclamation of Independence was virtually a defiance of the fear of brute force that seeks to throttle a nation's will to be free.

The Azad Hind Government functioned like all other civilized governments consisting of the following elements that are indispensable for the purposes of a state: (i) Territory, (ii) Population, (iii) Organization or Government, (iv) Sovereignty and (v) Diplomatic Recognition.

(i) *Territory*: On October 25,1943 Netaji leaves for Tokyo to attend the Greater East Asia Conference, where at a private interview with Gen. Tojo, he spoke about the handing over of the Andaman & Nicobar Islands to the Azad Hind Government. Netaji was an observer, but after his stirring speech, Tojo, while addressing the gathering announced that Japan will be handing over the Andaman & Nicobar Islands to the Provisional Government of Free India. The Islands were later renamed *Shaheed* (Martyr) and *Swaraj* (Independence). In February 1944 Lt. Col. Loganadhan took over as the Chief Commissioner of Port Blair. Netaji responded: "Like the Bastille in Paris, which was the first to be stormed in the French

Revolution, setting free political prisoners, The Andamans, where our patriots suffered, are the first to be liberated in Indians' fight for Independence. Part by part, Indian territory will be liberated...."

(ii) *Population*: The nucleus of the population under the Azad Hind State was formed when Col. Hunt, acting as a representative of the British Government, handed over 50,000 Indian troops to Major Fujiwara, and Major Fujiwara in his turn , acting as the representative of the Japanese Government handed over them to Capt. Mohan Singh. The fate of these 50,000 Indian troops roused the national consciousness of millions of Indians in East Asia. The personal allegiance to Netaji ultimately crystallized into allegiance to the Azad Hind State.

(iii) *Organisation or Government:* The Azad Hind Government functioned like all other civilized governments. Different departments discharged the legislative, executive and judicial functions of the government. And, in addition, the government undertook certain functions like Education, Public Health, Road-Construction etc. It maintained a regular institute for training people in Civil Services and from among these trainees recruited the officers for the Azad Hind Dal which was entrusted with the responsible duty of administering whatever territories were occupied by the Azad Hind Fauj.

The Azad Hind Government published an official gazette and brought out news bulletins called "Azad Hind" and "Jai Hind". The Congress flag was honoured as the flag of the Provisional Government of Free India. There was Azad Hind Bank, with its registered office at 97 Park Street, Rangoon, whose Director was Shri Dinanath. When the British Military authorities seized the Azad Hind Bank, it had the custody of substantial amount of money belonging to the Azad Hind Government.The amity and the goodwill which characterized the life under the Azad Hind Government, of men belonging to different religion and castes, bear clear testimony to the capacity and efficiency of the executive department of the Government. In maintaining the "law and order", the Executive had the fullest cooperation of the people. From the point of view of willing allegiance to the government and ready obedience to its orders, the Azad Hind Government was a true democracy. It was a democracy in spirit though not in form.

(iv) And finally whether the Azad Hind State possessed the supreme element of "statehood", namely Sovereignty. Sovereignty implies, in the first place, that the state should be supreme in internal matters, and secondly, that it should be independent of external control. Depending on the recorded evidence of the witnesses before the Court Martial affords clear proof of the fact that the Azad Hind Government was the only organization that could make itself obeyed by the people; and it is the fact of this obedience that makes a state internally supreme.

(v) The external sovereignty of a state is reflected through the state's foreign relations. The Allied news agencies had always referred to the Azad Hind Government as a puppet government of Japan. The fact remains that the first to give recognition to the Provisional Government of Azad Hind was Japan. On October 23,1943, two days after the proclamation of Independence by the Provisional Government, the Japanese Government issued a statement wherein they said, "The Japanese Government recognize the Government as the Provisional Government of Azad Hind and hereby declare that every possible assistance on its part will be afforded to the latter for the achievement of India's Independence." This was followed by similar recognition by Germany, Italy, Thailand, Philippines, Croatia, Manchuria and Burma.

The Japanese Foreign Office appointed Hachiya Teruo, the Envoy Extraordinary to the Provisional Government of Azad Hind in Rangoon. The British War Office records claim that Hachiya was appointed as the representative of the Japanese government to the Provisional Government of Azad Hind without any credential. It further claims that he would probably have the most intimate knowledge of any matter handled by the Japanese government and Chandra Bose. After the War, Hachiya was in the British custody and interrogated by the head quarters of SEATIC, Singapore. Hachiya's statements during the course of interrogation prove that the Japanese government did not appear to be in the habit of issuing credentials to its ambassadors in general, and an ambassador by the name of Kato Kochu was sent without credentials to the centre of the Provisional Government of Omsk in Siberia.

Kolesnikov, the former Major General of Warsaw Pact, and currently a diplomat in the Russian Embassy in Turkey mentions in his article "Bose strove to establish (relations) with the Soviet Leadership. With this aim in view he sent the authorized representative of the Interim Government, Kato Kochu, to Omsk with the rank of an Ambassador but without the proper Official documents. There is evidence to the effect that Kato Kochu reached Omsk."

After proclamation of the Azad Hind Government, Netaji tried through the Japanese political channels to get the PGI recognized by the Russian Government. Netaji's effort in this direction appears to have been sponsored and approved by the Japanese government. While in Tokyo Netaji approached the Foreign Minister of the USSR through the then Soviet Ambassador in Tokyo. The following letter is unearthed from the KGB Archive of Russian Federation.

Tokyo, the 16th November, 1943

To

His Excellency the Foreign Minister of the USSR

Your Excellency,

I have the honour to inform Your Excellency that in accordance with the will of all the freedom-loving Indians in India and abroad – and with the fullest support of all Indians residing in East Asia who number close upon three millions, and of their political organization, the Indian Independence League as well as with the backing of the Indian National Army now stationed in East Asia, the Provisional Government of Azad Hind (Free India) was established on the 21st of October, 1943, with its Head quarters temporarily at Syonan or Singapore.

In communicating this information to Your Excellency, I avail myself of this opportunity to express my sincere desire that there should exist between our two Governments and our two nations the most cordial relations of amity and friendship.

I also take this opportunity of assuring Your Excellency of my warmest esteem.

Yours respectfully,
Sd/
Subhas Chandra Bose
Head of the State, Prime Minister and Minister of Foreign Affairs of the Provisional Government of Azad Hind

From a paper, "The Declassified INA Documents from the Ministry of Defence", presented in March 1999, by Shri Pramod Mehra at the Netaji Institute of Asian Studies, Calcutta we find: "The recognition of the Provisional Government by the world powers viz. Japan, Burma, Germany, Italy, Thailand, Philippines, and Russia declared the firm resolve of the Provisional Government to execute their struggle for India's freedom."

Now the question arises as to how the USSR being a member of Allied Forces could give recognition to the Provisional Government of Azad Hind?

The Domei News Service of Berlin, reported: "A reception in Berlin in the 2nd week of November, 1943, was given on the occasion of the founding of the Provisional Government of India. Indians in Berlin were determined to give their utmost to liberate India. The Secretary of State Keppler, on behalf of the Reich gave a speech. The Japanese Ambassador General Oshima also spoke. The Head of the organization, Nambiar spoke about Subhas Chandra Bose."

... Bose sent a message from Japan for the occasion announcing that the Indian Provisional Government had declared war on Britain and the USA; and that as the German Government had recognized the Indian National Army, he had placed it under the German High Command and had appointed Nambiar as his Minister in Berlin."

The British Intelligence became very worried about the new developments in the Far East The vanguards in the Indian National Army reached Rangoon in the beginning of 1944. Full of glorious hopes and dreams, Netaji standing under the fluttering Tricolour gave orders to the INA to cross the Arakan and the Assam Mountains and to march on to the Red Fort at Delhi.

Arakan, Imphal and Kohima Operations

The Imphal and Kohima operation was the final offensive of the East Asia War, mounted by three Burma-based Japanese divisions, and one INA division. This was preceded by a diversionary attack on the Arakans. The campaign lasted from March 15 to July 9, 1944. The operation has often been compared to the operation Wacht am Rhein or the Battle of the Bulge, which was the final all-out drive launched by Germany towards Ardennes on the Western Front, from December 1944 to January 1945. Both the operations almost succeeded and both are termed "gambles" by the historians today. If the German push towards Ardennes was Wacht am Rhein, the Japanese-Indian thrust against Imphal might be called "Wacht am Chindwin."

Due to poor logistics, the Japanese forces were unable to complete their mission. The British launched their offensive in June 1944. The INA fought boldly and interfered with the crossings of the Irrawady and Mount Popa.

The moot question is – Did the Military Operations of the INA have an impact on the British to grant Independence to India? There are two prevalent opinions:

- *Opinion A.* The Military Operations by the INA had a marginal impact on the British mindset and did not affect the granting of independence to India.
- *Opinion B.* The British ruled India with the help of the Indian Armed Forces. The formation of the INA and its role in military operations resulting in the death of 24,000 INA soldiers shook the British mindset about its capability to govern with soldiers who had turned against the British Empire. They felt that it was

time to bid good bye before more mutinies made the situation untenable.

Prime Minister Clement Atlee of the United Kingdom was the person who took the decision to grant India her Independence. He felt that this was the primary reason for granting India her freedom from the British. Therefore, the INA was instrumental in getting India her independence.

"We should have but one desire today – the desire to die so that India may live ....the desire to free a martyr's death, so that the path to freedom may be paved with martyr's blood' ... Give me blood and I promise you Freedom".

Your promise came true, and now we promise to find the truth – What really happened to you Netaji.

Keynote Address

The Indian National Army (INA) and its Contribution to India's Independence

Chitra Ghosh

Opening a seminal debate on India's Independence from the British rule on August 15,1947, particularly on the role of Netaji Subhas Chandra Bose and the INA- where does one begin? A pacifist historian would probably put it at the date of return of Mohandas Karamchand Gandhi from South Africa. Gandhi was without any hesitation, the leader who evoked nationalist feeling in India. He was referred by Netaji as the "Father of the Indian Nation". In South Africa, Gandhi had learnt, not without extreme pain, that the colour of skin would create differences in attitude, thought and action, as he was thrown from the train at Petermartizbag by an Englishman. Gandhi's leadership created a variety of political views and actions in India. At the Ramgarh Conference of the newly formed Forward Bloc in 1939, Subhas Chandra Bose had opined that an ultimatum should be given to the Britain to leave India, as India should take advantage of the World War II, when Britain was facing a difficult situation, having lost Singapore, Malaysia, Burma and the Andaman & Nicobar Islands. At the same time, subjugated India had fielded a record of an All Volunteer Army of some 2.5 million men in occupied India to fight the Germans and the Italians in the western theatre of the War. They were being preferred by the English Military Commanders, as they proved both tenacious and steadfast in their occupation. On the other hand, the British forces were showing signs of war weariness. After the War, 11 of the 16 Divisions of the British Indian Army were disbanded. The 2.5 million strong Indian Army was rapidly downsized to 350,000 and the Jawans were further divided between India and Pakistan during the partition of the country. Further, no money was allocated to equip or modernize the army, which resulted in a humiliating defeat of the Indian Army in the Indo-Chinese War in India's eastern frontier.

When the World War began in 1939, India had contributed to England the largest All-Volunteer Army of 2.5 million men. They had been raised with conscription. These people, wanting to have an employment, were village people, uneducated and unsophisticated. They were easily made to realize that the Japanese and their allies were their national enemies. Bose was completely marginalized in the Congress and no one listened to what he had to stay. So, Subhas had to think and provide another way to achieve his dream.

On July 2, 1940, Bose staged a protest at the memorial of the Black Hole in Calcutta.

The Black Hole was a ruse created by the English against the last Nawab of Bengal, Sirajudaula. It was said that a large number of English men and women with children were pushed together inside a very small space, hardly enough for even the people to stand against each other and breathe, so that most of them died of suffocation.

At the same time, Bose was planning his escape as he was convinced that no purpose will be served to remain in custody for the entire War period. So, he gave to his nephew Amiya Nath a letter to be dispatched to Moscow, asking for help, but the Communist Party of India did not send the letter. On the other hand, the Kirti Kisan Party of NW Frontier Province (NWFP) helped him to escape. Persons like Bhagat Ram Talwar, who later turned into a double spy for both the British and the

Indians, Harminder Singh, Sodhi Achar Singh Cheena and Taja Singh Sutankar came forward to help.

In the early hours of January16-17, 1941, his nephew Sisir drove Subhas from his Elgin Road residence and without a break arrived at Bararee, where his eldest nephew Asoke Nath, who was working as a Chemist with Jardine Handerson, had a bungalow. Subhas posed as Mohammed Ziauddin, an Insurance agent. Arriving at Kabul, he was restricted as the future plan was not in hand. Bose hid in the house of Uttam Chand in Peshawar, till the Italians gave him a passport in the name of Orlando Mazzotta and he could ultimately reach Berlin through Moscow. But no help was given to him by the Russian authorities and even no one wanted to see him.

Bose arrived Berlin on April 2, 1941. His German contact was Admiral Von Trott. During this time the main activities of Subhas Chandra in Germany were threefold.

1. To secure a joint Axis Declaration on Indian Independence from Germany and Italy. He did not have success in this effort.
2. To set up a Free India Center for the cause of liberation of India and set up a Think Tank.
3. To start Radio broadcasts, which however he could only start as late as 1942.

Bose was able to meet the Foreign Minister Ribbentrop, who was friendly. But other than that there was no concrete help came from the Germans. So, Bose had to fight his own battle and this he did it by organizing the INA.

Comparatively, how did the Indian National Army under Subhas Chandra Bose fare in combat? They had neither sophisticated arms nor ammunitions, the training was hasty, they did not have enough food to eat to sustain themselves and often had to eat grass. On being asked by the Maj. Gen. Gray, GOC of the 20th Indian Division, whether or not it was madness on the part of the INA to continue to fight under such circumstances, Prem Sahgal replied that a revolutionary army lives on its spirit of madness, even though they may lack the wherewithal of a regular army. Let us see how far this madness took them to attain their goal and what was the spirit and nature of the leader who instilled this madness into them.

To instill the national feeling in the Jawans of the Indian National Army, who were very ordinary soldiers, Subhas Chandra introduced the following:

1. As the soldiers came from different religious background, a common solution had to be thought upon. So, "Jai Hind" was accepted as the slogan and Bose used rituals, customs and usages, which could build a united nation.
2. Rabindranath Tagore's patriotic song "Jana Gana Mana" was accepted as the National Song. It was translated in *Hindustani* and a marching tune was created. The militarization of the song was done by Netaji himself, so that a military band could play the tune.
3. *Hindustani* in Roman Script was accepted as the *lingua franca.*
4. Subhas Chandra Bose would henceforth be known as "Netaji", which was equivalent to "The Leader".

Thus, Netaji created a unity among these Indians who never had such experience in the past. They had served only as foot soldiers under the German command.

One has to start with the basic question. Was India ever a "Nation"? The answer will be an emphatic "No – for India is a country of many castes, communities, religions, languages, scripts and spoken languages. A resident of Kashmir has very little common with a Tamilian and a Keralite would be totally different from an Assamese. It was the first task of the leader to weave them into an organic whole. How could he do it? He had to imbibe into them the spirit of nationalism, so that they could feel as comrades in arm and fight together for the independence of the motherland.

Netaji insisted that the Indian League, which was organized in Germany, primarily from POWS, should get equal facility regarding pay, clothing, food, leave etc, as those enjoyed by the German units. The strength of the Legion grew in numbers steadily and the largest was the Annaberg Camp. Two original recruits showing promise were

Abid Hasan, who travelled with Netaji in the Submarine, when he went to East Asia and N. G. Swamy, who headed the intelligence branch of the INA. The Indians were placed under the command of Hauptman Harbig, who instructed them in morality and discipline.

In August 1942, the Legion was moved to Koenigsbruck, and they paraded in front of Netaji. They took oath to fight for India's freedom, with Bose giving them their standard, in tricolour of Saffron, White and Green, with a springing tiger in the middle. But there was a sad episode, Netaji did not have enough money and so he had to accept money from the Germans which made him unhappy. He tried to pay back the money after reaching Asia, where he got a lot of money and gold from the Indian Diaspora.

Because of the lack of funds, initially Netaji used to work only with his wife and Secretary Madame Emilie Schankl, but by January 1942 he had 25 Indian assistants and set up the Free India Office. He was given a Villa to stay and money for his daily use. In Germany, Netaji suffered hardship because of the paucity of funds. So the Indian Legion had to follow the dictates of the Germans, while in Asia, the INA was a full-fledged army.

As per the official recorded history of the INA, there were 1500 officers of different ranks, and 60,000 soldiers, of whom 26,000 were killed in combat. This makes the casualty figure of about 44 per cent which is awe-inspiring. The INA lost the war in Kohima and the Arakans, as they suffered from the lack of modern arms and ammunitions, a total lack of airpower bringing cover to the soldiers and they even had to go without food and sustain themselves by eating grass. They lost the war. Did Netaji come to Asia too late? Was he stuck in Germany for a longer time? But, was it not because of the INA and Subhas Chandra Bose that India became free in 1947.

The British authorities also made the big mistake. They put on trial at the Red Fort, which again was signified by Netaji as the ultimate destination to which the INA was to proceed, the three INA officers – Shah Nawaz Khan, a Muslim, Prem Kumar Sahgal, a Hindu and Gurbaksh Singh Dhillon, a Sikh. They signify the unity which the INA had created. The trial had to be abandoned and could not be continued as the country rose in revolt. Even Jawaharlal Nehru, who had never been to a court, though he was qualified as a Barrister in England, donned the Barrister's Gown and went with Tej Bahadur Sapru to defend the INA officers. Protests broke loose all over the country. The Naval officers of the RIN mutinied. It was followed by similar revolts in the Air Force and last but not the least, the army units at Jabalpur rose in rebellion. Around 40,000 British officers posted all over India, were eager to go back home. When the Earl of Mountbatten was sent to India as Governor-General, he could foresee what was coming and advised his home Government accordingly. But Mountbatten, adequately helped and advised by his wife Edwina, who entirely got control over Nehru, made the Congress agree to his proposal of partitioning the country.

I would like to mention here a vivid incident during which I personally was present. My Father, Sarat Chandra Bose was perhaps the only person who tried to prevent the partition of the country, realizing fully the pangs of sorrow that Bengal and Punjab will have to go through. He went from door to door, to everyone, beginning with Mahatmaji, to all the Congress and League Leaders. To his appeal, Gandhi's reply was – "Jawahar does not see me these days, Patel says no to whatever I say, Rajen Babu has kicked the ladder". Sarat Chandra Bose went to Jinnah, who said "get your Congress agree to your appeal, I shall not stand in the way to overrule it". As our car drove in, Fatima Jinnah opened the door and escorted us in. The Congress did not agree to my father's appeal. We came back home, and the Bengalees threw stones at Woodburn Park. It was a lonely dismal house. Riots had begun with ferocity in Noakhali and my father accompanied Gandhiji to the disturbed area.

But I have strayed from the original question and let us return to the INA. Netaji created a unified army, by taking momentary decisions. He mixed the people from different areas in India to stay in one camp; introduced one kitchen to give same food to everyone; both the disbanded army jawans incorporated in the INA and the drafted civilians, were given some training, stayed in the camps together and observed strict discipline.

Meanwhile, Gandhi and the Congress under his leadership, was not sitting quietly. In 1942 Gandhi declared the 'Quit India' Movement with the watchword "Do or Die", "Karo Ya Maro". The whole country responded unequivocally, particularly under the leadership of leaders like Jay Prakash Narayan, Aruna Asaf Ali, Sarojini Naidu and others. Police stations were burnt down, and atrocities committed on the Brtitish supporters. But, at the same time, the Congress was averse to the Japanese invasion. Viceroy Linlithgow reported to Churchill: "I am engaged here in meeting by far the most serious rebellion since that of 1857, the gravity and extent of which we have so far concealed from the world for reasons of military security". Netaji from East Asia sent gold and ornaments, which however went to people like Bhagat Ram Talwar, who handed them over to the British, so that none of it came to be any use.

There was another terrible tragedy. Rice was procured for the British army and the village people had nothing to eat. Bengal faced a disastrous famine with hungry people flocking to Kolkata and dying for a morsel of food on the streets of the metropolis. Netaji offered to send rice, but it was not accepted.

Perhaps, the most outstanding and unique creation of Bose was the Rani of Jhansi Regiment. Netaji always had immense respect and reliance on women. At the Calcutta Congress, held in 1928, under the Presidentship of Pandit Motilal Nehru, Bose had organized a Women's Volunteer Corps, under the leadership of Latika Ghosh, the niece of Sri Aurobindo.

The lady volunteers had marched alongwith men, wearing red-bordered saris and later on helped the delegates to seat, gave them water and supervised the kitchen, as was needed. In Singapore, Netaji organized a group of women under Capt. Laxmi Swaminathan, who was also given a seat in his Government. These girls were in their teens, left home, stayed in camps and were given military training. They did not want to be only the nursing unit of the army. Writing a petition in blood, they asked Netaji to send them to the front. They were sent. But as the INA faced defeat, the *Ranis* were also withdrawn from the front. They marched through jungles and swamps in utter hardship by foot, and Netaji walked with them, leaving his car behind. Janaki Thevar writes, "As Netaji pulled out his shoes, I could see his feet, red and full of blisters. But he had walked with us without a single word coming out of his mouth. Such was our leader".

The *Ranis* were disbanded and sent home. Unlike the INA soldiers, who after being captured were brought as prisoners, and made to stand in a straight line and shot … a treatment that was not allowed by the Geneva Convention on Treatment of Enemy Soldiers in a war. The same happened at Jhikargacha in West Bengal, to more than 16,000 INA soldiers.

That was not the end. Netaji had laid the foundation stone for martyrs at Singapore. When Nehru went to Singapore, at the residence of Mountbatten, Indians wanted him to go and place a wreath on the memorial. But Nehru refused to go. Moreover, at the order of Mountbatten the memorial was dynamited, so that no sign of it remained there. Nehru had even said : "When Subhas Chandra Bose returns I shall myself stop him with an open sword". Such was the enmity and hate for Subhas in the ranks of the Congress workers. The INA soldiers, who were able to come back to India, were denied entry the Indian army. They did not receive pension, gratuity or any compensation from the Indian Government. But those who opted for Pakistan had been incorporated in the army and given adequate pay and provisions.

In 1941, the Japanese were flooded by requests from the Indians in East Asia to bring Bose. Pritam Singh of the Indian Independence League was the first one to do that and then there were many others. When the Axis Powers did not vouch for a safe air journey to Bose, he asked for the submarine venture. Faced with a raging sea-storm, the German submarine Captain advised him to go back, to which Subhas Chandra replied "I haven't come all this way to go back. The submarine voyage took three months & was a test of endurance with a staunch diesel smell and no proper food. No one but no less than a person than Subhas Chandra Bose could have endured this privation.

On 12 June, 1943, the Japanese Radio announced the arrival of Bose in Japan. On June 19, Bose held his first press conference. On June 27, Bose arrived in Singapore, and Rashbehari Bose, who had till then been the leader of the Indians, handed over the power to Bose in October 1943. Subhas announced the formation of the Provincial Government of Azad Hind on 21 October, 1943 and declared war on England and America.

The INA was organized in the following manner:–

1. First Field Force Regiment commanded by Lt. Col. Hussain 3 Infantry Battalion; Machine Gun Company; Heavy Guns Battalion with 12 Bren Gun Carriers.
2. The Gandhi Guerilla Regiment, commanded by Lt. Col. Kiani.
3. The Azad Guerilla Regiment, commanded by Lt. Col. Gulzara Singh.
4. The Special Service Group to operate behind the advanced lines.
5. The Intelligence Group commanded by Lt. Col. Shankar Mallik.
6. The Reinforcement Group commanded by Lt. Col. Tajjamul Hussain.

The INA were soldiers to capture Indian troops and re-educate them to fight for India's Independence.

Of the six formations of the INA five were commanded by Muslims. Bose re-organized all the divisions and handpicked a few to form the "Subhas Brigade".

The Jawans of INA did not get any pay, but a small amount as pocket money to buy toiletries, cigarettes etc. When they advanced through the jungles, infested with flies, leaches, and even snakes, they suffered from lack of food, but there was only one direction to go. Such was the charisma of the leader. To keep their morale, there was Bravery Awards. With the motto Ittefaq, Itmad and Qurbani (Unity, Faith, Sacrifice), the INA moved on and fought the war.

Netaji felt the necessity of having land under the Provincial Government, so after the conquest of Andaman & Nicobar Islands by the Japanese, he made them hand over the 2 Islands to his Govt. and appointed Gen. Loganathan as the High Commissioner to govern the areas, renaming the Islands "*Shahid*" and "*Swaraj*" Islands.

There were the few bright sides of the dismal fight for it was a war between two very uneven sides.

To sum up, the contribution of the INA to Indian Independence, what could be better than to recapitulate the words of Clement Attlee?

On being asked by Mr. P. N. Chakrabarti, the then acting Governor of West Bengal–why England left India, which was to England the "Crown Jewel" of the Empire, Mr. Clement Attlee the former British Prime Minister had replied that it was because of Subhas Chandra Bose and his INA. What could be more impressive than these few words to evaluate the contribution of the INA to Indian Independence? Further, being asked – what was the contribution of Gandhi's "Quit India" movement, Attlee replied "minimal"!!

Military Evaluation of the Structure, Motivation and Combat Performance of the INA

Maj. Gen. (Dr.) G. D. Bakshi

The Azad Hind Fauj

Bose had initially planned to expand the INA to a size of 50,000 men. This was to be done by enrolling some 25,000 Indian POWs in Japanese captivity and also doing fresh recruitment from the Indian diaspora in South, East Asia. There are also reports that ultimately, Bose dreamed of a mammoth INA of some 3 million men. In this heavy reliance on vast masses of motivated manpower– he was so much like Mao- who had ultimately expanded the PLA to a record size of some 4.2 million men. However, by 1943, the Japanese were getting hard pressed in the Pacific theatre and the Japanese war-time economy was definitely showing signs of strain. They initially agreed to arm and equip a force of just 30,000 men. After the dissolution of the First INA, its General Head Quarters (GHQ) was replaced by two distinct organs:

- **Military Bureau**: One was the Military Bureau with Col. (later Maj. Gen.) J. K. Bhonsle as its Director. This was a policy formulation set up– something like a War Department functioning directly under the IIL. Bhonsle had his own staff. In many ways,therefore, it functioned somewhat like a Central Military Commission of Communist armies.

- **Army Command**: The other organ was the Army Command with Lt. Col. (later Maj. Gen.) M. Z. Kiani as its commander. Bose had earlier gained invaluable experience in raising the Indesche Legion in Germany and had a good idea of the German training and motivational methodologies. The bulk of his recruits was Indian POWs in Japanese prisoner camps.

It was not easy to create an INA out of the defeated British Indian Army. The INA had its roots in the British Indian Army that had been moulded over a period of nearly 200 years, first by the East India Company and then by the British monarch's pro- consuls, entirely to serve British imperial objectives. Sitanshu Das writes – the Army of Britain had been raised in India to ensure that there would never be another 1857 like revolt in the military. The British rulers had carefully studied the existing faultlines in Indian society. They had ensured that the internally divided British Indian Army would be held together by primarily two factors:

- First, by the *men's hereditary pride in their vocation of soldiering*. In most cases this was pegged on to the pride or *izzat* of the particular ethnicity/community on which that regiment was based and had its unique set of traditions, customs and practices. Thus, the Sikhs, Dogras, Kumaonis, Garhwalis, Rajputs, Jats, Ahirs, Punjabi, Muslims and Gurkhas etc. became the organizational basis for the establishment of class based fighting regiments of Infantry, Cavalry and Artillery. Over a period of time, each of these units became a corporate entity in its own right, repleat with histories that today stretch to 250 years and more. Each regiment and unit had its battle honours, flags, gudieons, awards of bravery and distinctive uniforms and regimental accoutrements etc. to foster and deepen the regimental and fighting spirit.

- The second factor was a sense of loyalty to the British Crown whose salt they had eaten– the concept of "*Naam, Namak, Nishan*" (Name, Salt, Flag), was the basis of its functional excellence and combat motivation. This was deepened by the oath of loyalty to the King Emperor or Queen and strengthened by the fact that being an officer or a soldier in British India was a matter of great prestige and the *British accorded pride of place to its soldiers by way of land grants (jagirs) and special care and responsiveness from the police and district administration.* (All this is now sadly ending) The Army recruitment/catchment areas from where these soldiers came were given priority for development by creation of canals and road and rail infrastructure, etc. The British Regimental Officers genuinely looked after and were dedicated to their men and went to inordinate lengths to learn the customs and traditions of the ethnic groupings/communities to which their men belonged. They usually spent their first annual leave touring the villages in their recruitment areas. The British Junior Officers also provided very competent leadership at the tactical level and always led from the front. This initial advantage, however, was badly frayed after the disastrous routs at the hands of the Japanese in Malaya, Singapore and Burma in 1942. In fact, in many cases the British Officers had callously abandoned their men when the chips were down. This did a lot to dent the carefully cultivated image of racial superiority.

Militant Nationalism as the Motivational Credo

Given the shortage of time that he had to field a fighting force, the simplest way out for Bose would have been to recreate British style organizational units. But, Bose was insistent that he would radically transform the organizational philosophy inherited from the British Indian Army to create mixed or All India All Class (AIAC) units that would seek combat motivation to fight, not from the ethnicity of their regiments, but from a far larger pan-Indian identity and make that the basis of militant nationalism. Such a pan- Indian identity did not have to conjured up from the blue. The fact is that it existed in a nascent form and Bose did his best to fan it to levels of incandescence. He had seen how the German and Japanese armies relied upon militant nationalism to fire up their soldiers for combat and how well this motivation worked on the battlefield. Thus, like in the Indesche Legion, he insisted upon raising mixed class or AIAC units for the INA. The men were usually mixed down to company level. In fact each company had a somewhat fixed grouping of classes (*eg*. Dogras and Sikhs or Jats and Ahirs or Jats, Gujars and Madrasis etc.). At the battalion level therefore, this resulted in an AIAC class composition. He put to use all the motivational tools he had seen in the Whermacht and the Imperial Japanese Army. This included rhetoric, propaganda, rallies, military music and community singing. The INA Flag was the Indian tri-colour with the Congress Charkha replaced by a Royal Bengal Tiger in the act of springing on a prey. It was a captivating symbol. Ultimately Bose, (the official history of the INA claims) was able to raise a force of some 1500 officers and some 60,000 men organized into three combat divisions. It also claimed that this force suffered a staggering 26,000 casualties during the War. The official history of the INA penned down by Capt. Yadav, unfortunately has its limitations. Less the first volume, all the rest are simply a Roll of honour, which too is unfortunately, incomplete. It is difficult to verify these figures from authentic muster rolls, because almost all the records of the INA were destroyed by them at the time of surrender (as per standard military practise before a retreat). There are therefore, little authentic written records of the INA per se for research. Reliance therefore has to be placed upon individual testimonies, wartime intelligence reports of the British and Americans about the JIFs- (or Japanese Inspired Forces) as also detailed interrogation reports of the INA personnel. One of the best written and most reliable accounts of the INA is by Maj. Gen. Mohammad Zaman Kiani, who was appointed Chief of the General Staff after the arrest of Mohan Singh and was later the Army Commander of the Second INA. Kiani comes across as a very competent and professionally sound officer and has left behind a very highly readable and well written account titled – "India's Freedom

Struggle and the Great INA". He had won the sword of honour at the Indian Military Academy, as also the gold medal for standing first in academic and military subjects. Most of the initial and post First INA re-organization of this force had been done by him. Another very good book on the INA is the American author Peter Ward Fay's– *The Forgotten Army* which gives an excellent and objective account of its combat performance. A third very reliable source is Joyce Chapman Lebra's- *Jungle Alliance: Japan and the Indian National Army*. The official history of the INA written by Capt. Yadav gives the following as the final organizational chart for the INA by the time when the war had ended:

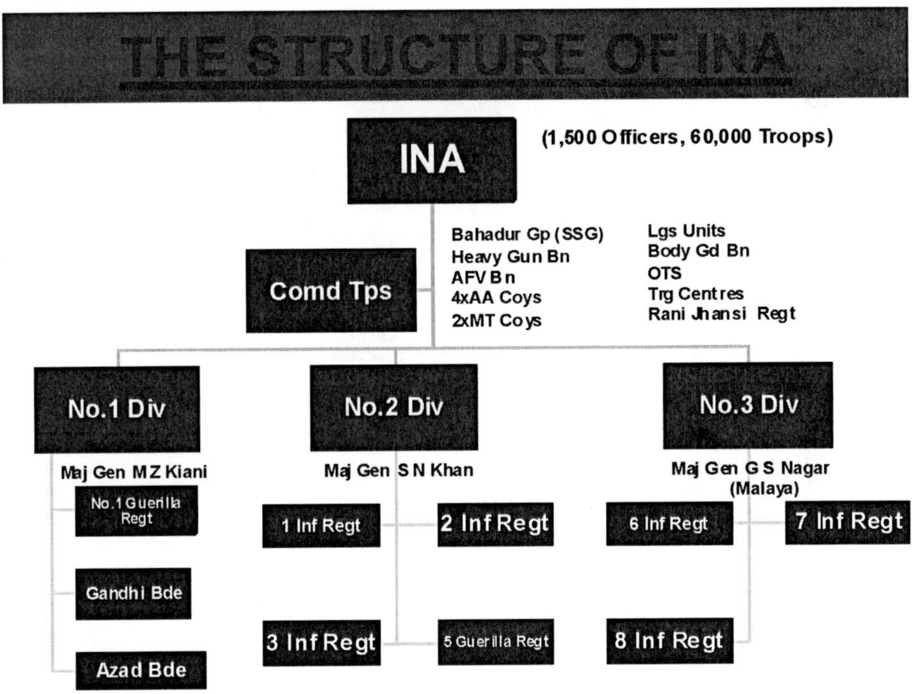

Thus the INA had a respectable size of three divisions, (a corps sized formation) besides a basal compliment of support units like an Armoured Fighting Vehicle (AFV) Battalion, A Heavy Gun battalion and four companies of anti-aircraft guns and two of Motorised Transport (MT) companies. These were available only at the army level and not at the divisional level (as was available to most of the modern armies of that period). It was, thus, a lightly equipped infantry force, that would today be categorized as' Light Infantry' (sans heavy integral fire- power). Besides it had logistics support units, a Body Guard Battalion, an Officers Training School and Recruit Training Centres. It was, therefore, a fairly modern and well organized, though not so very well equipped organisation. The paucity of equipment is really not understood, as there were huge stocks of captured British equipment. Possibly the supply of ammunition for these was a constraint. Two of the three combat divisions were led by Muslim officers– Major Generals Shah Nawaz Khan, and MZ Kiyani (who was also the army commander of the INA). The third was led by Maj. Gen. Gaur and was entrusted with the defense of Malaya. Bose had made officer selection for command clearly merit and seniority based and this carried credibility with the Force as being just and fair and based on professional criterion of past record and demonstrated performance. Thus, both Gen. MZ Kiani and Col. Shah Nawaz Khan (whom Bose handpicked to command the newly raised elite Subhas Regiment) were Sword of Honour winners from the Indian Military Academy. The Military Secretary's (MS) branch of the INA was obviously doing its homework and had put promotions on a scientific instead of a communal or casteist basis. This drastically improved morale and performance.

It was Bose who had insisted upon the formation of INA divisions, based upon his experience of the German Wehrmacht. Muslim and Sikh officers held some key appointments in this force and all men ate from a common *Langar* or cook house. This was a great improvement over the British Indian Army which still retained its separate cook houses for different castes/communities. One of the novel features of Bose's INA was an all women battalion called the Rani of Jhansi Regiment. Col. Lakshmi Swaminathan, a doctor, was its first commandant. Like Mao of China, Bose felt that 'women held up half the sky' and he was keen to give them equal footing and even wanted them in combat roles. This was well ahead of his times and the Japanese were most surprised and miffed by this experiment in women empowerment. They were indignant that a lot of energy and resources had to be diverted to protect and secure this unit in fast changing combat environments. They tried very hard to dissuade him, but this seemed an article of faith with Bose and he was adamant. Thus, Gen. Kiani records the following order of battle of the INA at the time when Bose had assumed charge:

The First Field Force Regiment

This was commanded by Lt. Col. S.M. Hussein. It had three Infantry Battalions, a Vickers Machine Gun Company, a 3 inch Mortar Company, the Heavy Guns Battalion (with nine 4.5" howitzers) and an Armoured Fighting Vehicles Battalion with 12 Bren Gun Carriers (all equipped from captured British weapons).

The Second (Gandhi) Guerilla Regiment. This also had three Infantry Battalions commanded by Lt. Col. I.J. Kiani.

The Third (Azad) Guerilla Battalion. Organised as above, this was commanded by Lt. Col. Gulzara Singh.

The Fourth (Nehru) Guerilla Regiment. Organized as above and commanded by Lt. Col. R.M. Arshad.

The Special Services Group. This was organized in small groups to be deployed all-along the Indo-Burma border at the outbreak of operations. These parties were to infiltrate behind the enemy lines, disrupt communications, create confusion and subvert Indian personnel of the British Indian Army.

The Intelligence Group. This was commanded by Lt. Col. Shaukat Malik. Their task was same as the SSG. However, they were designed to operate closer to the frontline and not operate as deep as the SSG.

The Reinforcement Group. This was commanded by Lt. Col. Tajjamul Hussein. This formation was to receive all the captured Indian Army Personnel during the fighting, re-educate them and prepare them psychologically to fight alongwith the INA for the liberation of India. British intelligence reports seem to confirm this organisation and ORBAT.

Change Over to Divisional Level Organisations. Gen. Kiani points out that out of the six formations of the INA at that stage – five were commanded by Muslims. It could be asked was this because he was then the Chief of Staff? (Did INA officers have a sub-conscious bias to rely more on their co- religionists? Mohan Singh had possibly given prominence to the Sikhs and after him the bias towards Muslim officers became somewhat apparent). Another reason for this perhaps, was the desertion of an entire Intelligence Group initially sent to Burma under Lt. Col. Gill. This caused quite a dent in Gen. Mohan Singh's standing with the Japanese. One Capt. M.S. Dhillon had commandeered an elephant and defected with his entire team. The Japanese were naturally most upset and Col. Gill had personally come under a serious cloud. Col. Gill was supposed to be close to Gen. Mohan Singh and this made the Japanese suspicious of his intentions. This had, for some time, put the poor Sikhs under somewhat of a cloud with the Japanese after this incident. British intelligence reports indicated this infighting amongst the three communities in the first INA. A far greater balance seems to have been restored in these matters, however, once Bose took charge. As stated, Bose had set this right by focusing on merit and demonstrated performance as the primary selection criterion for key posts. Thus, two key commanders were Muslim officers who had won the coveted Sword of Honour at the Military academy. (Gens. Kiani and Shah Nawaz).

Bose assumed charge as the Supreme Commander in August 1943. It was basically, a civilian appointment, but from then on, he began wearing the INA uniform, though without any badges of rank. One of Bose's first act on assuming charge was to raise a new guerilla regiment called the Subhas Regiment. This had the pick of the personnel of the existing three regiments (Brigades) and was placed under command Lt. Col. Shah Nawaz Khan- (later Maj. Gen.)– a sword of honour winner. Bose now designated the entire existing Army as the First INA Division and set about raising two more such divisions. Thus, to Bose goes the credit of reorganizing the INA on the standard combat Division basis on which all European Armies of that period were organized. The Indian staff had animated discussions with their Japanese counterparts on the Organisation and Staff tables as the Japanese had to provide the equipment. The Japanese officers insisted vehemently, on a very minimal, teeth to tail ratio. They ridiculed the western system of having outsized tail units with 3-4 men supporting each combat soldier on the front. All the weapons and equipment were from captured British stocks. The dry rations – Atta, rice, *dal* etc. were supplied by the Japanese Army free of cost. Fresh rations (vegetables, fruits etc.) were procured through the INA supply organisation. Thus the Indians had shown that they could do very well without British officers and given the many constraints they faced, had set up a fairly functional fighting and logistics support organisation.

Gen Kiani points out, there was no pay in the INA. All ranks however were paid a small amount as pocket money to buy cigarettes, soap and toiletries etc. Thus, he as an Army Commander, was getting just Rs. 400 per month! Even sans pay, this INA had fought far better than the British Indian Army had done in Malaya, Singapore and Burma when the air and sea power situation was heavily tilted against them. Had the INA been an all mercenary force that had joined purely for opportunistic reasons, it would have, as Gen Kiani points out, so correctly, disintegrated at the first contact with the British Indian Army. On the contrary, despite a terrible line of communication and dismal logistics support; without any air- cover and in fact with air- superiority heavily tilted against them and the Japanese Navy under great pressure on the high seas (which blocked most options of operational manoeuver from the sea flank), most of these units performed heroically and kept up with the hard marching Japanese Army.

The eminent American historian, Peter Ward Fay, writes in his most readable and voluminous history of the INA (The Forgotten Army) that in the operations in Imphal- Kohima the men of the first INA division suffered terribly from disease— especially Malaria, Diarrhea, Amoebic Dysentery, Scrub Typhus, deadly Naga sores that filled with maggots and above all from prolonged and painful starvation due to breakdown in supplies. There were, in addition, cobras and kraits and scorpions and above all the Hamadrayd or King Cobra that infested these hills. There were the blood sucking Leeches and the poisonous flies. There was the near total absence of medical facilities and even simple bandages and stretchers. The enemy had a pre-ponderance of air power and artillery and was well fed and well maintained by the air, even when cut off on the ground. In such terribly adverse circumstances, even the most well established Armies would have crumbled and surrendered in droves. The simple and honest miracle is that the men of the INA did not. It was a miracle of motivation and morale. British Military Intelligence Reports of that period honestly admit their astonishment that even in such disastrously adverse circumstances, most men of the INA held fast. In fact the British Military Intelligence Report summing up the operations of autumn 1944 noted laconically- "our expectations that large numbers of the INA would desert were not realized". It was the same in the Manipur basin. The July 1944 Intelligence summary, records that of the original 1600 men of the Gandhi Brigade only 650 were present for duty. But that was not because the rest had surrendered. Upto 30 Jun only a 116 out of 1600, that is just some 7.2% had surrendered or been captured. The rest were sick (but they held on doggedly – they did not surrender). Similarly in the Azad Brigade, in one battalion, the strength return at the end of June showed that out of a strength of approximately 600 men hardly more than 300 were present; 250 were sick, 12 had deserted, 3 had committed suicide and 3 were casualties." One reads these grim statistics and is appalled by the sheer scale and intensity of human suffering inflicted, not so much by the enemy but by the hostile elements (a Siachen like scenario at much lower altitude due to the dense and heavily forested terrain). This was doubly compounded by a completely broken down chain of logistics and supplies. Most armies would have mutinied or surrendered in droves in such circumstances. The miracle simply is that the INA did not. The fact that they held on in such grim circumstances speaks volumes of their motivation and morale and can be attributed entirely to the credo of militant nationalism.

Students of military history may kindly note that this Army was not receiving any pay but just pocket money. The Hygiene factors of motivation were abysmal. That despite this adverse combat and logistics situation, this INA still put up a stiff fight , and retained its organizational coherence virtually till the bitter end, is by itself a remarkable feat and speaks volumes about their intrinsic motivation and morale that had been generated by the technique of militant nationalism. A fighting retreat is one of the most difficult operations to undertake and the INA proved itself in such a retreat across the Chindwin and Irrawaddy rivers in Burma. In Mount Popa , it was to fight exceptionally well. It speaks volumes of the motivational methodology of Militant Nationalism that it had picked up from the German and Japanese armies. The degree of success achieved in such a short time frame in raising this force , integrating it and fielding it in a highly unfavourable and hostile combat environment, is indeed remarkable. I repeat, the *British and Australian and British Indian Army Divisions had disintegrated far more quickly in such adverse operational conditions with air and naval superiority entirely with the enemy during the fighting in Malaya, Singapore and Burma in 1942.* The Japanese had forced them all into an ignominious rout and surrender in just three months. The combined Japanese and INA Forces had launched a blistering attack in 1944 and almost succeeded in Imphal and Kohima. They then had to fight a grim, rearguard action that lasted almost a year and a half till Aug 1945 when atom bombs and the massive Russian intervention brought the war against Japan to a bitter end. I reiterate, that by the time the composite Japanese – INA force had launched its offensive in 1944, it had completely lost air and naval supremacy. Its lines of communications had become over – extended, whereas the lines of communication of the British had shortened immensely. Also they now had the support of the gigantic Military – Industrial complex of the USA. Despite this, the miracle is that the INA still put up a fairly credible combat performance, in such an adverse situation. Viewed in isolation from its situational context, some military commentators may categorize the combat performance of the INA as indifferent. I afraid they are missing the entire point. The combat performance has to be judged in the light of the highly adverse air and sea power situation of the composite Japanese – INA Force and its mind- boggling logistical constraints.

Composite Culture of the INA

The awards of the INA give an inkling of its composite culture where Urdu (Hindustani) was incorporated in a big way as a language of martial expression. Thus, it had bravery awards like 'Shaheed-e-Bharat', 'Sher-e-Hind', 'Tagma-e-Shatrunash', 'Tagma-e-Bahaduri', etc. Its motto was

Ittehad, itmad and *Qurbani-* (Unity, Faith and Sacrifice) which makes it far closer to the Pakistani Army's motto today (less the last factor of *Jihad fi Sabilullah-* added by Gen Zia ul Haq.)

THE COMPOSITE CULTURE OF INA

Awards

Shaheed e Bharat
Sher e Hind
Tagma e Shatrunash
Tagma e Bahaduri
Sardar e Jung
Shaheed e Bharat
Veer e Hind

Organisational Ethos

Bose was keen that his INA divisions should fight like regular Japanese Formations and play a leading combat role in the invasion of India. The first soldiers to set foot on Indian soil, he was insistent, must be Indians. The Japanese were hesitant. They had little experience till then, of the combat performance of INA formations and their morale in intense combat situations. They felt that Indian Officers had military experience only at the junior levels of platoons and companies in the British Indian Army. Very few of them had gained experience at the battalion level and almost none had ever held command of higher echelons. As such they wanted to use them for the Guerilla and scouting roles and to carry out intelligence and subversion operations to turn the loyalties of the Indian soldiers opposing them. There was considerable debate and discussion on the roles of the INA and Bose used his influence with the senior Japanese political leadership to have his way. He was insistent that his INA be treated absolutely as an Allied Force, equal in all respects to the Japanese Army. The Indian tended to be so prickly on the issue of prestige, that *the Japanese Army was forced to issue a pamphlet/ handbook to their units on how to deal with their Indian comrades who were apparently so touchy and quick to take offence*! Peter Fay writes in his book, The Forgotten Army, that the Japanese had issued a handbook that made no bones about the trouble that could be expected when dealing with Indians. Its aim was to tell the Japanese soldiers how they should "feel and act" when they encountered the "Indian National Army". It told them not to treat them as a Fifth coloum, nor a convenient source of coolie labour but men fighting for the freedom of their motherland, fighting a common enemy with a common purpose. In short an allied Army. The handbook cautioned– "Years of deceit, oppression and exploitation at the hands of the British have given them qualities of mind and patterns of behaviour that make them very difficult to handle." It catalogues a list of things that Japanese soldiers should never do. "Never strike an Indian. One blow will destroy years of kindness" also- "Do not tell lies. They have extremely good memories. They remember who said what and where and when and having laboured under British lies for so many years are extremely shrewd at discerning them." To all those who have propogated the myth that the Japanese were exploiting the Indians for their own purpose and like to label the INA as stooges of the Japanese, should read this Japanese Army Handbook on how to deal with the INA. It is a revelation and an eye-opener.

The simple fact is that because of the prestige of Bose and his very high standing with the Japanese hierarchy, the INA was treated far better than the Burmese National Army (BNA) for which the Japanese local officers had thinly disguised contempt. In hindsight, they were not wrong. The INA stood by them through thick and thin, whereas the BNA deserted them as soon as the British gained the upper hand and very cynically switched sides at the very last moment. Bose's INA was actually a hastily put together force from former Indian POWs and new recruits from the local Indian diaspora. As such the quality of units was not uniform. The local recruitment was all from the so-called non-martial classes – mostly the Tamil indentured labour. Yet they put up a fairly credible combat performance. The performance, in all honesty, did tend to be somewhat uneven and a lot depended on the quality of Indian officers who were placed in command. The KCIOs (Kings Commissioned Indian Officers) and Emergency Commissioned Officers (ECOs) tended to do well in combat assignments at levels two to three removes from what they had held earlier in the British Indian Army. It is the Viceroy Commissioned Officers (VCOs) who were at times found wanting due to reasons of age and lack of adequate command experience. Bose however, tended to view everyone through his personal prism of intense patriotism and at times felt let down by some elements of his command who tended to break down under stressful combat situations. Despite these limitations, his very dynamic and charismatic personality, had served to weld together this rag-tag outfit into a fairly cohesive and competent force that did put up creditable performances in the roles that were somewhat hesitatingly allocated to the INA by the local Japanese commanders. That they did so well in the overall circumstances when the tide of battle had turned and the advantages of air power dominance and better logistics, all lay with the enemy – is indeed a matter for surprise. This newly and hastily raised force held steadfast virtually till the bitter end. A great deal of credit must be given to the highly charged and inspirational personality of its Supreme Commander. There was no question of it buckling up like the BNA and opportunistically changing sides in the face of certain defeat. It fought to the bitter end and by and large retained its morale and cohesion through a very taxing retreat across Burma. In the phase two battles of the Chindwin river crossings and the battles of Mount Popa that came later, (and for which it was much better prepared), it would go on to do surprisingly, rather well.

Autonomy of Outcome

Few Commanders have had to lead their armies in such dismal and adverse circumstances. By the time that Bose got to lead his INA in real combat, the entire tide of war had turned against the Axis powers.

Towards the end of 1944 beginning of 1945, Germany had collapsed militarily. The Japanese offensive in North East India had turned into full scale retreat. Despite these highly adverse circumstances, the Composite Japanese – INA Force had almost pulled it off against a far stronger enemy with much shorter lines of communication and total command of the air, in the battles of Imphal- Kohima. In grueling forced marches of over 200 miles and more in such difficult jungle terrain, the INA formations had kept pace with Japanese Army units that were reputed to be one of the best Infantry soldiers then in the world. In fact, the whole world was then in thrall of the "Japanese Superman," who was unbeatable in jungle warfare. Then came the atom bombs on Hiroshima and Nagasaki and then the massive Russian invasion of Manchuria . Japan surrendered on 15 Aug 1945. It was all over. Despite this total collapse and unconditional surrender of his war – time allies, Bose displayed amazing tenacity of will. He exhorted his field commanders that the outcome of the Indian Freedom Struggle would be Independent of the final outcome of the Second World War. It was primarily essential that an Army of Indians was seen by their people as fighting for the freedom of India. Even if the INA just managed to engage the British Indian Army in a battle fought on Indian soil– it would be sufficient to trigger a tectonic plate shift in the collective Indian psyche. It would trigger the process that would hasten Indian freedom. The primary role of the INA was to catlyse the process of liberation. Whether it lost or won would be immaterial, the Indian people had just to see it fighting for their liberation and they would be inspired to rise and do the rest. As such the Indian liberation process would be autonomous of the outcome of the Second World War. Whichever side lost or won – India would be free. This did not happen immediately as strict war – time censorship by the British, had blacked out all news of the INA and its gallant actions. The North – Eastern theatre of operations was far removed from the Indian mainland and the Indian people had little clue of the significant role that the INA had played in this invasion. Fortunately, they got to know of it after the war, when the British, in a most foolish gesture of triumphalism, decided to tell the people of an INA they had beaten in the battles of Imphal and Kohima. They wanted to rub Indian noses in the sand and if needed, stage another psychological Jalianwala incedent to overawe the natives. What Bose had predicted so accurately, now came to pass in February 1946.There was an intense wave of outrage throughout the whole country. Indian men had come to form the largest volunteer army in the world – sans any conscription. This Army was now being de- mobilized after the war. That is the time when its loyalty to the racially arrogant British rulers snapped suddenly. The revolts first started in the Royal Indian Navy. They soon spread to the Royal Indian Air force. The British will to fight simply collapsed when the mutiny against the British spread to the Army. That was the end. Bose had been vindicated but by then he was lost behind the Iron Curtain. Maybe he was tortured to death. Maybe he died due to the harsh cold and the forced labour in a Russian Gulag. We do not know. Maybe the Quislings sold him out, we do not know for certain as yet. What we do know is – his beloved India was Free. However, all that was then in the womb of a highly uncertain future.

Notes on the Size & Structure of the INA

So, what then was the actual size of the INA? The official INA history claims a size of 1500 officers and 60,000 men. Considering that it was a three divisional sized force and the standard division in the Second World War had a strength of some 20,000 men, it all works out rather neatly. The problem is that as per British Intelligence Reports, the INA divisions were not up to full strength. Yes, but even then the INA had a sizeable number of Command troops – the Bren Gun Carrier and Artillery Battalions and several MT Companies, Air Defense Companies and Engineer/Pioneer companies, besides Signal and Logistical elements. Besides, there were also the Recruit Training Centres, The Officers Training School (OTS), The Women's Battalion and the Body Guard Battalion. So, what then was the actual strength of the INA?

British Military Intelligence (MI) Assessment of INA-10 November 1944

The British War Office has declassified its MI Assessment of 10 November 1944 and provides a detailed assessment of the INA strength in 1944 after Bose had reorganized the INA. The document states –

"In 1942 we estimated that about 15,000 POW (Prisoners of War) might have been suborned, or more possibly coerced into joining the INA. A revised estimate is 41,500. This is based upon the reports of agents and escapees. The latest Axsis broadcast claims a strength of 200,000. As the total number of POW the Japanese had was 70,000, this figure could be attained by extensive recruitment of largely indifferent civilian material". Thus, the British Intelligence estimates are somewhat tentative. Hard intelligence indicates a strength of some 41,500. This was when the INA had just its First Division of four brigades and the Second Division had almost completed raising. Subsequently, a Third INA Division was added. Even if an under-strength division is catered, it could still have a strength of some 7000-10,000 on the lower side. So, a final INA strength of some 51- 52,000 is plausible. The INA official history figure of 60,000 therefore is perhaps not too wide off the mark, as the British Indian Army's MI report itself does not discount higher figures.

Rash Behari Bose and Subhas Chandra Bose Life, Thought and Action in Comparative Perspective

Sumit Mukherjee

The spectacular achievements of the Indian National Army, commanded by Netaji Subhas Chandra Bose, have attracted the attention and interest of historians, scholars and researchers. While the life of Subhas Chandra Bose was replete with breath taking adventures, it was equally so with Rash Behari Bose who invited Subhas to come over to East Asia and assume command of the INA. The life of Rash Behari was most fascinating and the incredible way he evaded imprisonment a number of times and ultimately escaped from India disguised as P.N. Tagore, compares favourably with the Great Escape of Subhas from house arrest on January 16, 1941. Unfortunately, the life and work of Rash Behari has not received requisite emphasis and no comparative study of the same with respect to Subhas Chandra Bose has been produced so far in historical perspective. The present paper is a modest attempt as a comparative analysis of the life and thought of the two prominent Indian revolutionaries in East Asia. It endeavours to establish that the two Boses had a meeting of minds not only with regard to the idea of revolution and agenda of struggle for India's freedom but also their vision of independent India. While Subhas was not a political thinker or system builder in the strict sense of the term, yet, he did have a reflective and thoughtful orientation and articulated his thoughts about post Independence India, albeit incompletely, in his book *The Indian Struggle.* Rash Behari was predominantly an activist and his hectic political career left him little scope for thoughtful reflection, but he too had certain clear-cut ideas about India's future which bore a striking resemblance to those of Subhas. Moreover, their revolutionary inheritance was identical and their outlook on British rule and conception of the most feasible and effective strategy to achieve India's freedom were akin in many respects. They have been criticised as utopian revolutionaries who dreamt of the impossible. However, on closer scrutiny of historical facts, it appears that they were pragmatic rather than utopian who provided an ingenious and novel agenda for India's emancipation from British imperialism.

Inheritors of the Same Legacy

Rash Behari Bose was the trusted comrade of the famous revolutionary of Bengal, Jatin Mukherjee, also known as Bagha Jatin, who ought to be remembered not for his heroic self-immolation in the battle of Buri Balam in 1915, but for his new and dynamic revolutionary line which envisaged armed struggle through mass awakening and incitement of a spirit of revolt in the British Indian Army which was the strongest bastion of British Colonial Administration. Aurobindo Ghosh prior to his departure to Pondicherry held identical views. He held both Jatin Mukherjee and Rash Behari Bose in high esteem. Subhas considered Aurobindo his spiritual Guru, as stated in his letter to Sarat Chandra Bose, though Aurobindo's retirement from political life disillusioned him. Probably, he did meet Jatin Mukherjee once during his student days in a mess at 3, Mirzapur Street, Kolkata, as testified by Narendra Narayan Chakravarti.[1] However, at that point of time, he was not inspired by any revolutionary fervour as he was under the influence of Suresh Chandra Banerji who was devoted to non-violence and constructive work. From the testimony of the noted revolutionary Bhupendra Kumar Dutt of *Jugantar* group, it is known that once when he was relating to Hemanta Kumar Sarkar, a close friend of Subhas, how Jatin Mukherjee who seemed to be the embodiment of the Emancipated Soul of the *Gita,* inspired them with the ideal of self – sacrifice for the freedom of their country, Subhas who was present on the occasion, was visibly moved and was stunned into silence.[2] It is not known for certain, whether he was influenced by Bagha Jatin's idea of revolution at that point of time, though his grandson Prithwindranath Mukherjee claims that after a night's reflection, Subhas asked Bhupendra Kumar Dutt to inform Bagha Jatin that he would follow his path. No such testimony has been provided by Dutt himself and the above claim is most doubtful. At the same time, it is a fact that Subhas had great admiration for Bagha Jatin and while presiding over a function in memory of the latter at Albert Hall, Kolkata on September 9, 1929, paid respectful tributes to him.[3] When and how he became acquainted with Bagha Jatin's life and work cannot be ascertained, because he did not have the opportunity of coming into close contact with him which Rash Behari had.

Jatin Mukherjee foresaw the imminence of the First World War, and contemplated the idea of organising guerrilla warfare for a massive insurrection against the British Government. He also wanted to ensure the participation of the soldiers of the British Indian Army in this uprising and established contacts with the soldiers of Fort William in Kolkata. He also envisioned a Provisional Government in India, exactly as Subhas did later on in East Asia. Rash Behari Bose envisaged an all India upsurge with the co-operation of the British Indian Army almost at the same time, and Bagha Jatin was also a party to it. The date was fixed for February 19, 1915, but it was nullified by an act of treachery. On May 12, 1915, he escaped to Japan with the intention of sending arms to India with which the mass movement would be translated into reality. Jatin Mukherjee planned to obtain arms from Germany, but the ship Maverick which was supposed to pick up arms from another ship Annie Larsen was unable to do so, and was captured at Java and thus frustrating his hopes. Bagha Jatin subsequently died a martyr's death on September 9, 1915, after a heroic fight in the Battle of Buri Balam in Baleswar. While his martyrdom deserves to be treated with reverence, the historical significance of Jatin's life lies in his idea of inciting revolt in the British Indian Army. After 1915, the Indian National Congress did not adopt any agenda for eliciting the sympathy of the armed forces.

In none of the movements led by Gandhi, was there any attempt to damage the loyalty structure of the armed forces. It has been rightly stated that, 'The attempt to make the army and the police loyal, was seldom tried by the Congress. Muhammed Ali had attempted to create disloyalty among Muslim regiments, but to no avail. Only those in the underground movement attempted to win over the army but even they did not gain much success. The real success was achieved only later in Malaya by Netaji Bose.'[4] Not only Jatin Mukherjee and Rash Behari, but also the revolutionaries like Madam Cama, Shyamaji Krishna Verma, Raja Mahendra Pratap etc. strove for the mobilisation of international sympathy and support for India's freedom struggle and were prepared to accept foreign help for the Indian cause. Here, Subhas fell in line with them and the INA upsurge was a continuation, affirmation and vindication of the legacy of Bagha Jatin, Rash Behari Bose and others. Thus, Dr. Jadugopal Mukherjee has stated in a letter dated June 16, 1951 that Subhas Chandra Bose's effort was a reenactment of the 1915 drama staged by Jatin Mukherjee. [5] It can be asserted in the same vein that the INA venture was the final attempt to fulfil the unrealized dream of Rash Behari Bose, which was by no means utopian. Sir Charles Teggart, the Police Commissioner of Bengal who paid respects to Bagha Jatin in the Battle of Buri Balam, has admitted that while the visionary was stronger than the realist in the character of revolutionaries, like Jatin Mukherjee, their driving power was immense. Moreover, if 10,000 soldiers had been able to receive training in the Burma-Thailand border and shipment of arms to Chittagong had succeeded, England might have lost in the First World War. [6] It is also a historical fact that Jatin Mukherjee met Rash Behari at Dakshineswar and asked him whether he would be able to capture Fort William and the latter answered in the affirmative. He immediately cultivated rapport with Mansa Singh of Fort William and it is a matter of conjecture as to what would have happened had this materialised. It was also in consultation with Jatin Mukherjee that Rash Behari made strenuous efforts to incite rebellion in the armed forces in North India. With the escape of Rash Behari to Japan and the martyrdom of Jatin Mukherjee, the agenda of enlisting the support of the armed forces and striking at the strongest point of the power base of British Imperialism, was consigned to oblivion. The INA upsurge signified the resurgence of this legacy.

Cementing of the Revolutionary Bond between Rash Behari and Subhas Chandra Bose

It is known that Rash Behari wrote a letter to Subhas after his election as the Congress President in 1938, where he expressed his faith in the latter's leadership. Rash Behari had been keeping track of the developments in India after his escape to Japan, and the largest single factor which strengthened his confidence in Subhas was his disillusionment with Gandhi and the efficacy of the method of non- violent struggle. In April 1934, Rash Behari wrote that "Subhas Chandra Bose is a prominent leader of India's independence movement and is highly respected by the Indian youth."[7] He added that the Indian residents in Japan unanimously supported Subhas. Gandhi's role at the Second Round Table Conference of 1931, in London, was severely criticised by Rash Behari. In an article entitled 'Concessions by Gandhi and India's Independence Movement' in *Nihon Shinron,* he said that Gandhi was an admirer of England within his heart. From around this time, he began to pin his hopes on Subhas.[8] Explicating the limited efficacy of non- violence, Rash Behari wrote in *Nihon Nihonjn* that Gandhi's ideology was important as a first step to create awareness among the masses but non- violence had its limitations in India's independence movement. [9] Then, again in his article 'India and Gandhi' in *Gakan,* in April 1929, Rash Behari provided a singularly dispassionate analysis of Gandhi, saying that 'in India, sacrifice has always been highly rated from the older days. Mr. Gandhi perhaps cannot be rated highly as a scholar, as a politician or as an eloquent speaker, but his greatest asset is his spirit of sacrifice. The intellectuals monopolised the independence movement till Gandhi emerged on the Indian political scene. Based on his personality, he visualised the independence movement. The credit goes to him. Even today Gandhi's name is known widely among the poorest of the poor living in the remotest of areas. It is a big mistake to regard Gandhi just as a politician; he is a religious leader and a humanist. His objective was not just the independence of India, but that of the entire mankind, to guide it to happiness.'[10] This largely reflects the spirit of Subhas's attitude and response to Gandhi. Observing the 75th birth anniversary of Gandhi on October 2, 1943, Subhas had said, 'It is no exaggeration to say that if in 1920, he had not come forward with his new weapon of struggle, India would perhaps have been still prostrate. Since, 1920, the Indian People have learnt two things from Mahatma Gandhi, which are the indispensable preconditions for the attainment of independence. They have first of all, learnt national self respect and self confidence as a result of which, revolutionary fervour is now blazing in their hearts. Secondly, they have now got a country wide organization which reaches the remotest village of India.'[11] Then again in the concluding part of his Presidential Speech at the Haripura Congress, Subhas paid an eloquent tribute to Gandhi saying that, 'We need him for the cause of India's independence. What is more, we need him for the cause of humanity. Ours is a struggle not only against British Imperialism but World Imperialism as well, of which the former is the keystone.' [12] In 1940, Rash Behari expressed his preference for Subhas ahead of Gandhi first in *Miyako* on July 4, 1940, saying that, 'Gandhi is a person whom I respect, but he is an Indian saint and a person of yesterday while Subhas Chandra Bose is the person of today' and then again in *Yomiuri-Chugai Nippo*, the very next day, saying that, 'I think Subhas Chandra Bose is an even better politician than Gandhi.'[13] While neither Rash Behari nor Subhas belittled the significance of Gandhi's role in India's freedom struggle, they both were irrevocably convinced that India's emancipation would not be achieved under Gandhi's leadership. Thus, Subhas in his assessment of Gandhi's role in the freedom movement said with dispassionate candour that, 'Mahatma Gandhi has rendered and will continue to render phenomenal service to his country. But India's salvation will not be achieved under his leadership.[14] This was also what Rash Behari Bose felt in the heart of his hearts. It may be noted that on September 21,1922, Rash Behari wrote a letter to the editor of *Young India* where he asked incisively whether a single instance could be cited where foreign rule has been established with the consent of the people. He contended that there was nothing in between freedom and subjection. Thus, it was necessary to sever all connections with the

English. It has been stated rightly that Subhas realised this after 1939 which resulted in his confrontation with the Gandhian Wing. However, Gandhi himself appears to have realised it in 1942 when he gave the call for 'Quit India'.[15] This belated realisation is considered by some to be Gandhi's gift to Subhas who had by then left India. In fact, it was also a belated vindication of Rash Behari Bose.

We are On the Same Boat Brothers: Reaffirmation of Rash Behari's Faith in Subhas Chandra Bose

In 1938, Subhas Chandra Bose was elected as the President of the Indian National Congress. In a letter to him from Tokyo dated January 25, 1938, Rash Behari Bose congratulated him heartily saying that he was proud of Subhas and expected him to give a definite lead to the Congress for the attainment of the goal of Independence. He wanted the Congress to be transformed from an evolutionary to a revolutionary body. He also argued forcefully against making a fetish of non- violence. He remarked sarcastically that 'The non-violent atmosphere is simply making Indians womanly men. No nation in the present world should think of non- violence if it wants to exist as a self-respecting member of the world.[16] This was a most derogatory dig at Gandhi because despite all its limitations, non-violence did not make the Indians effeminate or weak. It was a doctrine of soul-force which was a source of strength, not weakness. Even Subhas never denigrated non-violence as a gospel of weakness. Rash Behari had a valid point when he said that "Our difficulty had been the 'other worldliness' dinned into our ears for such a long period. Instead of 'other worldliness', we must have 'this worldliness' first as Swami Vivekananda preached. *Daridra Narayans* should be fed, clothed and sheltered first. Let them have the enjoyment of the world first. Then we can talk of heaven." Though Rash Behari's letter was intercepted by British intelligence and did not reach Subhas, yet had he received it, he would have found in it, the most resonant reverberations of his own thoughts. He had himself observed that India's material and political downfall was caused by her "inordinate belief in faith and in the supernatural, her indifference to modern scientific development, her backwardness in the science of modern warfare, the peaceful contentment engendered by her latter-day philosophy and adherence to *ahimsa* carried to the most absurd length' [17] It is noteworthy that Subhas was critical of the exaggeration of the value of non-violence and did not castigate it as a creed of cowardice. He came very close to Vivekananda who too in his book *East and the West* took the Indians to task for constantly thinking about death and the other world. Like Rash Behari, Subhas too was imbued with the spirit of service for the *Daridra Narayan* and in a letter to Bhupendra Nath Banerjee from Mandalay Prison, he went to the extent of saying that he could forsake the work of the Congress, but not the service of South Calcutta Sevasram, which gave him the opportunity to serve the *Daridra Narayan* which none else could provide. [18] Subhas also shared Rash Behari's conviction that 'the Congress should agitate for control of the army first, all branches of the army. Education, sanitation, etc. can never make us free. Indians should first of all be masters of the army. They must secure the right to bear arms.' In the aforesaid letter Rash Behari urged the Congress to have a world outlook. Subhas expressed this most appositely in the last sentence of his Haripura speech saying that 'India freed means humanity saved.' Rash Behari further advised the Congress not to indulge in anti-Japanese movements saying that Japan was a friend of India and other Asian countries, and warned that a time may come when England would shake hands with Japan and control India, pointing to Japan, the anti - Japanese activities of the Indians in Japan's hour of trial. Presently, she was the eyesore of England and "International situation should be studied and utilised for India's benefit and interest. we should make friends with Britain's enemies. This should be our foreign policy. Sentiments should find no place in actual politics. Interest is always the basis." Though Subhas did not read this letter, his Haripura address reflected its spirit at every point. He stated clearly that India's foreign policy should not be influenced by the internal politics of any country or the form of its state. He referred to the Soviet example of making alliance with non-Socialist states. In a letter to Jawaharlal Nehru dated March 28, 1939, Subhas said in the same vein as Rash Behari, Foreign policy is a realistic affair to be determined largely from the point of view of a nation's self-interest. Take Soviet Russia, for instance. With all her Communism, she never allows sentiment to dominate her foreign policy. That is why she did not hesitate to enter into a Pact with French Imperialism when it suited her purpose. The Franco-Soviet Pact and the Czechoslovak-Soviet Pact are instances in point. Even today, Soviet Russia is anxious to enter into a Pact with British Imperialism.'[19] Thus, like Rash Behari, Subhas too had a pragmatic streak in him and was repugnant to ideological inflexibility. This was in striking contrast to Nehru who had a pathological hatred for Fascism and the Axis powers. The recurrent theme of Subhas's policy, particularly after re-election as the Congress President in 1939, and even as the leader of the Forward Bloc after his expulsion from the Congress, was the emphasis on the urgency of utilising the international situation to India's advantage. It may be recalled that in an article in *Hindustan Standard* on November 22-24, 1938, Rash Behari criticised the erstwhile Congress leadership for its one sided opposition to countries like Italy, Germany and Japan. He wrote, 'For the last few years, especially after the outbreak of the Sino-Japanese conflict, it has almost become a fashion for some of the Congress leaders to attack and condemn and abuse the Fascist countries indiscriminately. They do not know what harm they do to the cause of India's freedom. India's foreign policy ought to make as many friends as possible and to avoid creating enemies. Particularly they should follow the principle 'England's enemy is our friend'. They fail to take cognisance of the fact that by creating enemies of the first class Powers in the world, they simply help the British and the prolongation of the British rule in India. Britain supported Ethiopia against Italy. In fact it was a British instigation which led Ethiopia to offer resistance to Italy. When Britain found that her policy was not conducive to British interests, she at once changed her policy and sacrificed Ethiopia to court the friendship of Italy. The Sudeten problem of 1938 is the latest instance of how Britain changes her policy to her own interests by securing the good will of strong powers whether they are Fascistic or Democratic States. In international politics, self interests always play the most important part. It is not ideals however noble they may be, but actual material interests that determine the foreign policy of a nation."[20]

Likewise, Subhas too excoriated the British policy of appeasement on occasions more than one.

Rash Behari also made the point that 'For a subject country, dictatorship is absolutely necessary in a freedom movement. As in the time of war, dictatorship is indispensable, at present in India's struggle for freedom, dictatorship is equally indispensable. Democracy is all right in peace time, but if it is observed in war time, disaster may surely overtake that country.' Subhas expressed identical views long ago in a letter to his friend Hemanta Sarkar on September 25, 1915, saying that 'Germany has found an answer to the problem of adjustment of individual freedom with state control as in peace time the people enjoyed unfettered freedom but when the call came, all renounced freedom and presented themselves obediently and ready with arms.'[21] Notably, neither Subhas nor Rash Behari subscribed to the idea of unbridled dictatorship represented by Fascism and Nazism, but were in favour of emulation of certain positive traits of their national character. It may be noted here that when after his emergence as Netaji, Subhas gave the call for total mobilisation, he literally demanded that the affluent people should surrender their cheque books to the Provisional Azad Hind Government. In the course of his speech at the All Malai Chettiar and Other Merchants Conference on October 25, 1943, Subhas declared that 'Legally speaking, there is no private property when a country is in a state of war. The Government has absolute right over the lives and properties of its people during such emergencies.' [22] He also sounded a note of warning for some rich Indians who complained of harassment and were changing their nationality to evade financial contributions. There were also some who thought of paying the promised sum in small instalments so that evasion would be easy at some point of time. To them, Netaji's message was loud and clear. 'We have to carry out total mobilization voluntarily if possible, by compulsion if necessary'. Here, he did sound like a dictator but the allegiance he received from the people was spontaneous and not under duress, because everyone knew that Subhas demanded not a penny for himself but for the freedom of his motherland. The people never considered him a tyrant or oppressor but rather as the epitome of sacrifice and patriotism. He was the visible embodiment of the spirit of Rash Behari and the latter invited him to come over to East Asia because he knew that they both were travellers on the same boat.

The New Helmsman in East Asia: Predecessor Greets the Successor

It is claimed by some that Savarkar, the prominent Indian revolutionary showed to Subhas, a letter written by Rash Behari and advised him to leave India and to organise an armed struggle against British Imperialism from outside. The eminent historian Uma Mukherje has testified to Bose's meeting with Savarkar at Bombay in 1940, but has nowhere referred to Rash Behari's letter.[23] It is however likely, that Subhas realised that he would be inevitably imprisoned by the British and if he escaped, the opportunity would not be wasted. On January 16, 1941, Subhas escaped from house arrest and proceeded first to Kabul, then Berlin where he built up the Indian Legion. However, he failed to elicit the support of Hitler for the Indian cause. In 1942, he had a telephonic conversation with Rash Behari who had been made the President of the Indian Independence League in East Asia, but deprived of supreme power. Japan too was not initially very interested in inviting Subhas to come over to East Asia. Japan felt that Gandhi and his Quit India Mvement was sufficient to arouse anti-British feelings in India. When Rash Behari conveyed the Japanese position to Subhas over the telephone, he replied that if Rash Behari and Japan felt that Gandhi would be able to deliver the goods, they were destined to be disappointed, because Gandhi was always prone to compromise. He was not a dynamic, revolutionary leader. It would be a big mistake to inflate Gandhi's stature because ultimately Gandhi would never side with Rash Behari.[24] Eventually Japan did accede to the idea of inviting Subhas to come over to East Asia, and after a perilous journey in a German submarine from Kiel on April 29, 1943, Subhas boarded a Japanese submarine at Madagascar. Thereafter, he reached Singapore on May 6, 1943, from where he flew to Tokyo. Then, on July 4, 1943, Rash Behari Bose handed over the charge of the President of the Indian Independence League in East Asia saying 'I have brought for you this present. Srijut Subhas Chandra Bose needs no introduction to you, to India or the world. He symbolizes all that is best, noblest, the most daring and most dynamic to the youth of India.' The rest is now history. The allegation that Subhas disregarded the advice of Rash Behari and went to Germany first and then to East Asia, is totally wrong, because it was the initial reluctance of Japan which precluded his early arrival in East Asia. There is however every reason to believe that had he arrived in East Asia a year earlier when the war situation was more in favour of the Axis Powers, the independence of India would have been expedited.

The Founder and the Builder: Twin Pillars of India's Freedom

It has been contended that it was Rash Behari and not Subhas who was the founder of the INA and it was he who really inspired it. While it is indubitably correct that Rash Behari laid the foundation of the INA and prepared the groundwork for its spectacular exploits under Subhas, it should be clarified that Subhas's role in transforming the INA into a genuine fighting force, was no less significant. It symbolised the fulfilment of Rash Behari's unrealised dream and the completion of his incomplete task. Both were indispensable to each other. While ensuring for Rash Behari, his due recognition, one should be careful not to belittle the contribution of Subhas. It was Rash Behari who launched the first concerted drive to build up a movement consisting of Indian soldiers and expatriates in East Asia. Subhas built the INA on the foundation provided by Rash Behari. Dr Syama Prasad Mookerjee has rightly stated that Subhas was not the creator of the INA but filled up its leadership vacuum.[25] It may be asked, what would Subhas have been without the INA? Perhaps he would have remained obscured from prominence, and it was only as Netaji that he rose to Olympian heights. However, it is an equally interesting question to ask, what the INA would have been without a leader of his stature? History has already delivered its judgment.

References

1. Narendra Narayan Chakravarti, *Netaji Sanga Prasanga,* Vol. 2, Grantha Prakash, Kolkata, 1966, p. 48.
2. Bhupendra Kumar Dutt, 'Chatrajibane Subhas Chandra' in Samar guha et al, Jayasree, *Netaji Subhash Chandra Basu Janmasatabarshiki Smarak Grantha,* Jayasree Patrika Trust, Kokata, 1999, p.28.
3. *Liberty,* September 10, 1929, p. 8.
4. Wilhem Von Ponchhammer, *India's Road to Nationhood-A Political History of the Subcontinent,* Allied Publishers, New Delhi, 1981, p. 461.
5. Jadugopal Mukherjee, *Biplabi Jibaner Smriti,* Academic Publishers, Kolkata, 1983, p. 562.
6. Amales Tripathi, *Swadhinata Sangrame Bharater Jatiya Congress,* Ananda, Kolkata, 2000, p.78.
7. *New Asia,* Nos. 11-12, April, 1934.
8. Takeshi Nakajimi, *Bose of Nakamuraya, An Indian Revolutionary in Japan,* Promila and Co. Publishers, New Delhi and Chicago, 2009, p. 190.
9. *Ibid.*
10. *Ibid.,* p.191.
11. Vithalbhai Javeri and Soli Batliwala ed. *Jai Hind,* Janmabhoomi Prakasan Mandir, Bombay, 1950, p. 50.
12. Subhas Chandra Bose, *Crossroads,* Netaji Research Bureau, Kolkata, 1981, pp. 27-28.
13. *Nakajimi* n.viii, p. 227.
14. Sisir K. Bose *et al.*, *Netaji Collected Works* Vol 2, Netaji Research Bureau, Kolkata, 1981. p. 333.
15. Bijon Bihari Basu, *Karmabir Rashbehari,* Radical Impression, Kolkata, 2017, pp. 109-110.
16. Bose, *op.cit.*, p. 412.
17. Bose , *op.cit.*, p. 126.
18. Subhas Chandra Bose, *Taruner Swapna,* Ananda Publishers limited, Kolkata, 1986, p. 48.
19. Bose, *op.cit.*, p. 117.
20. Benoy Kumar Sarkar, *Political Philosophies since 1945.* Motilal Banarasidas, Lahore, 1942, pp. 337-38. **[357-58]**
21. Bose, *op.cit.*, p. 170.

22. Verinder Grover ed. *Subhas Chandra Bose,* Deep and Deep Publications, New Delhi, p. 380.
23. Uma Mukherjee, *Two Great Indian Revolutionaries,* K.L. Firma and Mukhopadhyay, Calcutta, 1966, p. 158.
24. Milan Hauner, *India in Axis Strategy, Germany, Japan and Indian Nationalists in the Second World War,* Klett Cotata, Stuttgart, 1981, p.544.
25. Umaprasad Mukhopadhyay ed., *Shyamaprasader Diary O mrityuprasanga,* Mitra O Ghosh, Kolkata, 1991, p. 68.

Origins of the INA: A Critical Analysis

Kaushik Roy

Introduction

Most of the scholars dealing with the origin of the Indian National Army (INA also known as the (*Azad Hind Fauj*) focus on the larger than life personality of Subhas Chandra Bose. Actually, Subhas Chandra Bose created the Second INA. The First INA was formed by Captain Mohan Singh. Mohan Singh's First INA comprised of the Prisoners of War (PoWs) captured by the Japanese in South-East Asia (mainly in Malaya/ Malaysia and Singapore) during 1941-42. Despite Bose's attempt to broaden the social base of his Second INA by recruiting South Indians from the Indian diaspora in South-East Asia, the core of even the Second INA remained the Indian PoWs. Support from Imperial Japan made possible the genesis of both the First and Second INA. This paper based on archival evidence drawn from the various archives of United Kingdom and Australia examines the structural defects in the Indian Army in the context of the first half of the Second World War which resulted in the ex-Indian soldiers joining the INA.

Structure of the Indian Army

Before the beginning of World War II, the Indian Army had 150,000 personnel. Within India, there was tremendous enthusiasm for joining the army in Punjab.[1] From May 1940 to September 1941, 5,200 officers (of them 1,400 Indians) were recruited along with 550,000 Indians as rank and file. On an average, monthly recruitment was 50,000. On 1 October 1941, the strength of the Indian Army came to about 820,000. Of them, 264,000 officers and men were serving overseas.[2] The Indian Army was a multi-religious poly-ethnic force. On 1 February 1942, of the 690,000 men in the Indian Army, there were 341,000 Hindus (including 57,000 Gurkhas), 239,000 Muslims, 72,000 Sikhs and 38,000 belonging to the other communities.[3]

Who joined the Indian Army and why? The Martial Race ideology shaped the recruitment of the Indian Army. According to the Martial Race ideology, only some communities hailing from particular regions were martial in nature due to biological and climatic reasons. The ideologues of Martial Race theory claimed that cold hilly frontier regions gave birth to martial people. Further, due to Aryan conquest of India at the dawn of history, asserted the Martial Race ideologues, only the Aryan communities had martial skill. The rest of the Indians were unmartial. The martial races for the British officers were Pathans, Punjabi Muslims, Sikhs, Garhwalis, Kumaunis/Kumaonis, Gurkhas, Dogras, Jats, Rajputs and Marathas.[4] Annually, five to six million Indians died due to disease. Malnourishment and disease due to general poverty actually made many Indians unsuited for military service.[5] The low standard of physique due to malnutrition as a result of poor agrarian economy was another obstruction as regards mass recruitment.[6] But, the Martial Race theory's spokesmen explained it through the lens of racial degeneration and climactic factors. The Martial Race theorists were not eager to recruit men from the urban centres. The Martial Race theorists believed that only peasants should be recruited in the army. And the small peasants joined the Indian Army mainly due to economic inducements.[7]

Pre-combat motivation refers to the factors which led one to join the army. And in-combat motivation refers to the reasons which enable a soldier to encounter the dangerous fire filled battlefield. The British in India for political reason never resorted to conscription. Military service in British India remained voluntary. Most of the Indian soldiers were long service volunteers. They were attracted to military service due to pay, pension and gratuity in the context of colonial underdevelopment.[8] The Indians were quasi-mercenaries. It would be wrong to argue that all the Indian social groups joined the army for pay only. For instance, the *Tiwanas* (Rajput Landlords) from Shahpur District in Punjab and *Garewal Jats* from Ludhiana District of Punjab joined the army because military service was considered honourable in their communities. Ethnic pride, clan, class and territorial ties motivated the men within the Indian units. Most of the *jawans* being illiterate and semi-literate had left us with few written materials about their military experiences. For the Pathans, fighting prowess was related with pride of their clans. The Punjabi Muslims stressed their *izzat* (personal honour). Historian David Omissi writes that *izzat* refers to honour, reputation, credit and prestige. Fame was linked with *izzat*. If a man performed valorous deeds which raised his *izzat*, he might be spoken of and remembered even after his death. The soldiers were also aware that they should fight well to uphold the prestige of their battalions.[9]

The British built upon such sentiments and created ethnic units. The British being an alien ruling power could not use the national sentiment of the Indians. So, they had to utilize the hereditary fighting traditions of a caste or a tribe to sustain the morale of the Indian soldiers. The Indian Army thus encouraged the tribal prejudices and caste exclusiveness. The British officers' technique of motivating the Indian soldiers was to pamper their parochial vanity and respecting the peculiarities of different communities.[10]

The Indian infantry battalions were organized as class units and as class company units. A class battalion comprised of a particular ethnic group from a particular region. The Gurkha Rifles were class units. A class company unit comprised of two to four ethnic communities organized in the different companies. For instance, the 2nd/35th Sikhs was a class company battalion. It had two Sikh Companies and two Jat Companies. Another class company battalion was the 2nd/72nd Punjabis which had two Sikh Companies, one Pathan Company and one Punjabi Muslim Company.[11] The different ethnic groups were not mixed within a company. Each ethnic community in a particular company was officered by Viceroy's Commissioned Officers (VCOs) drawn from that particular community. The VCO functioned as a link between the junior British commissioned officers and the *jawans*. The VCOs lead platoons and sections and also managed the interior economy of the units. Class units were more cohesive and combat effective. However, the British maintained class company units as part of their *divide et impera* policy. As Lieutenant-General G.N. Molesworth (Deputy-Chief of the General Staff, India) puts it: '… absence of homogeneity in India as regards race, religion, language which militates against mixing of classes indiscriminately. Northerners are foreigners in the south and vice versa.'[12] Organization of the different communities within a battalion prevented the emergence of any potential anti-British feeling within the different Indian communities. And the British continuously encouraged competition among the different communities within a battalion. Commanding class company unit was a problem as the British officers had to be fluent in the different vernaculars of the men. Still, the British maintained them as a part of political security. So, the British made a compromise between political security and military efficiency. Expanding the class community battalions was time consuming. The recruits just cannot be inducted wholesale in the units. Different communities had to be integrated in the different companies and to officer them VCOs of a particular community was required in a particular company.

Nirad C. Chaudhuri, a Bengali scholar asserts that the caste system within the Indian Army was more rigid than that which operated in the Indian society. The different ethnic groups were distributed in various units in such a way that they retained local communal and tribal loyalties.[13] Stephen Peter Rosen an American political scientist writes that the British separated the Indian Army from Indian society, by constructing regiments from a number of self-contained inward looking military communities with their own languages and habits. These self-contained units were separated from each other linguistically, sociologically and geographically.[14]

Again, the policy of the Government of India (GoI) was that men from a particular locality should be serving in a particular unit. The aim was to allow the friends and relatives serving in the same battalion. One assumption was that a *jawan* would think twice of displaying cowardice for the fear that it would be reported by his peer group back in his village where he would then lose face. Soldiers who had behaved dishonourably in the battlefield might also feel shame when they returned home. Omissi writes that shame was infectious and could be passed from the soldier to his immediate family. The people of his village would be disgusted by his shameful behaviour.[15] Second assumption was that men who knew each other would develop a better cohesion and would fight well. Sociologist, Anne Hoiberg writes that group cohesion was strong when individuals knew each other and had similar background experiences.[16] The Indian regiments had the characteristics of being an extended family. Family connections existed among many members of a particular regiment. Many men followed their grandfathers, fathers and brothers into the regiments.[17]

Discontent in the Indian Units at Malaya

The 9th and 11th Indian Divisions were stationed in Malaya in 1941. The 9th Indian Division which comprised of the 8th and 22nd Indian Brigades had many *jawans* whose mother tongue was not Urdu. Verbal communication not only between the British officers and the Indian soldiers but even among different groups of Indian soldiers were a problem.[18] One aspect of the commanders' function is to inspire and motivate the men to fight and die.[19] Inspirational leadership raise and sustain morale.[20] The *jawans* were willing to follow their officers to death if the latter had won their trust.[21] Due to the war time expansion of the Indian Army, many British officers without any knowledge of the vernaculars of the *jawans* and lacking military experience were inducted in the Indian battalions. The newly commissioned inexperienced British officers without any means of communicating with the Indian troops and the new VCOs and NCOs (who in several cases failed to communicate even among themselves) failed to win the trust of the men they commanded and to inspire and motivate them in the battlefield.

In May 1940, it was decided that to obtain the maximum efficiency in the new units as quickly as possible, the existing units were to be 'milked' of trained personnel. It was accepted that this would result in the existing units to be in a fluid state for some time.[22] Officers, NCOs and the privates need to stay together long enough to create a feeling of belonging and pride and to establish a relationship of trust which is an essential component of combat effectiveness.[23] But, milking increased personnel turbulence which in-turn reduced combat effectiveness. This process of milking was going on in the Indian Army on a large scale when the Japanese struck in Malaya in December 1941.

Further, the Indian units in Malaya were not trained for Jungle (forest) warfare. The 5th/11th Sikh Regiment of the 22nd Indian Brigade left Quetta in April 1939. All the officers commanding the companies were Indians. Harbakhsh Singh commanded the Manjha Sikh Company. The personnel of the 5th/11th were not *jungle* savvy. They were afraid of snakes.[24] The marshes in Malaya were filled with leeches and mosquitoes. And huge snakes hung on the undergrowth and slithered on the ground. Cobras, pythons and kraits were common. In addition, there were hornets and scorpions.[25] Jungle fear was not unique among the 5th/11th Sikhs. While moving through the jungle, the personnel of 4th/19th Hyderabad (12th Indian Brigade) were horrified to find themselves covered with leeches. The 28th Indian Brigade (2nd/1st, 2nd/2nd and 2nd/9thGurkhas) was raised in April 1941 in Secunderabad and trained for duty in the Middle East,[26] but was send to Malaya. As the troops were settling down at Ipoh, they were visited by staff officers of the 3rd Indian Corps. Brigadier W. Carpendale the commanding officer (CO) of the 28th Indian Brigade noted: 'I asked if unit representatives could be sent to a Jungle Warfare School. Was informed that such a School did not exist, and that it was not proposed to start one.'[27]

Let us see the state of weaponry of the Indian units. On 29 June 1940, the Secretary of State for India warned about the Indian contingents that these forces though considerable, were extremely weak in artillery and in automatic weapons.[28] In July 1940, the Chiefs of Staff Committee had warned that the troops from India were on a lower scale of equipment compared to the standard level. The danger was that such troops might get involved in serious fighting. India could not provide mortars and anti-tank (A/T) rifles to the newly raised units. And due to Britain's own needs and shipping difficulties, the War Cabinet was unable to equip these newly raised units fully.[29] The 5th/11th Sikh Regiment was not issued any A/T mines. The Vickers-Berthier which replaced the Lewis Gun and Sten Browning guns alongwith 3-inch and 2-inch mortars plus anti-personnel mines were issued to this unit just before the Japanese invasion. So, one can presume that the men just did not have much chance to train with their new 'toys'. Again adequate numbers of Bren Guns were not available. So, many Indian infantry units continued to use the Lewis Gun mounted in twins on a tripod for anti-aircraft (AA) purpose. However, these guns proved worthless in actual combat as they stopped firing after the first burst.[30]

The 28th Indian Brigade had no training in using A/T rifles. In early September 1941, the brigade concentrated at Ipoh. Carpendale then requested ammunition to enable the troops to practice firing their weapons, but the ammunition for mortars and Bren Guns was received only in late October 1941. However, no tracer ammunition was supplied. So, the brigade was not able to carry on AA practice firing.[31] Only in early November, each company in this brigade received two 2-inch mortars and the full complement of Bren Guns. Carpendale grimly noted: 'It is considered that the majority of the men had to go into action having fired only the minimum amount of rounds from their weapons. Under such conditions can they have had the confidence in their weapons that they should have had?'[32]

The Indian officers were angry due to the obstructions placed in the path for entry of Indian cadets to the commissioned officer ranks in the Indian Army. While one group of historians (who could be categorized as Imperialists) argue that the British were following a grand plan in slowly Indianizing the officer corps of the Indian Army, the other group of scholars (who could be labelled as Nationalists) assert that for controlling India, the British always wanted to keep the commissioned officer corps in the Indian Army a 'white preserve'. The

Raj was afraid, continue the nationalist historians that opening up of the commissioned ranks to the Indians would result in loss of British control over the principal coercive apparatus of the *Raj*. The nationalist historians opine that only due to the pressure of World War II and lobbying by the nationalist politicians, the Indian Army's officer corps was Indianized. Between 1919 and early 1939, only 250 Indian officers were commissioned. Again, the British prevented subordination of the British officers to the Indian officers by separating the units earmarked for Indianization. Also, the Indian officers were discriminated as regards command of squadrons and companies. Once the Second World War erupted, the Indian Army started expanding which raised the demand for officers. Not only were the British cadets inducted in the expanding British Army and to replace officer casualties due to the ongoing war, but the British officers from the Indian Army were also taken away to fill the officer slots in the British Army. Then, the floodgates opened for the Indians to join the commissioned ranks. Many Indians were also granted emergency commissions. Emergency commissions were also granted to British civilians from the Dominions in order to check the volume of entry of the Indians. In October 1939, there were 396 Indians in the officer corps. In January 1940, their numbers increased to 415 and in January 1942, the figure stood at 596.[33]

In 1941, the Indian Army was slowly Indianizing its commissioned officer corps and the commissioned university educated urban middle class Indian officers were politically conscious. They were vulnerable to wider political opinion. The morale of the Indian commissioned officers was seriously dampened by the racial discrimination of the British. There was a strict colour bar between the white men and the Asians in Malaya. Harbakhsh Singh writes: 'Everything for the whiteman was exclusive – clubs, swimming pools, buses, railway carriages, and even sheds against rain.'[34] Like Harbakhsh, Mohammad Zaman Kiani of the 1st/14th Punjab Regiment also noted the issue of racial discrimination. Kiani was General Staff Officer (GSO) III in the 11th Indian Division's Headquarters at Sungei Patani. He mentions that there was a European club in Ipoh in which the Asians were not allowed to enter.[35] After the Battle of Jitra (11 December 1941), many Indian officers and *jawans* from Kiani's unit would join the Japanese sponsored INA. When the 5th/11th Sikhs was deployed in Malaya, the Raja of Perak invited only the British officers for a dinner party. And the CO of the battalion Lieutenant-Colonel John Parkin went with the British officers for the dinner. This act somewhat embittered the Indian officers of the unit.[36]

Also, the issue of higher pay of the European soldiers disheartened the Indian personnel.[37] While a *jawan* received Rs 25 per month, a British private got Rs 75 monthly. While an Indian lieutenant got Rs 400 (inclusive of all allowances) monthly, a British lieutenant was paid per month Rs 600 plus allowances.[38] Occasionally, the British officers misbehaved with the VCOs.[39] There were cases of friction between the British officers and commissioned Indian officers also. The British officers behaved rudely with the Indian commissioned officers senior to them and the British soldiers did not salute the Indian officers.[40] And in Malaya, the junior British officers superseded senior Indian commissioned officers.[41]

Mohan Singh, a commissioned Indian officer of 1st/14th Punjab rightly noted that patriotism had nothing to do with combat motivation of the Indian Army. Its efficiency was based on discipline and tradition.[42] Mohan Singh described his feelings during the beginning of World War II in the following words:

> 'Our brave soldiers, who were going to be committed in various battlefields, in the East or the West were to fight as mercenaries, were not even supposed to know why the war was on.... We had not forgotten the bitter experience of World War I.... The British victory achieved through the untold sufferings of the Indian soldiers, further strengthened the chains of our bondage.... The fact was that Britain was not as strong in 1939 as it was in 1914, on the other hand, India had gone stronger many folds in the wake of World War I. We seemed to be in a better position to demand our rights. By this war, I thought, India was bound to gain, whatever the outcome.'

Kiani opines that most of the Indian commissioned officers were driven by pride in their profession rather than patriotism. Their sympathy lay with the Germans. The officers hated to serve in inferior position as subjects of the British. They understood that they were not fighting for their own-selves but for the British cause. And vaguely they believed that with the defeat of the British, things would change for better in India. After the British surrender at Singapore, Kiani joined the INA and rose to the position of major-general. The unfavourable conditions of the poor Indians compared to the labouring classes of Malaya further embittered the Indian commissioned officer corps. Kiani in his memoirs writes that the unskilled labour in Malaya earned eight times more than their counterpart in India. And the conditions of the lower middle class in Malaya were much better than those of India. They wondered why the condition of India under British rule was so bad compared to that of Malaya.[43]

Back in India, despite the rising tide of nationalism, Viceroy Lord Linlithgow was against any devolution of power to the Indians. On 21 January 1942, Linlithgow in a telegram informed the Secretary of State for India:

> 'I take very seriously, too, in reaching my conclusions… that further transfer of power would give marked encouragement to Quisling activity. Recent report from military authorities in Eastern India is to the effect that there is a large and dangerous potential fifth column in Bengal, Assam, Bihar and Orissa, and that, indeed, potentiality of pro-enemy sympathy and activity in Eastern India is enormous. Sarat Bose has been a lesson…. But Cabinet will, I think, agree with me that India … have no natural association with the Empire.'[44]

Sarat Bose was Subhas Chandra Bose's brother and the latter would later join the Axis powers. Linlithgow continued that India was in the British Empire because it was conquered by force and in case of a British defeat the Indian political leaders might be willing to make terms with the victor.

Even though most of the *jawans* were illiterate and semi-literate rustics, still they were somewhat influenced by the wider political currents in India. One of the dominant 'martial' groups of the Indian Army was the Sikh Community. The Sikhs were somewhat disturbed by All India Muslim League's (AIML) Pakistan Resolution of 1940 which was issued with the encouragement of Linlithgow. The Sikhs were concerned about their future due to AIML's demand of Punjab to be incorporated within the separate Muslim homeland of Pakistan. The Sikhs doubted the *Raj's* support in securing their interest.[45] And the personnel of the 1st/14th Punjab were not keen for overseas service. They believed that this war was not India's war. India was not threatened at this time either by the Japanese or Germans or Italians. Moreover, the Indian leaders were not consulted before the Viceroy declared war on behalf of India against the Axis powers. The *jawans* believed that they were being exploited by the British.[46] And this battalion would be one of the first to defect to the Japanese after the disastrous Battle of Jitra.

And the Japanese added fuel to the fire. Japanese agents were active in Singapore. They started a propaganda regarding the bad treatment of the Indian troops by the British officers. Their attempt to subvert the loyalty of the Indian troops had some effect. The 4th/19th Hyderabad had sailed from India for South-East Asia in August 1939 as part of the 12th Indian Brigade. Lieutenant Muhammad Zahiruddin of this battalion displayed anti-British activities. His assumption like that of Mohan Singh was that the Second World War would last long enough to exhaust the British Empire which in turn would enable the Indians to turn the British out of India. He was sent back to India. On 7-8 May 1940, there was trouble in the A (*Ahir*) Company and it spread to B (*Jat*) Company. The *Ahir* soldiers shouted slogans for Zahiruddin's reinstatement. The *Ahir* Company was disarmed. Finally, Major K.S. Thimayya (who in post 1947 India would become the Chief of Army Staff), commander of D Company handled the situation well and restored normalcy in this battalion.[47] Loyalty in the Indian units was on razor's edge just before the Japanese invasion of Malaya.

Conclusion

The Indian Army was a network of caste, clan and tribal ties. Structurally, it was unready to undergo a mass expansion due to the demands of the 'Total War'. In the specific context of Malaya in 1941-42, it was untrained for *jungle* warfare and underequipped. Further, massive expansion of the Indian Army due to the demands of the global war and the resultant entry of inexperienced British officers weakened the loyalty bonds between the *jawans* and the British officers. Encouragement by the Japanese officials and Indian politicians, racial discrimination by the British plus continuous withdrawals and defeats in the course of fighting in the Malayan Peninsula resulted in the sword arm of the *Raj* turning against its white masters. The demoralized and dejected Indian soldiers then went for the only 'rational' course of action left to them. Of the 60,000 Indians who surrendered in Singapore on 15 February 1942, about 45,000 joined the INA which offered them better treatment and a new ideological cause of fighting for their country.

References

1. Enclosure to the Private Secy. to the Viceroy, Letter no. 5178, 16 Sept., 1939; From the Secy. District Soldiers Board, Etawa to the Assistant Recruiting Officer, Lucknow, no. 418/SB, 21 Sept., 1939, L/WS/1/136, Oriental and India Office Collection (OIOC), British Library (BL), London.
2. Memorandum by the Secy. of State for India, 30 Jan., 1942, WP(42)54, Cabinet Papers (CP), Nehru memorial Museum and Library (NMML), New Delhi.
3. Communal Strengths of the Combatant Groups on 1 Feb., 1942, L/WS/1/456, OIOC, BL.
4. Note by General Molesworth on Indian Army Recruitment, 21 July, 1943, L/WS/1/136.
5. Nirad C. Chaudhuri, 'The Martial Races of India', Part 4, *Modern Review*, vol. XLIX, no. 2 (1931), p. 221.
6. Note by Molesworth on Indian Army Recruitment, 21 July, 1943.
7. Nirad C. Chaudhuri, 'The Martial Races of India', Part 3, *Modern Review*, vol. XLIX, no. 1 (1931), p. 79.

8. Sri Nandan Prasad, *Expansion of the Armed Forces and Defence Organization 1939-45* (Calcutta: Saraswaty Press, 1956), pp. xxviii-xxix.
9. David Omissi, *The Sepoy and the Raj: The Indian Army, 1860-1940* (London: Macmillan, 1994), pp. 77, 79; *Indian Voices of the Great War: Soldiers' Letters, 1914-18*, Selected and Introduced by David Omissi (Basingstoke: Macmillan, 1999), pp. 31, 41-2, 50, 53-4, 57-8, 126, 142, 157-58, 191, 236, 268-69, 294, 319.
10. Chaudhuri, *'The Martial Races of India'*, Part 4, p. 218.
11. Army Despatch from GoI, 11 Jan. 1918, L/WS/1/456.
12. Note by Molesworth on Indian Army Recruitment, 21 July, 1943.
13. Nirad C. Chaudhuri, 'The Martial Races of India', Part 1, *Modern Review*, vol. XLVIII, no. 1 (1930), p. 45.
14. Stephen Peter Rosen, *Societies and Military Power: India and its Armies* (New Delhi: Oxford University Press, 1996), p. 195.
15. Omissi, *The Sepoy and the Raj*, p. 83.
16. Anne Hoiberg, 'Military Staying Power', in Sam C. Sarkesian (*ed.*), *Combat Effectiveness: Cohesion, Stress, and the Volunteer Military* (Beverly Hills: SAGE, 1980), p. 232.
17. *Burma 1942: Memories of a Retreat, The Diary of Ralph Tanner, 2nd Battalion The King's Own Yorkshire Light Infantry*, R.E.S. Tanner and D.A. Tanner (Gloucestershire: The History Press, 2009), p. 53.
18. War Diary of 9th Indian Division, G. Branch, Training Instruction of 1941, 21 April, p. 7, 553/5/22, Australian War Memorial (AWM), Canberra.
19. Gary Sheffield, 'The Challenges of High Command in the Twentieth Century', in Gary Sheffield and Geoffrey Till (eds.), *The Challenges of High Command: The British Experience* (Hampshire: Palgrave Macmillan, 2003), p. 3.
20. Mungo Melvin and Stuart Peach, "Reaching for the End of the Rainbow: Command and the Revolution in Military Affairs", in Sheffield and Till (*eds.*), *The Challenges of High Command*, p. 201.
21. Ronald Lewin, *Slim, The Standardbearer: A Biography of Field-Marshal the Viscount Slim* (1976, reprint, London: Pan, 1978), p. 138.
22. Prasad, *Expansion of the Armed Forces and Defence Organization 1939-45*, p. 58.
23. Guenter Lewy, 'The American Experience in Vietnam', in Sarkesian (*ed.*), *Combat Effectiveness*, p. 103.

24. Lieutenant-General Harbakhsh Singh, *In the Line of Duty: A Soldier Remembers* (New Delhi: Lancer, 2000), pp. 85-6, 89.
25. H. Gordon Bennett, *The Fall of Singapore* (1944, reprint, New Delhi: Natraj, 1990), p. 7.
26. Report on Operations of 11 Indian Division in Kedah and Perak by Brigadier W. Carpendale, CO 28th Indian Brigade, p. 1, L/WS/1/952, OIOC, BL.
27. Report on Operations of 11 Indian Division in Kedah and Perak by Carpendale, p. 1.
28. Memorandum by the Secy. of State for India, 29 June, 1940, COS(40)504, CP, NMML.
29. Memorandum by the Chiefs of Staff Committee, 25 July, 1940, WP(40)291, CP, NMML.
30. Singh, *In the Line of Duty*, p. 91.
31. Report on Operations of 11 Indian Division in Kedah and Perak by Carpendale, p. 1.
32. Report on Operations of 11 Indian Division in Kedah and Perak by Carpendale, p. 6.
33. Lieutenant-Colonel Gautam Sharma, *Nationalisation of the Indian Army: 1885-1947* (New Delhi: Allied, 1996), pp. 79-81, 105, 107-8, 154-55, 165, 177, 184.
34. Singh, *In the Line of Duty*, p. 91.
35. *India's Freedom Struggle and the Great INA, Memoirs of Major-General Mohammad Zaman Kiani* (New Delhi: Reliance, 1994), pp. 14-5.
36. Singh, *In the Line of Duty*, pp. 92-3.
37. Report on the Fall of Singapore, G.W. Seabridge, p. 5, 25 April, 1942, WP(42)177, CAB/66/24/7, Public Record Office, Kew.
38. Chandar S. Sundaram, 'Soldier Disaffection and the Creation of the Indian National Army', *Indo-British Review*, vol. 18, no. 1 (1990), p. 157.
39. *India's Freedom Struggle and the Great INA,* p. 43; Srinath Raghavan, *India's War: The Making of Modern South Asia, 1939-1945* (New Delhi: Penguin, 2016), p. 286.
40. *India's Freedom Struggle and the Great INA,* pp. 42-3; Sharma, *Nationalisation of the Indian Army*, p. 195.
41. Raghavan, *India's War*, p. 285.

42. Mohan Singh, *Soldiers' Contribution to Indian Independence* (New Delhi: Army Educational Stores, 1974), p. 41.
43. *India's Freedom Struggle and the Great INA,* pp. 1, 13, 15-6.
44. Telegram from Viceroy to the Secy. of State for India, 21 Jan., 1942, WP(42)43, NMML.
45. Raghavan, *India's War*, p. 183.
46. Singh, *Soldiers' Contribution to Indian Independence*, pp. 45-46.
47. K.C. Praval, *Valour Triumphs: A History of the Kumaon Regiment* (Faridabad: Thomson Press, 1976), pp. 102-03; Sundaram, "Soldier Disaffection and the Creation of the Indian National Army", pp. 155-56.

Bose in Southeast Asia and His Negotiations with Japan– His Assessment of the Way Operations Would Result in Freedom for India

P. K. Chakravorty

Introduction

Subhas Chandra Bose was a leader who had extremely good knowledge of the British having lived in England, married a German and finally spent time with Adolf Hitler while the Second World War was being fought. His interactions with these people led him to believe that the British were not keen on giving Independence to India. India was the jewel in the British Crown which once given up would make Britain lose their status as a World Power. Therefore, they would leave India only when they were compelled as a result of revolt by the military forces who were their keepers of India. Keeping this as the Concept, Bose worked for a military plan to shake the British in their thought that they could continue to govern India and deny her its Independence.

The same has been aptly summarised in the conversation that occurred post-Independence in the Governor House of Kolkata between the British Prime Minister Clement Atlee and the Governor of West Bengal, Justice Chakraborty. Prime Minister Atlee clearly stated that the single reason for his decision to grant transfer of power to Indian people was Subhas Chandra Bose. This does provide crucial evidence to the importance of the need for military challenge to the British Empire. Indeed Bose was right that military operations by the Indian National Army would threaten the British of their capability to govern India.

Bose in South-East Asia – His Assessment

The *Azad Hind Fauj* referred as the Indian National Army (INA) was formed by the Indian Nationals fighting for her Independence in Bangkok, in June 1942. Its aim was to secure India's Independence with the aid of Japan. The INA was formed by Rash Behari Bose under the command of Captain Mohan Singh. The organisation was formed by Prisoners of War who had fought against the Japanese in their offensive against Malaya, Singapore and Burma. Neither Rash Behari Bose nor Captain Mohan Singh had the charisma which was needed to motivate the newly raised organisation and the same collapsed by December 1942.[1] Captain Mohan Singh was arrested and the Prisoners of War returned to their Camps.

Rash Behari Bose realised that a charismatic leader was needed to organise the INA. He invited Subhas Chandra Bose to take up the leadership. Bose was then in Germany working out a military strategy to liberate India from the British. In February 1943, Subhas left Germany from Kiel port in a submarine. After an arduous journey, he finally reached Tokyo in June 1943. Bose was able to influence the Japanese leadership, who promised the Independence of India after the War. Thereafter, he reached Singapore where Rash Behari Bose handed over the leadership to Subhas Chandra Bose. He became the President of the Indian Independence League and Indian National Army. Addressing a huge meeting on 04 July 1943, Rash Behari said, "In your presence today I resign my office and appoint Desh Sevak Subhas Chandra Bose as President of the Indian Independence League".[2]

Subhas Chandra Bose was not another leader in the freedom struggle, but a towering personality and maverick who provided an alternative concept of Indian nationalism that sprung up before the Second World War. While the rest engaged in civil disobedience, Bose felt that the only effective way to gain Independence was through military means. It is pertinent to note that when Bose took over the INA, the support was overwhelming from the Indians in places like Malaya, Singapore, Burma, Thailand, Vietnam and also Indians from the East Asian region.[3] On 05 July 1943, Bose formally reviewed the INA and announced its existence to the World. On 06 July General Tojo received a Guard of Honour from the INA. Bose pro-actively planned a three divisions force for the INA and persuaded Japanese to undertake operations in Arakan as also Central Burma so as to capture Kohima and Imphal leading to the rail head at Dimapur. On 13 July, 1943, Bose had discussions with the Commander-in-Chief of the Southern Expeditionary Force, Field Marshal Terauchi, on the planned Japanese operations. Terauchi offered restricted role to the INA in gathering intelligence and assisting navigation. Bose told Terauchi that the Japanese should only supplement the Indian effort and liberation of India by the Japanese would not be appropriate. Terauchi agreed that one INA regiment for the campaign as a test case. The success of this regiment would lead to employment in offensive operations of the entire force. Bose was keen on three divisions and was able to motivate people to join in big numbers. He gave his famous battle cry, "*Dilli Chalo*."

Subhas Chandra Bose was a revolutionary of greater stature than Rash Behari Bose and his value was apparent to those Japanese who met him. His leadership of the Overseas Indian Community was undisputed. The Japanese observed that Bose was convinced that the only way to expel Britain from India was through use of force. Bose had a charismatic personality which had an immediate impact on Chief of Staff Sugiyama, Foreign Minister Shigemitsu and Prime Minister General Tojo.[4]

On 27 July, 1943, Netaji Subhas Chandra Bose left Singapore for a tour of the East Asian and Southeast Asian countries. The prime objective of this tour was to enlist moral and monetary support for his movement from other countries, as well as the resident Indian communities. He was given a rousing reception in Rangoon. From Rangoon Netaji went to Bangkok and met Thai Prime Minister, Pilbulsongram. He won the moral support of Thailand and tumultuous ovation from the Indian

Community. He then flew to Saigon and addressed the Indians there. Returning to Singapore for a brief rest, he flew to Penang to address a rally of 15,000 Indians. Everywhere, he held his audience spellbound for hours with his superb oratory, and at the conclusion of his speech the people raced to reach the platform and pile up all they had before him – a total of two million dollars. This scene was repeated over and over in towns and cities all over Southeast Asia, when Netaji stood before thousands of people like a prophet, addressing them for the cause of India's freedom. Merchants, traders, businessmen and women came forward everywhere and donated their wealth and ornaments in abundance, to enable their leader to fulfil his mission.

In his plan for total mobilization, Netaji had outlined a grandiose scheme for an army of three million men. However, the immediate target was set at 50,000. The major part of this number would be from the Indian Prisoners of War and the rest from the civilian volunteers. According to Bose's plan there would be three divisions from thirty thousand regulars and another unit of twenty thousand– mainly from the civilian volunteers. The Japanese authorities informed Netaji at that time that it could provide arms for thirty thousand men only. However, by 1945, it was authoritatively known that the actual strength of the INA rose to greater than 45,000 men. After completing the task of reorganising the Indian Independence League, launching preparations for revolutionising the army, and after conducting a successful campaign to mobilise the support of the Indian communities throughout Southeast Asia – a phase which lasted from July to October 1943, Netaji turned towards formation of the Provisional Government of *Azad Hind* (Free India). This had to be done before the Army could be sent for action in the battlefield. This government was officially proclaimed in Singapore at a mass rally on 21 October 1943, where Netaji was unanimously elected as the Head of the State and The Supreme Commander of the Indian National Army.

The Provisional Government of Free India had five Ministers, with Netaji as the Head of the State, Prime Minister and Minister for War and advisers representing the Indian communities in East Asia. The first momentous decision which the new government took was its declaration of war on Britain and the United States, which was decided on the night of 22-23 October. Recognition of the Provisional Government came quickly from nine countries– the Axis powers and their allies. The Japanese Army promised all-out support for the Provisional Government.

Towards the end of October 1943, Netaji flew to Tokyo again to meet Tojo and to attend the greater East Asia Conference. Since, India technically did not fall within this sphere, he attended as an observer. He made an impressive speech at the conference, stressing the creation of a new Asia where all vestiges of colonialism and imperialism would be eliminated. The Japanese navy had captured the Andaman & Nicobar islands in the Bay of Bengal during the early months of war.

As a result of Netaji's requests, Prime Minister Tojo announced at the conference that Japan had decided to place the two islands under the jurisdiction of the Provisional Government of Free India, thereby giving it, its first sovereignty over a territory. The ceremonial transfer took place in December, and Netaji named Lieutenant Colonel Loganathan, an officer in the Medical Services, as the chief commissioner in charge of the civil administration of the islands. Soon thereafter, preparations began for sending the army to the front and moving the provisional government headquarters to Rangoon, in Burma. In the meantime, Netaji announced the formation of a women Brigade within the INA, and named it "Rani of Jhansi Regiment," after the celebrated queen of Jhansi, Laxmibai, who had led her soldiers against the British in an uprising during the First War of Independence in 1857. Coincidentally, Lieutenant Colonel Lakshmi was placed in charge of this regiment by Netaji. In November it was agreed between Netaji and the Japanese military headquarters that the INA first division and the civil and military headquarters would move to Burma in January 1944.

Success of Bose's Strategy in Persuading the Japanese and the Impact it had on the British

It was not an easy task to convince Bose to persuade the Japanese that the INA was to be involved in military operations. It was through his persuasive skills at all levels of the Japanese Government and Armed Forces that they were able to launch the INA in combat. As a matter of fact there was a hesitation to launch the operations as the Japanese were reasonably satisfied with their conquests in Asia and due to logistic reasons were reluctant to undertake the Manipur and Arakan Campaign. Bose was able to convince the Japanese on all aspects which was an extremely difficult task.

Being a charismatic leader, who believed in patience, persistence and persuasion, Bose used his persuasive qualities to convince staff officers, field commanders and political leaders right up to the Japanese Prime Minister on the issue of launching the Manipur Campaign. The Japanese weighed the pros and cons. Militarily, it was fighting through difficult jungle terrain followed by numerous logistic problems and possibly difficulties in providing Air support. However, one thing weighed in favour of the INA, this was the need for a Japanese victory after their reverses in the Pacific theatre. As it happens in all countries the political leadership has the last word, and the Prime Minister of Japan General Tojo agreed to undertake the Manipur Campaign. For Bose it was putting all cards on the table to ensure that the British were attacked on the frontiers of India to ensure that psychologically they felt insecure to continue in India once they were attacked by the Japanese and the INA.[5]

The Imphal Campaign has been described as the bloodiest battle of the Second World War. The INA lost 24,000 personnel and fought remarkably against the British. Colonel Claude Hugh Toye was an officer in the British intelligence during the Burma Campaign and had interrogated the INA Prisoners of War as a part of the Combined Services Defence Intelligence. He scripted his views in the book, *The Springing Tiger*, which brings out the courage and motivation of the INA. Despite having limited firepower, they rose to the occasion and undertook all their missions with Elan, Pride and Military precision.[6]

Assessment

At the outset, let us be clear that the British were in no mood to leave India so long as they could control the nation by using its native inhabitants.

There was no drain of British manpower and economically they were at a great advantage having a big country with rich natural resources under their rule. Britain ceased to be a world power, the day they granted India her Independence. Civil Disobedience is an issue, they could control through the Indian policemen and soldiers of the Indian Army. Bose understood this aspect due to his stay in England and his intimate contact with the Europeans. Rightly, the first war of Independence in 1857 shook the British East India Company and compelled the Government to step in. Accordingly, when the Second World War broke out, Bose initially tried to work out a plan with Germany. Having realised the geographical difficulties *vis-a-vis* Germany, he moved in for a coalition with Japan. During the interview with a few living INA veterans, they stated that Bose always assured them that their struggle will lead to India's freedom.

The difficult part for Bose was to make the Japanese agree to undertake the offensive against Imphal and Kohima. It was equally difficult for Bose to convince the Japanese that they should allow the INA to fight in battalion sized units and take part in active combat and not merely be used in a reconnaissance role. Bose wanted to prove to the British that Indians were loyal to India rather than the British Crown. The formation of the INA and their subsequent operations comprehensively drove in this point to the British. To continue to remain in India in a state of questionable loyalty of Indian soldiers would be incorrect and insecure. Bose appreciated these issues correctly, resulting in the British transferring power in August 1947.

Conclusion

The nation owes its Independence to Bose and the INA. Strategically, Bose was great in planning and execution. He correctly visualised that the British were not going to leave India unless they were threatened militarily. Thereafter, he strained every sinew in persuading the Japanese and raising the INA.

Thereafter, he ensured that the INA was involved in combat. They fought well under extremely difficult conditions. There were heavy casualties and this was the price they paid for our independence. Bose was a visionary who achieved his political aim. The nation remains indebted to him for our independence.

References

1. Sankalp India Foundation, "Formation of Indian National Army," www.sankalpindia.net
2. A Mani and A. P. Ramasamy, "Subash Chandra Bose and the Indian National Army, A South East Asian Perspective," www.apu.ac.jp/rcaps/uploads/fckeditor/.../RJAPS_V22_Mani_Ramasamy.
3. S. Priyadarshini, "Role of Subash Bose and the Indian National Army," www.historydiscussion.net/ historyof.../role...indian-national-army/2611.
4. Joyce C. Lebra, *Japanese Trained Armies in South East Asia*, Heineman Educational Books (Asia) Limited, Hongkong and Singapore, 1977, pp. 28-29.
5. Yasmin Khan, "The Raj at War: A People of India's Second World War." 6 Col. Claude Hugh Toye, *In the Springing Tiger*, First published by Cassell Publishers London in 1959 followed by Jaico Publishing House in India in 2008, pp. 177-178.
6. Col. Claude Hugh Toye, *In the Springing Tiger*, First published by Cassell Publishers London in 1959 followed by Jaico Publishing House in India in 2008, pp. 177-178.

The First and the Last INA Headquarter of Free India

M. Jugindro Singh & Y. Madhu Singh

To a patriot, there is no sweeter and soul stirring word than 'liberty'. It is only liberty that gives him comfort without compromise and to him any amount of sacrifice is worth achieving it. Subhas Chandra Bose belongs to this category. His Love for motherland was intense, genuine and super-supreme. Even the sacrifice of thousands of life would not please and he did the same.

As to the achievement of freedom, he held views, diametrically opposite to that of Mahatma Gandhi. Mahatmaji believed in non-violence but Netaji doubted it. Gandhiji wedded to his principle of non-violence and Subhas Chandra Bose instituted 'by all means'.

The very first meeting between the two front ranking personalities exhibited the difference. At that time, Mahatma Gandhi was a mature politician, best known throughout the length and breadth of Indian Sub-continent whereas Subhas Chandra Bose was in the prime of his youth covering only twenty four springs and least known. His only credibility was his inscrutable resignation from much coveted and lucrative ICS post. Gandhiji could not well convince the young mind and heart. Even his best words and explanations failed to clear the doubt of the practicability of non-violence. The second meeting between the two also did not fare better and proved to be even worse than the previous one. On his honest question that if he would bless his soul stirring independent movement, he had to remark, " If your conscience tells you that this is the best time to striking out, go ahead and do your best. If you come out successful, I shall be the first to congratulate you". It was the last meeting of the Indian 'pilgrim' with his revered great soul. Netaji did not come back in flesh and blood nor could Gandhiji congratulate him. He died without death and had become a legendary. But he could not be defeated and his eternal faithful INA heroes earned freedom to present unalloyed independence to Mahatmaji and his non-violent soldiers. Away from his motherland he went to Kabul under disguised name; reached Italy through the USSR and then to Berlin. From Berlin he was transferred to the east at the German cost. He underwent a 90-day perilous journey by submarine; reached Penang and then Tokyo by air on May 16, 1943. The unformidable Himalayan Ranges, inhospitable terrain, strict surveillance, waves of unpredictable oceans and towering characters in the persons of Mussolini, Hitler, Hirohito and Tojo could not check, rather gave the way to his ultimate wish for freedom struggle of India. Prime Minister Tojo had to assure "...to extend every possible assistance to the cause of India's Independence". By the end of December, 1943, Subhas Chandra Bose and his Indo-Japanese forces strongly supported by the INA heroes were at the threshold of Indian subcontinent, and ready for final showdown of freedom struggle.

Netaji Subhas Chandra Bose made a fervent appeal to all the freedom lovers of India, and particularly Manipur, to extend unstinted support to the liberating forces which had already strengthened at the border of India to march all the way to New Delhi crossing Manipur. The appeal made an impact upon the heart of Manipuries and was well received.[1]

OPERATION – U

The Battle of Imphal was conceived by the top ranking officers of the Japanese Imperial Army as early as in 1942 but had to be postponed for the time being. The proposal was renewed when Japan was threatened to strike out from Asian Mainland in the middle of 1943.

The executive order for operation of the Battle of Imphal christened as 'Operation U' was issued in the early part of January, 1944. Though delayed for some days, the offensive was scheduled to start in the first week of March.

The operation was entrusted with the command of Gen. Mutaguchi who prepared the whole plan along with his senior officers. According to the plan the operation was to be carried out by three Imperial Army Divisions.

1. 33rd Division under the command of Lt. Gen. Yanagida had to open surprise attack on 17th Division of Allied Forces by way of cutting Tiddim Road at Tengzang and proceed to Imphal. Another detachment under the command of Major Gen. Yamamoto was to advance up to Kabaw Valley towards Tamu.
2. Lt. Gen Yamauchi the Commander of 15th Division had to cross the Chindwin and proceed to the north-west of Imphal. Another Division was to proceed to Kanglatongbi to cut Imphal-Kohima Road.
3. Lt. Gen. Sato Commander of 31st Division had to proceed direct to Kohima and capture it before reinforcement.

The Japanese Offensive on Tiddim Line

On the night of 7/8 March, 1944, the headquarter of the IV Corps at Imphal received an alarming news of about 50 Indo-Japanese forces crossing the Manipur River. The local villagers of Maulnuam also confirmed the report and their presence continued considerably. On page 3, March 9, hostility opened at Tongzang area. The Allied positions at Phaitu and Richmond Park were also attacked; pushed to Tuitum (RP 1217) on March 14; administrative area at Milestone a 09 was threatened; the nucleus of Tiddim line connection was also cut off.

The situation, thus, sharply deteriorated and had to retreat in batches towards Imphal. Quickly the Indo-Japanese forces dug up themselves along the line of Tiddim road and blocked the retreat of the 17th Indian Division towards Imphal. Already Lt. Gen. G. Scoones commanding IV Corps ordered to withdraw on March 13. The Divisional Engineers finding no alternative, had to blew up as many as 5 strategic bridges and planted about 400 booby traps to check speedy advancement of Indo-Japanese forces. Indo-Japanese were handicapped further by the excellent air raids and tanks of the Allied forces. But the quick advancement of the INA forces destroyed all calculations and controlled a long stretch of 100 miles out of 162 miles by the end of March. All along the hill track of southern hill ranges of Churachandpur District and all the villages of Bishnupur district upto Potsangbam, adjacent to the District Hd.Qtr., Bishnupur Camp passed into the hands of invading forces. Thus, the Allied forces reinforced at Bishnupur Camp and throughout the whole of four next months, pitched battles were fought in and around Bishnupur, Toubul, Kwaksiphai, Potshangbam, Ningthoukhong, Moirang, etc. between the two belligerent military camps at Bishnupur and Moirang.

Flag Hoisting at Moirang

It was April 14, 1944. A warm sunny day of *Sajibu Cheiraoba* (Vaisakhi Day), Moirang looked like a deserted village. Many families of Moirang had already evacuated and left to take shelter at Thanga, Ithing, Sendra, Mamang-Ching, Omba-Ching, Khongjaingamba-Ching, etc. They were quite alarmed, tensive and painsive at the outbreak of Indo-Japanese forces. They hardly knew that Moirang was going to open a glorious chapter in the freedom struggle of India. The day before, Shri M. Koireng Singh and some of his close associates who where active members of Mahasabha[2], spent a sleepless night to witness the withdrawal of the 17th Division towards Bishnupur and remained in hiding under the Lamkhai Bridge. In the morning, (1) M. Koireng Singh, (2) L. Sanaba Singh, (3) K. Kanglen Singh, (4) M. Mani Singh and others went to Tronglaobi to meet the advance party of Indo-Japanese Forces and had lengthy discussions on the course of action. At about 5 p.m. Col. Saukat Ali Malik, Commander of the Bahadur (Intelligence) Group assembled at Moirang Kangla and planted the Tri-Colour Flag with Springing Tiger as emblem at the historic Moirang Kangla in a ceremonial manner as a mark of liberation of Moirang and its neighbouring villages from the British Imperialism. Moirang Kangla[3] is the place where kings of Moirang Salai lineage were coroneted ever since Phang-Phang-Ponglenhanba, the first ever ruler of Moirang Princely State in 52 BC. Col. Saukat Ali Malik, the commander of Bahadur Group (intelligence Wing of the INA) addressed the gathering and was translated into Manipuri version by M. Koireng Singh. The gist of version was, "... *The Provisional Government of Azad Hind had declared war on England and America ... The Indian National Army with unstinted support of the Japanese Government has now crossed the Indo-Burmese border and in the course of its struggle for the liberation of the people of India from the British yoke... we have now reached Moirang, the ancient citadel of Manipur. Our commitment is to march to Delhi and unfurl the Tri-Colour Flag there at LAL KILLA. Many had died on our way to reach here (Moirang) and many would die on our way to Delhi. However, expulsion of the enemy from the sacred soil of India is a compulsion for us... Freedom of india is very near, near at hand; we shall win it and we shall have progress and prosperity of the people of India after it... So, give us your hands; your collective efforts should cause India free from slavery.*"

As many as fifty participants including the Indo-Japanese Forces were assembled at Moirang Kangla. They were thrilled to learn that their hometown was liberated from the yoke of the British Imperialism and were appealed to donate either in cash or in kind to the liberating forces. They happily and readily volunteered to donate rice, paddy, grains, vegetables etc. and some of them enrolled themselves as voluntary corps under the leadership of Col.S.A.Malik.[4] In the evening at about 5 pm, the Indo-Japanese Forces were led to the residential building of Shri H. Nilamani Singh at Konjengbam Leikai, Moirang, and opened the first Headquarter of the Indian National Army of free India. The involvement of K. Kanglen Singh and M. Koireng Singh with the local volunteers was very timely, impressive and praise-worthy. They were able to donate as much as 80 mounds of rice, 40 mounds of dry fishes at the first instance, and were piled up at the outhouse of K. Kanglen Singh for distribution elsewhere. From the record, it is learnt that a large amount of food-grains was transported by head-loads, *Kangkots* (sledge) and bullock carts to Sunusiphai-Phubala where a column of Indo-Japanese Forces stationed.

By 27 April, the entire stretch of plain area of Imphal Valley passed into the hands of liberating army, except the strong and key positions of Allied forces in Bishnupur and Imphal. There were heavy dogfight battles in and around these key positions. It became clearer that the Indo-Japanese Forces could not succeed a speedy and quick win over the Allied Forces. At such a critical juncture and precious moment, the contribution of Moirang and the active members of Nikhil Manipuri Mahasabha is exemplary and bear the testimony of patriotic zeal and fervour.

INA Headquarter at Moirang

The building of the Headquarters of 1944, which was once the residential building of the late H. Thambaljao Singh father of H. Nilamani Singh,[5] is still standing today testifying the brunt of machine gun tides and bomb splinters. The adjoining houses and structures provided a very advantageous location from military point of view. The entire area covers five acres of land and surrounded in all directions by well-thatched roofs of houses in traditional style. Only the northern part opens to the wide stretch of Loktak Lake. Half a kilometre from the only living and busy Road Tiddim, which connects Tiddim (now in Myanmar), with the state capital Imphal through the dense forest in between. The inaccessible swampy portion along the fringes of Loktak Lake proved to be a good place for hideouts and provided either to sneak into the thick floating biomass of Loktak Lake or into the dense jungles in the nearby hill ranges.

The residential house of the late H. Lukhoimacha Singh is separated from the headquarters by a small stream Lt. Ando and other officers and members of Hikari Kikan were accommodated. A little away of, about 20 feet, from the headquarters on the left side, there was a large pit which was turned into Bunker. It was constructed well ahead of the outbreak of Indo-Japanese offensive. It was fully camouflaged by thick wooden beams and again strengthened with mud. The pit was about 30 feet in length and 20 feet. in breadth, perhaps the biggest and the safest bunker. Finally, the bunker was occupied by the Indo-Japanese Forces.

The Headquarter was well roofed by thick GI sheets and thick mud ceilings, flanked by two granary houses full of paddies (kei- Manipuri language) and the barrack of the Hikari Kikan on the left side. On the east, it was bordered by I.V.R and on the north a stream, the residential house of Late Lukhoimacha was on the south where the Indo-Japaneses forces and Hikari Kikan groups took shelter.

On the eastern side of the Inter-Village Road, there was also another one big pond covering an area of (12 x 20) feet. It was enclosed by green leaves and branches of tree and a tank was garrisoned there . The main area of the Hadquarter covered a larger part of 800 feet in length and 400 feet in breadth.

Structures of INA Headquarter

INA Headquarter was constructed in traditional Manipuri style (Manipuri Sang-Gai). It is consisted of 7 parts i.e.:

(1) LAININGTHOU SANAMAHI (FAMILY DEITY)
(2) EMA LEIMAREL (MOTHER GODDESS)
(3) JATRA YUMBI (MAIN PILLAR)
(4) KITCHEN FIREPLACE
(5) PHUNGA MEIPHAM (FIREPLACE)
(6) CHENGPHU (GRAIN & OTHER STORAGE)
(7) MAIN FRONT DOOR

It was well founded at the plinth level of about 2 ft. 6 inches in height. The height of the residential house was about 10 ft. above the plinth level upto the ceiling; breadth 11ft. and length 21 ft. The area of veranda was (16x21x10)ft. and consisted of Naktha (Women Handloom Place), Manggol (Central part of the veranda) and Phamen (Elders resting place). The other rooms were Ningol-Ka (Daughter's Room), Lukhum-Ka (Son's Room), Leimarel-Ka (Mother's Room), Phamen-Ka (Father's Room), Chakhum-Ka (Kitchen) and Sanamahi (Family Deity).Their location and room area was as big as enclosed.

The kitchen room was constructed at the far end of the residential building on the left side.

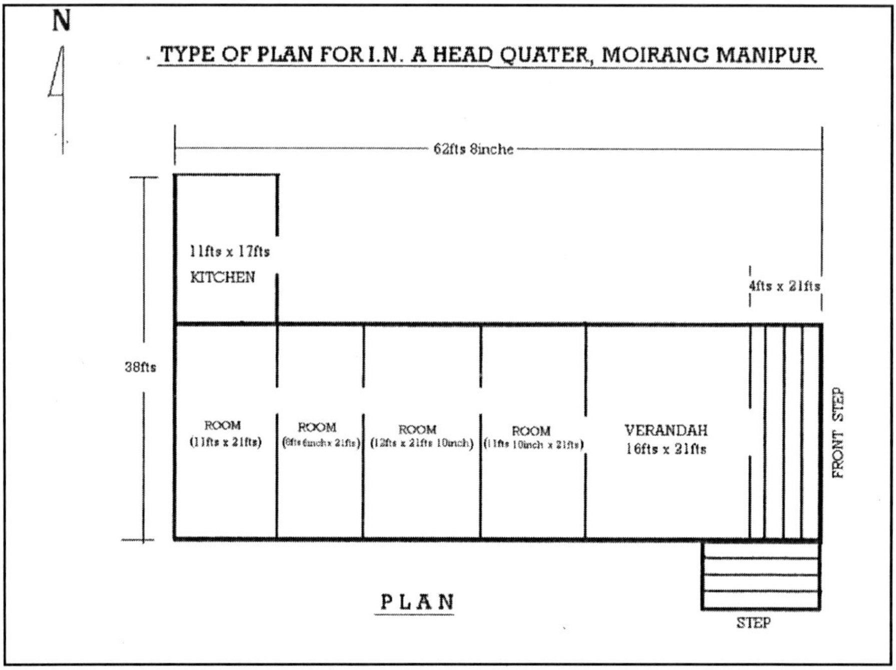

Circumstances Leading to the Establishment of INA Headquarter at Moirang

Towards the end of April, 1944, the advancement of the INA forces was checked by the reinforcement of strong Britishers fortified at Bishnupur. They were held up to the south of Imphal Valley, Bishnupur, and had to put up strong resistance and blocked at Maibam Lokpa Ching, Oinam cutting each other's line of communications. The fate of Indo-Japanese Forces hung in balance situation and face unsurmountable position. They were threatened total disconnection of communication, poor supply of men, arms, ammunitions and food. Forced non-stop march for a long distance of more than 2,500 miles away from Singapore without any rest, coupled with lack of warm and comfortable dresses and proper food exerted heavy pressure on their physical and mental health. Besides, inhospitable land, difficult terrain, continuous exposure to extreme weather condition and brunt of the battle front further deteriorated their moral and effective fighting capacity.

ROOM LAYOUT OF INA Hd. Qtr. - 1944
MOIRANG KONJENGBAM LEIKAI

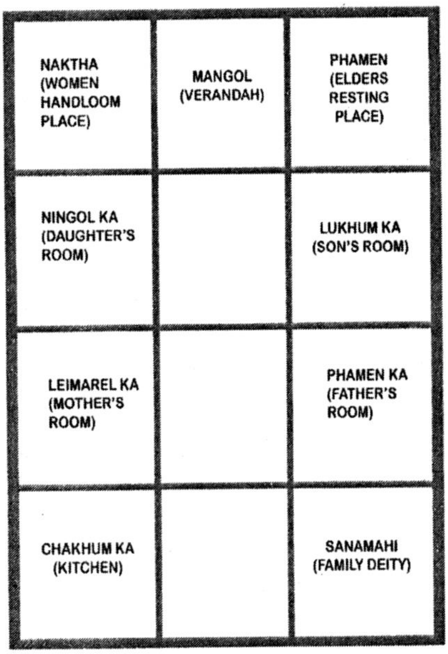

TRADITIONAL PLAN OF MANIPURI HOUSE

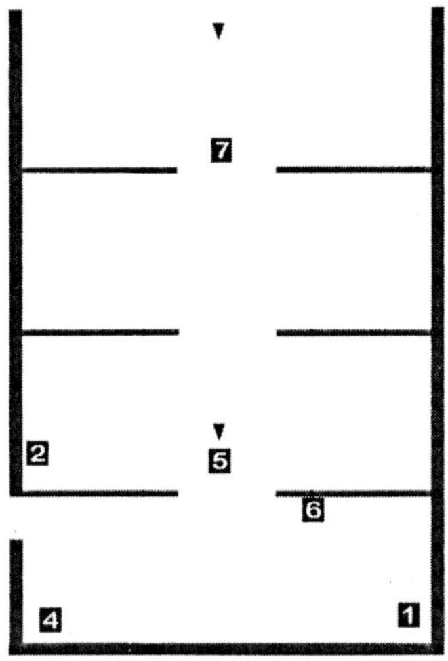

1. LAININGTHOU SANAMAHI (FAMILY DEITY)
2. EMA LEIMAREL (MOTHER GODDESS)
3. JATRA YUMPHAM (MAIN PILLAR)
4. KITCHEN FIRE PLACE
5. PHUNGA MEIPHAM (FIRE PLACE)
6. CHENGPHU (GRAIN & OTHER STORAGE)
7. MAIN FRONT DOOR.

SECTION OF EXISTING I.N.A HEAD QUARTER,MOIRANG MANIPUR

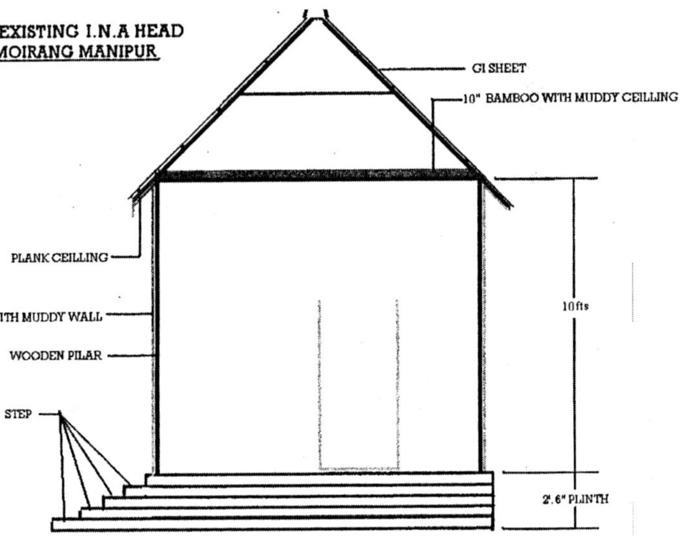

SECTION

TRADITIONAL MANIPURI HOUSE STRUCTURE

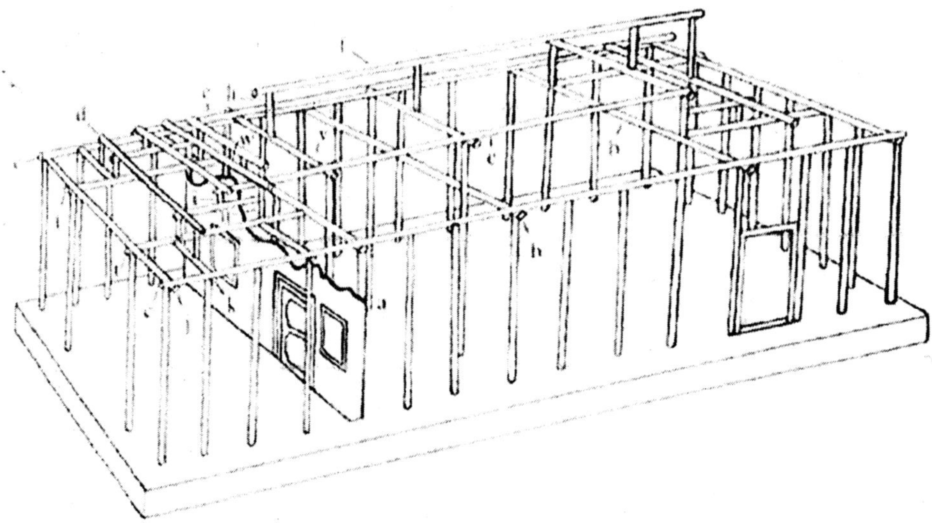

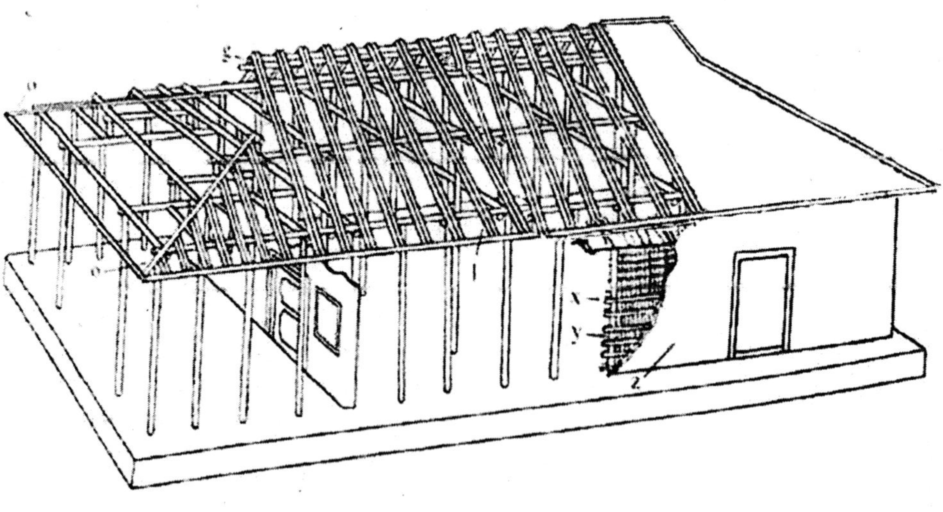

At such a critical juncture, the comfort of INA headquarters and service-minded natives strongly enthused with the patriotic zeal and flavour, proved to be a soothing balm to the uncompromised heroes who preferred death to surrender and chose bayonet when their machine guns stopped rattling for the want of bullets. The native people served in every capacity– as informers, porters, providers of service in espionage activities or as advance parties, and in terms of food. It seemed to be a prophetic word, full of wisdom of the great leader who died without death, the fact that once the INA heroes stepped on the sacred soil of India, they would be received with heroi's welcome, and the magic of the Britishers in India would be soon melted away. The INA headquarters at Moirang served the very purpose and that too in all possible ways and means. In the face of the threat of total deadlock of the lines of communication, the INA headquarters facilitated the INA men to have some rest and provided some comforts under the strongly fortified barracks, the safest hiding place in the bosom of Loktak Lake, shielding from bullets under the cover of GI sheet and improvised ceiling; provided dispensary and nursing services with provision for first aid, medical treatment and medication; treated them with hot and ready food, warm clothes like a home away from home. In the words of Shri M. Koireng Singh, a local INA hero and freedom fighter, "without the co-operation and involvement of the local people how three divisions of Nippon army and one Brigade of the INA who entered Manipur without ration could continue heavy fighting for three months against the mighty Allied Frces ".

The fierce battle with hand to hand offensive were fought in and around Moirang, Ningthoukhong, Toubul, Potsangbam, Tronglaobi, Gothol and Thoya in between the month of May, June and July and continued till the withdrawal on July 15, 1944. The surrounding areas of Moirang was declared 'enemy zone' by the British and shoot - at - sight order was issued and Shri K. Gopal Singh, L. Sanaba Singh, H. Nilamani Singh and M. Koireng Singh were declared traitors. All the 17 members of Nikhil Manipuri Mahasabha (13 members who came down from Imphal and 4 members from Moirang) were black-listed. The scorched earth policy was extended to all the villages from Torbung

(Phougwakchao Ikhai) to Ningthoukhong area. The areas between Moirang and Ningthoukhong were heavily bombed; many civilians were killed and injured; almost all the trees and bamboos were uprooted. Just in Moirang itself, more than 1,000 houses were set ablaze leaving aside five or six houses where the INA headquarter and the office of Hikari Kikan were set up, alongwith barracks, store house of grain, food and food kitchen, dispensary which met their needs, served their purposes and provided services and of course, where the Indo-Japanese Forces and the INA soldiers took shelter.

Conclusion

In its surface value, the flag hoisting event and the opening of INA headquarter of Free India is just a glimpse of the personality of Netaji all rolled into one. As the holy *Upanisad* aptly says 'where the boundaries disappeared, the oceans become drop, and drop turns into ocean'. The venture invites micro level study to explore more and examine certain historical facts and testimonies as is clearly exhibited by the INA headquarter, Moirang, which is still braving the brunts of battle. Still many queries are to be answered.

Was it planned? If not, why was the residential building with all unique features like GI sheet roofing, bullet and bomb splinters proof improvised mud ceiling, granaries, nature looking ready barracks, etc. built well-ahead of mid thirties of the twentieth century?

References

1. S.K. Bose, (ed.), *A Beacon Across Asia*, New Delhi, 1973.
2. N.G. Jog, *In Freedom's Quest*, Poona, 1969.
3. Kusum Nair, INA, Mumbai, 1946.
4. Jeofrey Mathews, *The Re-conquest of Burma 1943-1945*, Dehradun, 1966.
5. Sir Geaffrey Evans and Anthony Bret-James, *Imphal: A Flower on Lofty Heights*, London, 1965.
6. S.K. Bose, (ed.), *Proceedings of the International Netaji Seminar*, 1973.
7. National Seminar on Netaji and INA, Moirang, 1985.
8. M. Manindra Singh, (ed.), Souvenir, *75th Birth Day Celebration of Netaji Subhash Chandra Bose*, Imphal, 1972.

9. H.C. Shobha, (ed.), Souvenir, *Netaji Bal SenaVidyalaya*, Moirang 1997.
10. M. Manindra Singh, (ed.), Souvenir, *Golden Jubilee Celebration of Azad Hind Government*, Imphal, 1993.
11. Y. Modhu Singh, (ed.), Souvenir, *80th Birth Anniversary of M. Koireng Singh*, Moirang, 1995.
12. M. Manindra Singh, (ed.), Souvenir, *Birth Centenary of Netaji Subhash Chandra Bose*, Imphal, 1997.
13. Mairembam Sanjeeb, Shri. M. Koireng Singh gi Punshiamasung Thabak
14. Manipur Sahitya Samitti, *Thoubal Journal*, March and September 2004.
15. Dr. K. Sushila Devi, (ed.), *INA: Through the Lens of History*, Imphal, 2015.

Notes:

(1) *(a)*The message was brought by Dr.Gulapchand Singh the Medical Officer of Government Hopsital at Sungoo and handed over to Thokchom Angou Singh of Singjamei. Thirteen members of the Nikhil Manipuri Mahasabha, the only political party in Manipur which had identify ideology and objective with the Congress Party went to Moirang secretly. The members of Mahasabha working together with the members of Mahasabha , carried out espionage activities and collected a large quantity of ration. The supply of ration for over 1 lakh of Indo- Japanese Army for three months is a big contribution of the Manipuris to the war effort.*

(M. Koireng Singh, Ex-INA Freedom Fighter, Ed. Manipur's Contribution to the freedom struggle of the Country) Manipur Today, Special Issue Independence Day 1985.- DIPR Government of Manipur.

(b) Shri Hijam Irabot Singh, popularly known as NetaIrabot, was the president of Nikhil Manipuri Mahasabha in 1938. The Mahasabha became the first political party in Manipur that demanded a full responsible and representative government in state. "*The Mahasabha was affiliated to the State People's Conference under the Chairmanship of Dr. Pattavi Sitaramia*". (Shri M. Koireng Singh-Manipur's contribution to the Freedom struggle of the country).

(2) (a) Under the charge of his inflammatory speech on 7 January, 1940 to wage war against, he was arrested under section 124 (A) Indian Penal Code and put behind the bars for three years. He was transported to Sylhet jail now in Bangladesh. After three years he was released from the jail

in1943 but was denied entry into Manipur by and order passed in the Durbar.

The circumstances forced the leader to go underground. Longjam Bijoy, a close friend who worked with him, went to Cacharfo a rendezvous with the leader. A revolt was thus the Indian National Army of Subhas Chandra Bose against the British rule. As this was announced in the nation papers, the Government of India started rounding up several persons in Manipur. (H. M. BAREH- ENCYCLOPAEDIA OF NORTH-EAST INDIA Volume III Manipur; page no. 9-10).

(b) *"The British authorities suspected that the members of the Manipur PrajaSanmeloni and its active workers were collaborating with Netaji Subhas Chandra Bose against the Government. The Suspicion had been confirmed through the broadcasts of the All India Radio and some leading paper of the day. Many of the suspected activities of the Party were arrested and kept in the Langthabal Military Jail. They also charged Irabot for the establishment of connection with the INA and a case was lodged against him in 1944 in the court of the Assistant Magistrate under section 90 of the Defence of India Rules. The case No. was 987C. The case was continued for three months and Irabot was put in the Jail. Later in 1945, he was released from the Jail.*

(P.M. Singh, Editor Bhagyabati Patrika, Karam Manimohon Singh- *Ed.* NetaIrabot, a revolutionary page no. 158).

(3) (a) *"Sarva Shri L. Sanaba Singh, K. Kanglen Singh, M. Koirengsingh with some people went to Tronglaobi and met Col. S.A. Malick leader of the Intelligence group of the INA. Planted the Tri-Colour Flag on the 14th April 1944 at about 5 pm at Moirang Kangla, the sacred soil of India for the first time as a liberated area". – H. Nilamani Singh.)*

(L. Basanti Devi, Seminar paper – Origin growth and fall of the oirangpirincipality in South Manipur Valley) *"The actual founder of the Moirang Principality was Phang- Phang Atengpa,… His date as suggested by the Moirang scholars is 52 BC to 28 AD."*

(b) "It was only during the reign of Iwang Puriklai Phang- Phang Ponglenhanba, the 8th King of Moirang who was coronated on the throne of the kingdom of Moirang in 52 BC that Eputhou Harouba was started to have been performed for the first time by human worshipper."

(H. C. Shobha – Authour of Moirang and Ebudhou Thangjing, -Chapter 3 and President of MoirangThangjing Yageirel Marup)<M

(c)

যশীং	মিং		পাল্লম্বা মতম	চহী যশী ং
১।	ঈরাং পুল্লাই ফাং-ফাং	খৃ: পূ:	৫২-খৃ: ২৮	৮০
২।	" " তেনহৈবা	খৃ:	২৮ - ৭৮	৫০
৩।	" "লাইফাজেং	"	৭৮-১৩০	৫২
৪।	" " উরা ভাংভোই	"	১৩০-১৮৫	৫৫
৫।	" " সনা লখ্বা	"	১৮৫ - ২৩৬	৫১
৬।	" " লাইয়ুপুন্নিবা	"	২৩৬ - ২৯৭	৬১
৭।	" " তুশেম্বা	"	২৯৭ - ৩৩৭	৪০
৮।	" " থংবাই কোংদিং	"	৩৩৭ - ৩৮৭	৫০
৯।	" " থী কু নাচাউবা	"	৩৮৭ - ৪৪৭	৬০
১০।	" " নুঙনাং তোম্বা	"	৪৪৭ - ৪৯৬	৪৯
১১।	" " খোকথৈ লান্থবা	"	৪৯৬ - ৫৩৩	৩৭
১২।	" " উরা কোংয়াম্বা	"	৫৩৩ - ৫৭৪	৪১
১৩।	" " থী য়াং গী চাউবা	"	৫৭৪ - ৬১৪	৪০
১৪।	" " কোক্বা নুংহু ইরাং	"	৬১৪ - ৬৬২	৪৮
১৫।	" " চরনবা	"	৬৬২ - ৬৯৮	৩৬
১৬।	" " থাঙ্গ ইফেন লানথবা	"	৬৯৮ - ৭৩৯	৪১
১৭।	" " আংদোল থুবা	"	৭৩৯ - ৭৮৪	৪৫
১৮।	" " লাইগী ংথু	"	৭৮৪ - ৮২৫	৪১
১৯।	" " যমেম্বা	"	৮২৫ - ৮৬৭	৪২
২০।	" " কোইরেনবা	"	৮৬৭ - ৯১৭	৫০
২১।	" " কাবা-পুরাং	"	৯১৭ - ৯৮২	৬৫
২২।	" " ঈথাই কাইরেম্বা	"	৯৮২ - ১০২৩	৪১

... ৬

("Moirangthem Nodia, *Ed.* Moirang Salai {Moirang Clan} Secretary, Thangjing Yageirel Marup and Author of a book – "Chronology of Moirang Kings")

4. Statements of the Freedom Fighters :-

(a)

2 / मणिपुर के आजाद हिन्द सेनानी एक श्रद्धांजली

श्री एम कोईरेंग सिंह

श्री एम. चाओयाईमा सिंह के पुत्र श्री एम कोईरेंग सिंह का जन्म विष्णुपुर जनपद में मोयरंग के थाईम्बम लईका में 1915 में हुआ था। वे 1933 में निखिल मणिपुरी महासभा के सदस्य के रूप में सक्रिय राजनीति में आये और फिर 1944 में आजाद हिन्द फौज में सम्मिलित हुए। वे मणिपुर राज्य कांग्रेस के संस्थापक सदस्यों में से थे।

श्री कोईरेंग 1948 में मणिपुर राज्य विधानसभा के सदस्य बने। 1952 में इलेक्टोरल कॉलेज के सदस्य और 1955 से 57 तक मणिपुर राज्य कांग्रेस के अध्यक्ष रहे। वे 1957 से 1962 टैरीटोरिल काउन्सिल के भी सदस्य रहे और 1962 में पुनः चुने जाने पर इसके अध्यक्ष बने।

श्री कोईरेंग 1963 से 1969 तक मणिपुर के मुख्य मन्त्री रहे। इन्हें 1972 में पुनः विधानसभा का सदस्य चुना गया। वे 1979 में जनता पार्टी की मणिपुर इकाई से अध्यक्ष बने और 1980 में फिर विधायक चुने गये। 1985 में इन्हें पुनः विधायक चुना गया।

मणिपुर के आजाद हिन्द सेनानी एक श्रद्धांजली / 69

श्री खुमबोंग मायुम जुगेश्वर सिंह

थांग मेईबाण्ड लांऊ संगपुटेल लेइकाई, इम्फाल के निवासी श्री खनिंगबो ऊआओ सिंह के पुत्र श्री खुमबोंग मायुम जुगेश्वर सिंह का जन्म 1926 में हुआ था। बचपन से ही जुगेश्वर को राजनीति का चाव था। ये 1939 में प्रजा सोम्मिलोनी में सम्मिलित हुए और फिर इसी वर्ष चावल आन्दोलन में भी भाग लिया जिसे नूपी लाल कहा जाता है।

1944 में इन्हें श्री एस. इबोहल सिंह के माध्यम से नेताजी सुभाष चन्द्र बसु का एक पत्रक मिला जिसके द्वारा आजाद हिन्द फौज के बारे में जानकारी प्राप्त हुई। जब मोयरंग स्वतन्त्र करा लिया गया तो ये वहीं 1944 में ही कर्नल एस.ए. मलिक की कप्तान में फौज के खुफिया विभाग में सम्मिलित हो गये। जब फौज को पीछे हटना पड़ा तो ये भी उसके साथ ही यांगून चले गये। ये वहीं तब तक कार्य करते रहे जब कि 1 अप्रैल 1945 को म्यांमार पर अंग्रेजी सेनाओं का अधिकार नहीं हो गया।

यद्यपि जुगेश्वर छुप गये तथापि 8 जुलाई को इन्हें म्यांमार रक्षा नियम 26 के अन्तर्गत गिरफ्तार कर लिया गया। इन्हें यांगून जेल में रखा गया। जब 1946 में फौज पर अभियोग समाप्त हुआ तो इन्हें भारत लाया गया। इसी वर्ष इन्होंने मणिपुर में अखिल भारतीय कांग्रेस की स्थापना में योग दिया।

(b)

मणिपुर के आजाद हिन्द सेनानी एक श्रद्धांजली / 3

श्री सारूंगबाम इबोहल सिंह

श्री सारूंगबाम अंगाहल सिंह के पुत्र श्री सारूंगबाम इबोहल सिंह का जन्म 1920 में पश्चिम इम्फाल जनपद के सिंगजामेई में हुआ था। इनमें जन्म से ही राष्ट्र भक्ती के भाव भरे थे। इन्होंने 1940 में मणिपुर प्रजासोम्मेलोने में सम्मिलित होकर मणिपुर अवज्ञा आन्दोलन में भाग लिया था।

जब 14 अप्रैल, 1944 को आजाद हिन्द फौज द्वारा मोयरंग को स्वतन्त्र करा लिया गया तो इबोहल मोयरंग गये और फौज में सम्मिलित होकर कर्नल एम. ए. मलिक की कमान में खुफिया विभाग में काम करते रहे। इन्होंने मोयरंग के युद्ध मोर्चे पर तीन महीनों तक काम किया। जब फौज यांगून लौट गई तो इबोहल भी उसी के साथ म्यांमार की राजधानी चले गये और संयुक्त सेनाओं द्वारा म्यांमार पर भी अधिकार कर लिये जाने तक स्वतन्त्र भारत की तदर्थ सरकार के अधीन आजाद हिन्द आन्दोलन में भाग लेते रहे।

जब 1 मार्च, 1945 को अलाईड फोर्सेस ने यांगून पर अधिकार किया तो इबोहल को युद्ध बन्दी बनाकर यांगून केन्द्रीय कारागार में डाल दिया गया। इन्हें लालकिले में फौज पर चले मुकद्दमे के उपरान्त ही छोड़ा गया और ये 23 मार्च 1946 को यांगून से चले।

इसी महीने की 28 मार्च को बंगाल आई.एन.ए. रिलीफ कमिटी (बंगाल आजाद हिन्दी फौजराहत समिति) द्वारा इनका भव्य स्वागत किया गया। ये अप्रैल 1946 में मणिपुर पहुँचे।

इबोहल 1946 में कांग्रेस में सम्मिलित हो गये। ये मणिपुर राज्य कांग्रेस के पश्चिम अंचल के महासचिव बने। 6 अक्टूबर 1947 को मणिपुर के महाराजा के विरुद्ध मणिपुर में एक उत्तरदायी सरकार की स्थापना के लिए सत्याग्रह आन्दोलन चला तो इबोहल ने उसमें बढ़-चढ़कर भाग लिया।

इबोहल 1979 से अखिल भारतीय स्वतन्त्रता सेनानी संगठन की मणिपुर इकाई के महासचिव भी रहे और राष्ट्रीय संगठन की कार्यकारिणी के सदस्य बने। साथ ही इबोहल मणिपुर कांग्रेस कमेटी (ई.) के स्वतन्त्रता सेनानी कक्ष की नगर जनपद इकाई के संयोजक भी रहे।

(c)

16 / मणिपुर के आजाद हिन्द सेनानी एक श्रद्धांजली

श्री ओकराम जोगेश्वर सिंह

श्री ओकराम जोगेश्वर सिंह का जन्म 15 नवम्बर 1909 को इम्फाल में हुआ था। अत्यधिक गरीबी के कारण ये केवल कक्षा 9 तक ही अपनी पढ़ाई कर सके। 1932 में ये इम्फाल के 4थी बटालियन असम राईफलन मिलेट्री अस्पताल में नियुक्त हो गये। इसी दौरान सौभाग्य से इन्हें डिब्रूगढ़ से कम्पाउण्डर का कोर्स करने का भी अवसर मिल गया। राजनैतिक जीवन में ये महात्मा गांधी से अत्यन्त प्रभावित थे जो देश को विदेशी शासन से मुक्त कराना चाहते थे।

जब जापानी विमान इम्फाल पर बमबारी कर रहे थे उन दिनों जोगेश्वर सिंह मोयरंग में चिकित्सा विभाग में पदस्थापित थे। 1942 के अन्त में नेताजी ने स्वतन्त्रता संग्राम को सशक्त करने का सेना को जो आह्वान किया उसने इनके दिलों में नयी ऊर्जा और उत्साह का संचार कर दिया। फिर इन्होंने मोयरंग में आजाद हिन्द फौज को अपनी सेवा समर्पित कर दी। इस दौरान इन्हें अनेक कठिनाइयों का सामना करना पड़ा।

अंग्रेजी सरकार ने इन्हें राजद्रोही और 'फौज' का भक्त माना। 24 जुलाई 1944 को इन्हें अंग्रेजों द्वारा गिरफ्तार कर लिया गया और एक रात मोयरंग में रखकर इम्फाल कारागार भेज दिया गया, जहाँ से भारतीय अध्यादेश अधिनियम 37/43 की धारा 26 के अन्तर्गत 14 फरवरी 1945 तक जेल में रहे। 15 अगस्त, 1972 को जोगेश्वर के अवदान को स्वतन्त्रता सेनानी के रूप में मान्यता प्रदान करते हुए ताम्रपत्र प्रदान किया गया। सरकार की ओर से इन्हें 300 रुपये प्रतिमाह पेंशन भी स्वीकार की गई।

66 / मणिपुर के आजाद हिन्द सेनानी एक श्रद्धांजली

श्री थोकचोम अंगोऊ सिंह

इम्फाल के सिंगजामेई माथाक थोकचोम लेईकाई निवासी श्री थोकचोम अंगोऊ सिंह का जन्म 1889 में हुआ था। ये जन्मजात नेता, महत्त्वपूर्ण स्वतन्त्रता सेनानी और न्याय तथा समानता के पक्षधर थे। इनका अधिकांश जीवन मानवता की सेवा में ही व्यतीत हुआ था।

1939 में तत्कालीन अंग्रेजी प्रशासन की नीतियों के विरुद्ध महिलाओं के लोकप्रिय आन्दोलन के दौरान इन्हें प्रजा सोम्मिलोनी का प्रतिष्ठित नेता होने के नाते 24 घण्टों के लिए इम्फाल पुलिस थाने में बन्द रखा गया था। 1942-43 के दौरान ये प्रजा सोम्मिलोनी के अध्यक्ष बने थे।

इन्हें 4 मार्च 1944 को म्यांमार में फौज के एक कप्तान द्वारा नेताजी सुभाष चन्द्र बसु द्वारा हस्ताक्षरित एक पत्रक मिला। ये अपने कुछ मित्रों के साथ कर्नल एस. ए. मलिक की कमान में आजाद हिन्द फौज के मोयरंग मोर्चे के खुफिया विभाग में सम्मिलित हो गये।

फौज के म्यांमार में पीछे हट जाने के समय ये उसी के साथ यांगून चले गये, जहाँ इन्हें अंग्रेजी सेना ने गिरफ्तार कर लिया। युद्धबन्दी के रूप में इन्होंने अनेक यातनाएं झेलीं। इन्हें 17 फरवरी, 1946 को आजाद हिन्द फौज के सभी युद्धबन्दियों के साथ छोड़ दिया गया तो ये उसी वर्ष 8 अप्रैल को मणिपुर पहुंचे। इन्होंने मणिपुर की टैरीटोरियल काउन्सिल के सदस्य के रूप में 1957 से 63 तक जनता की सेवा की। लेकिन मित्रों में सत्ता के लिए बढ़ते संघर्ष को देखते हुए इन्होंने राजनीति छोड़ दी और सन्त हो गये। 30 नवम्बर 1976 को एक सन्त के रूप में ही इनका स्वर्गवास हुआ।

(d)

मणिपुर के आजाद हिन्द सेनानी एक श्रद्धांजली / 17

श्री लाईशराम इराबोत सिंह

इम्फाल के केईशामपत मुतुम लेइका निवासी श्री लाईशराम खोमदान के पुत्र श्री लाईशराम इराबोत सिंह का जन्म 1920 में हुआ था। इराबोत बचपन से ही मणिपुर के विविध राजनैतिक सामाजिक आन्दोलनों में अत्यधिक रुचि लेने लगे थे। ये 1939 में मणिपुर प्रजा सम्मेलनी में सम्मिलित हो गये जो असम राज्य का एक मात्र राजनैतिक दल था।

श्री इराबोत ने मणिपुर के चावल आन्दोलन में भाग लिया जिसे लोग '1939 नूपी लाल' कहते हैं। 1944 में इन्हें भी एस. इबोहला सिंह के हाथों मिले नेताजी के एक परचे के माध्यम से आजाद हिन्द फौज की जानकारी मिली। जब आजाद हिन्द फौज ने मोयरंग को मुक्त किया तो ये 14 अप्रैल 1944 को कर्नल एस.ए. मलिक के नेतृत्व में 'फौज' में सम्मिलित हो गये। जब फौज को पीछे हटना पड़ा तो ये भी उसके साथ यांगून चले गये और जब अन्य फौजियों को अंग्रेजी सेना द्वारा गिरफ्तार किया गया तब तक म्यांमार में कार्य करते रहे। 1 मई 1945 को यांगून पर एंग्लो अमरीकी सेनाओं का अधिकार होने पर ये भूमिगत हो गये। लेकिन इन्हें उसी वर्ष 8 जुलाई को गिरफ्तार करके यांगून के केन्द्रीय कारागार में युद्ध बन्दी के रूप में रख दिया गया।

लालकिले में फौज पर चले मुकद्दमे के बाद इराबोत को 1946 में जेल से रिहा किया गया। उसी वर्ष इन्होंने मणिपुर में भारतीय राष्ट्रीय कांग्रेस की स्थापना में योग दिया और पार्टी के सक्रिय कार्यकर्त्ता के रूप में काम करते रहे।

(e)

जनाब नकी अहमद चौधरी

श्री अल्हज मौलवी अरिरूल्लाह के पुत्र जनाब नकी अहमद चौधरी का जन्म 1914 में मणिपुर के मुस्लिम गाँव केईखु में हुआ था। इन्होंने नेताजी सुभाषचन्द्र बसु के चमत्कारिक नेतृत्व में हिन्दुस्थान की स्वाधीनता के लिए आजाद हिन्द फौज की मुहिम में मणिपुर का नाम रौशन किया था। मैट्रिक करते ही श्री अहमद चौधरी ने राजनैतिक और सामाजिक आन्दोलनों में भाग लेना आरम्भ कर दिया था। ये निखिल मणिपुर महासभा के सदस्य बने थे और नूपी लाल में भी 1939 में भाग लिया।

दूसरा विश्वयुद्ध आरम्भ होते ही ये ब्रिटिश इण्डिया आर्मी में सम्मिलित हो गये। इन्हें 1941 में जापानियों का मुकाबला करने के लिए सिंघापुर भेजा गया। अंग्रेजी सेनाओं द्वारा जापानियों के समक्ष बिना शर्त समर्पण कर देने पर इन्हें आजाद हिन्द फौज में सम्मिलित होने का अवसर मिला। ये 16 फरवरी 1942 को सिंघापुर में फौज से जुड़े और फौज के साथ हिन्दुस्थान में इम्फाल की ओर बढ़ते हुए मोयरंग तक आये।

इन्हीं की टुकड़ी ने मोयरंग पर विजय प्राप्त करके अप्रैल 1944 में भारतीय तिरंगा फहराया था। मोयरंग में ये एक बम विस्फोट में घायल हो गये। जापानियों को साथ फौज का मोयरंग में पतन होने पर 16 अगस्त, 1944 को इन्हें अंग्रेजी सेना ने गिरफ्तार कर लिया और मल्टन जेल में रखा गया। जेल में इन्हें 'ब्लैक कॅप्टिव की श्रेणी दी गई। ये 8 मई, 1946 को ही रिहा किये गये। श्री अहमद इम्फाल में मणिपुर कांग्रेस कमेटी (ई) के स्वतन्त्रता सेनानी कक्ष के सदस्य भी रहे।

Courtsey; Director, Directorate of Art & Culture, Govt of Manipur.

(5) ***<u>IMPORTANCE OF INA HEAD QUARTERS</u>:-*** *"...The southern part of Manipur from Ningthoukhong was under the Control of the INA with its Headquarters at Moirang for three months till July 15, 1944. The building of the Headquarters belonged to Shri H. Nilamani Singh, freedom Fighter which s tands till today. The surrounding areas of the Headquarters was declared 'Enemy Zone' by the British". – M. Koireng Singh.*

(H.C. Shobha, *Ed.* Souvenir, Netaji Bal Sena Vidyalaya, Moirang 1997 and author of "IputhouThangching and Lai Haraoba& chief editor of annual publication of Thangjing Yageirel, Moirang").

(a)

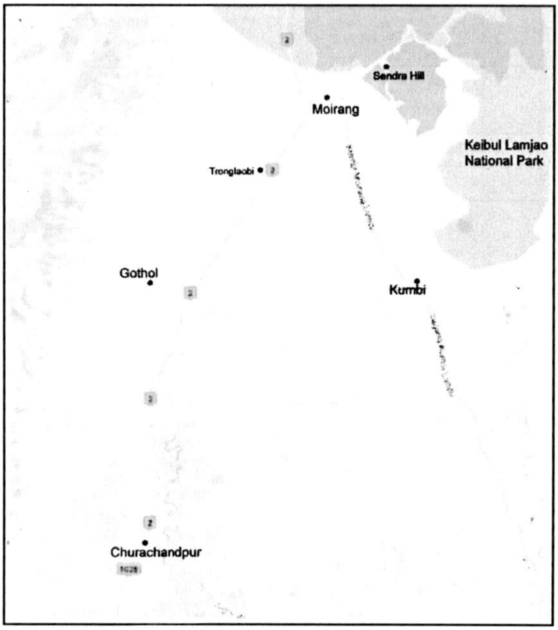
Sendra Hill
Moirang
Keibul Lamjao National Park
Tronglaobi
Gothol
Kumbi
Churachandpur

(b)

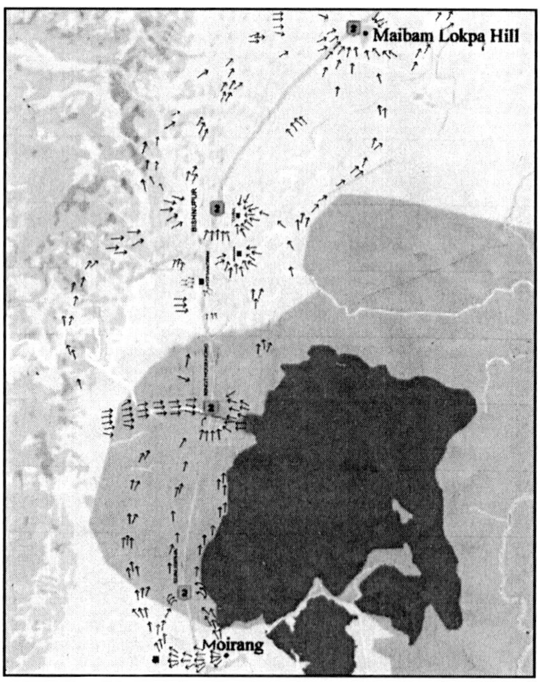
Maibam Lokpa Hill
Moirang

(c)

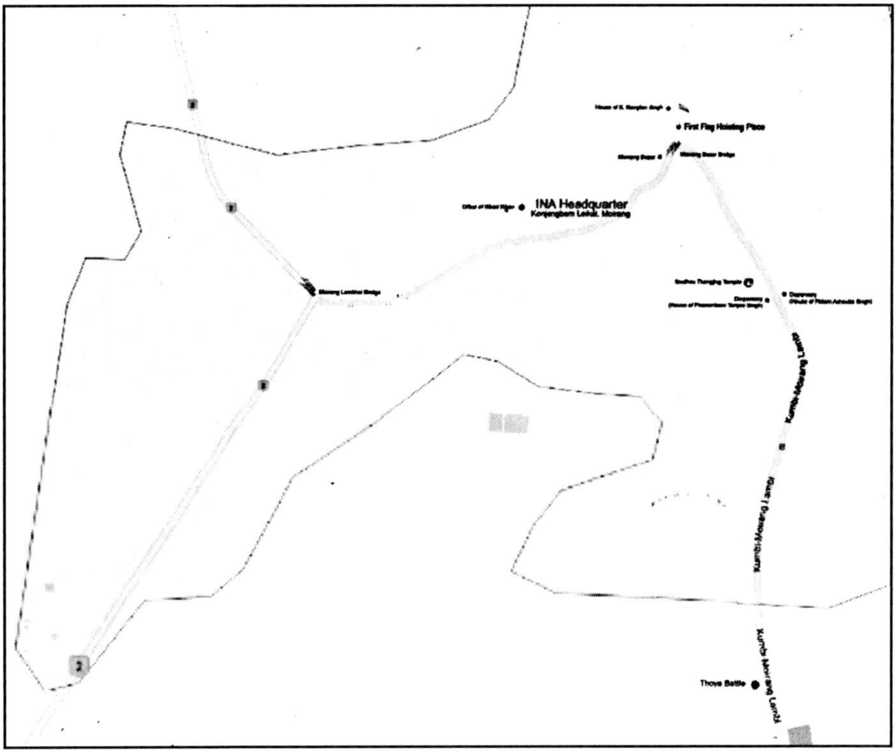
First Flag Hoisting Place
INA Headquarter
Konjengbam Leikai, Moirang
Kumbi-Moirang Lamb
Thoya Battle

The First INA Administered Village in Naga Hills in India and It's Significance Towards the Battle of Kohima

Er. Vekho Swuro

Introduction

While writing on,"*The Discovery of Netaji Subhash Chandra Bose Delhi Chalo Last Camp in Nagaland*", my interest towards Netaji Subhas Chandra Bose and Indian National Army (INA) movement for India's Freedom developed greatly. I travelled across villages interviewing eyewitnesses even after publication of the book and in the process I heard stories that were not found in books. It is for this reason that I felt the need for people to hear those stories of the heroes who gave their lives and services for the great cause of India's freedom.

The formation of INA and its forward Mission

In the year 1943, Bose revived the INA movement, which was founded in 1942 in order to liberate India from the British rule that has rippled across the nation and abroad. In September 1943, Netaji selected a regiment considered as the cream of INA to spearhead and advance into India, known as "Subhas Brigade". Major General Shahnawaz Khan was selected to command this Brigade, which took part in the Arakan, Haka and the Vicinity of Kohima.

In 1944, the INA together with the Japanese Army begins Operation 'UGO', moving its troops across the Chindwin River and towards its objectives; Imphal, Kohima and Delhi. On 15th March, they crossed the Chindwin River with their plan to reach railhead at Dimapur, traversing the Naga hills and from there go to Delhi *via* Assam with their slogan, "Delhi Chalo". It is important to remember that the British had started surveying the Naga Hills from 1922 and came up with the maps in 1943. As per Vikenyu Naga's (a Naga British Labour Commander) account, one Naga man stole the map and gave it to the Japanese, which helped the latter to map all the important villages, mountains, rivers and different routes in their own language. With the map in hand, they were earnestly looking forward to meeting some Nagas from the Naga Hills guiding them from Myanmar to Kohima. During this time, the Imperial Japanese Army and the INA led by Netaji already had a working relation.

A.Z. Phizo mentioned that he had no idea about how the Japanese came to know that he and his brother were Nagas. But Japanese came in search of them and asked them for help. The Japanese officers invited his brother and him at the very first meeting to talk and brought a map of Nagaland, showing all the minute details of villages, mountains, rivers and different routes. It was also during this meeting where they were introduced to the INA leader Subhas Chandra Bose. It is evident that with the maps and co-operation from the people they became even more confident to enter the Naga Hills probably taking the British Inspection Bungalows (BIB) as their reference point en-route to Kohima.

The Japanese troops crossed the Chindwin River under two Japanese Lt. General *Viz*. Mutaguchi of the 15th Division of Imphal sector and General Kotoku Sato of the 31st Division alongwith INA; General Shah Nawaz Khan and its Supreme Commander Subhas Chandra Bose. As narrated by the eyewitnesses they came to the Naga Hills from Kharasom and Jesami through the British bridle path with horses carrying rations, weapons, guns and bullets. General Mutaguchi's 15th division headed towards Imphal and the 31st Division went towards Ukrul, Kharasom and Jesami. They reached Jesami and Kharasom around 28th March

1944 and from there they entered in three direction in the early morning to attack the British allied force of the 1st Assam Regiment, camped at Jesami and by 1st April the INA and the Japanese troops won the battle and occupied their camp.

While General Sato and the INA General Shahnawaz Khan moved towards the northeast route through a very popular bridle path from Burma to Kohima, constructed by the British government and travelled by the Bangladeshi refugees for the first time in the month of November 1943 *i.e.* Losami, Chizami IB, Mesulumi, Pfutsero, Kikruma, Chakhabama towards Kohima. Bose with a number of INA and Japanese troops alongwith the captured 1st Assam Regiment at Jesami went through the eastern route towards Kohima *via* Phek IB, Khuza, Mutsale and Ruzazho, which was the shortest route among all others from Burma to reach Kohima (Approx. 447 km aerial distance *via* Google map). After a week long stay at Ruzazho village, they moved to Suthozu, Yoruba, Chozubaand, Chesezu where Bose had his camp overseeing Kohima battle. Some of the soldiers directly passed through the Chindwin River towards Zunheboto and Tuensangarea as the rear front of northeast security.

Netaji and Ruzazho Village

According to the accounts by eyewitnesses, one year prior to their arrival some spy came through the village placing milestones with the BIB as their main reference path. The route was not so popular as compared to the rest, which probably might not be even in the British list of threat or watch out list, and that made it more strategic for his troops to pass through with the already tension and battle going on the other side *viz.* Imphal sector, than Ukrul, Chizami-Pfutsero and Kohima, while the other sectors were heavily engaged in battle he came through the safest way *via* Ruzazho village. Probably that is why Bose not only passed through the village but also stayed for a week, making it the first administered village by appointing many villagers into his government.

On reaching Ruzazho village, Bose called all the villagers for a meeting to a place called *Methochophezho* at the village's northern gate. As the meeting was about to begin the British jet flew above them making the INA and Japanese troops as well as Bose to lie on the ground and also instruct the villagers to hide, but to the innocent villagers it appeared silly and they did not pay heed to it. Later, their meeting was relocated to a place under a bamboo grooves near the village gate. Bose addressed the villagers and promised to develop and improve the village conditions: roads, schools and industries. Raising his sword he said,"I will defeat the Britishers and the Indian Government will deliver and make developments in the best way".

On asking if the village had any literate person, the villagers responded by naming Shri Poswuyi Swuro as the lone candidate. Subsequently, Bose without any hesitation asked for his consent to be the DB (Dobashi) in that area. Poswuyi too agreed to his request and his name was written down in his personal diary. He further opened his invitation to the villagers to stand for the post of Gaun Bura (GB) chief of khel/clan in the village where Nine men stood up and were appointed accordingly. They are: (1) Mr. Vekhwuyi Swuro, (2) Mr. Satsoyi Sapuh, (3) Mr. Selhuyi Veswuh, (4) Mr. Kahunyi Swuro, (5) Mr. Pulhucho Swuro, (6) Mr. Soyira Swuro, (7) Mr. Khrukahi Sapuh, (8) Mr. Nekahisapuh, (9) Mr. Rachoyi Swuro. The rest of the village youth volunteered as labourers to carry their stuffs from one place to another. Few days later Poswuyi led the INA and Japanese troops to Satakha (approx.50 km from Ruzazho) and fought the British troops, on their way back, the British troops ambushed them and one Naga INA guide was killed. The graveyard still remains in Dzulha Village.

The village vowed to support and fight for freedom in every possible way with utmost sincerity and honesty. The simple nature of the villagers can be known through some of the outsiders who observed and wrote about the Nagas. For instance, Hutton wrote that, "Nagas have fine qualities; simple, cheerful, colourful, humorous, courteous and hospitable". Petermaster also remarked that the Nagas are distinguished by some noble qualities; their pledge word can always be trusted and they are ever ready to devote themselves for the common safety.

It may be mentioned here that, according to eyewitnesses by the time they reached Ruzazho, their rations were almost exhausted. As per some of the accounts given by nearby villages, at times the INA used to pay *Azad Hind Fauj* currency as the cost of their rations but usually they appealed them to donate rations through the appointed GBs. Others accounted that the Japanese troops would come and forcefully take their domesticated animals, rations and chickens from the villagers. The appointed GB's also gave their best by taking them around, surveying different areas risking their lives. In fact, the whole villagers in one way or the other contributed towards the cause of freedom of India by volunteering as labourers; transferring heavy loads of INA goods to different locations while some engaged in building their camps. Not only did the villagers unsparingly gave away their choicest vegetables, domesticated animals and paddy as ration to INA but also travelled from village to village on foot in search of rations for them.

Probably, Netaji found the villagers very simple, honest, charming and hospitable and camped in the village for a week. He also made an outpost camp just above the village opposite the BIB, a strategic place overseeing Kohima and its surroundings. However, the British got the information and bombed that camp after a week, possibly making it one of the first camp bombed in Nagaland after reaching the Indian Soil. According to the witnesses, even while they stayed in the village they formed a kind of layer where Bose stayed in the Centre guarded by the INA, many of them wearing turbans, the next circle by the INA and Japanese troops and third layer mostly by the Japanese. They also shared that their food and eating habits were different.

Significance of Ruzazhomi's contribution towards the battle of Kohima and Indian freedom from a distance, a village might not sound a big deal compared to the many battles and the struggles INA fought. However, delving deeper into the strategies Netaji had come with, it makes so much more sense and significant. Bose intentionally came through this village it being the shortest route, and considering the location it became one of the most strategic places for his team to camp, which could have led him to appoint the villagers into his government to work alongside.

It is pertinent to mention that, before the World War II, many Nagas became closely associated with the British and were already working with them. Many Naga villages were not co-operating with the

INA allies the Japanese as they were forceful in their action towards the people by ordering, demanding and taking their things against their will. Hence, Bose being a highly educated leader would have been aware of the situation well in advance and the hospitable gesture he received from the Ruzazho village would have made him stay there to build relationship and trust in order to further their support for the noble cause as its ambassadors. His strategy worked well as appointed GB's, DB's and interpreters played a major role in taking them around to different locations for setting their camps and propagating Netaji's vision to liberate India from British *raj* by convincing the neighbouring villages. It became even more evident as they would go to various villages to collect their rations for the INA. As written by many authors, one of the major factors faced by their allies (the Japanese) and even INA was shortage of ration and when they came to the village it was told that they did not have enough rations with them. Thereby, the villagers played a major role in collecting and storing their ration for the onward journey to Kohima.

Ruzazho also stands at the strategic place with BIB surrounded from the North at Chepoketa, West at Suthozu just above the village and Dzulha on the West side. Hence, had the Ruzazhomi decided not to cooperate with the INA at this juncture, the story of INA's attempt at liberating India from the clutches of the British upon entering Naga soil from Burma would have taken a different course with BIBs in close proximity. The villagers contributed immensely towards INA's fight for India's freedom physically, morally and providing enough rations for them to move forward to Kohima battle for her independence.Though Netaji might have lost the war he won the hearts of the people by sowing the seeds of love and earned respect from them for which he is remembered with great esteem to the present day. In the author's view, the villagers went beyond their reach to help Bose and INA to fight for India's freedom.

Conclusion

It is sad that Bose and the INA lost the battle. Nonetheless, he gave the courage to the Indians to be free from the British *Raj*. The impact was so great that it challenged the minds of the Indians, and the momentum grew even stronger gaining more attention in the later years after the War. Many historians and writers commented that, riots and rallies of the masses in support of the INA, and violent confrontations between the masses and the police which broke out everywhere throughout India, challenged the British. This situation also led to major conflicts within the British army where the British Indian army started ignoring the order from their British superiors resulting in outbreaks of mutiny in major cities like Madras (Chennai), Pune, Jabalpur and Mumbai. The British became helpless day-by-day, as the uniting Indians, both within the army and public, grew nationwide in support of the INA vision. The passion and courage among men and women to be free from the British Raj also grew as well.

These developments shook the strong foundation of the British *Raj*, which in the later period of time led them to realise the situation and understand that they could not contain the forces that had already been stirred in the hearts of the people by the great leader Subhas, and ultimately to leave India by giving them freedom.

It no longer remained just a speculation but a confirmed fact, that the effects of the INA and Bose's activities on the British Indian Army and the Bombay Mutiny was the most important reason behind the British decision to relinquish the Raj in India, as has been echoed by Atlee, the then British Prime Minister, while reflecting the factors leading to the British exit from India. Hence, it is commendable that the Government of India is looking into the affairs of the INA and honouring their great contribution for the freedom of India in the best possible way. The GoI also must look at those villages, which contributed immensely towards the INA and Indian Freedom movement. Suggestion may also be made to even set up a national heritage in memory of the first INA administered village at Ruzazho.

References

1. Hutton, J.H. (1885-1968). *The Angami Nagas*. London: Macmillan & Co., 1921.
2. Khan, Shah Nawaz, The INA Heroes: *Autobiographies of Maj. Gen. Shahnawaz, Col. Prem K. Sahgal [and] Col. Gurbux Singh Dhillon of the Azad Hind Fauj*, Lahore: Hero Publication, 1946.
3. Keane, Fergal. *Road of Bones: The Epic Siege of Kohima 1944*. London: Harper Press, 2011.
4. Nagi, Rev. Savito. *Kohima Rhiiu Rii Kralakeshii.* Kohima: N.V. Press, 2015.
5. Reid, Sir Robert. *History of the Frontier Areas Bordering on Assam 1883-1941*. Delhi: Eastern Publishing House, 1983.
6. R. Petermaster. *The Living Race of Mankind.* London: Hutchinson & Co., 1920.
7. Zinyu, Mhiesizokho. Phizo and the Naga Problem. Kohima: N.V. Press, 2014.
8. Web Source- http://www.towardsfreedom.in/site/Indian_National_Army.

Subhas Chandra Bose, Indian National Army and Rajputana States

V.K. Vashishtha

Subhas Chandra Bose (1897-1945), a socialist and an ardent revolutionary who emerged parallel to Mahatma Gandhi, as a leader of the protagonists of armed struggle with foreign aid for the liberation of India from British imperialism. As a pragmatist, Subhas Chandra Bose regarded the Sabarmati Ashram as retrogressive as it ignored "physical culture and military training," abhorred modernism and industrialization, while he saw no utility of Ashrams in political life, and in the scheme of creation of "a new India at once free, happy and great."[1] In contrast to this, he acclaimed the "philosophy of activism" of the Pondicherry centre which prompted "for ceaseless and unselfish action." He argued that "the best way to conquer nature is to fight her, and it is weakness to seek refuge in contemplation when we are hemmed in all sides by dangers and difficulties".[2] Hence, he advocated for organising an armed struggle in India with foreign aid to win freedom for India as was followed by revolutionaries all over the world. He was convinced by his experience that the British Government would not grant freedom to India, and would never surrender "to persuasion or moral pressure or non-violent resistance." He clearly visualized that "it was impossible to organize an armed struggle in India without some help from outside help from our countrymen abroad, as well as from some foreign power or powers."[3]

His diagonally opposite views to Gandhi's non-violent struggle for the Independence of India, mobilized him to reorganize the Indian National Army (INA) after the assurance of support from the Imperial Government of Japan and the opportune time of breaking of the Second World War for the struggle of India's freedom. Even after the surrender of the INA men on the Indo-Burma border and subsequently, the news of the death of Subhas Chandra Bose, almost all the political parties and people across India came to the rescue of INA officers and INA prisoners. At last, the sustained political pressure of the Congress since the passing of Quit India Resolution coupled with the escalation of disaffection in the ranks and files of British Indian Army under the spell of INA, triggered the British Government to grant expeditiously Independence to India on 15 August, 1947. Thus, even in its reversal, the INA appeared victorious by accelerating the process of liberation of India from British thralldom. This contribution of INA to the Independence of India prompted the Indian nationalists to acclaim Subhas Chandra Bose as "George Washington of India."[4]

In the light of growing popularity of INA all over India, the present paper attempts to study the impact of Subhas Chandra Bose and INA in furtherance of the process of political awakening among the students and Praja Mandal leaders of nineteen Princely States of Rajputana. Besides, it elucidates the sacrifices of INA recruits of these States in the battles of Arakan and Imphal. On top of this, the paper deliberates over the role of INA officers in associating its soldiers with the Praja Mandal movements for the establishment of responsible governments in Rajputana States. This change geared the INA soldiers into the mainstream of national movement and converted them into the votaries of non-violence.

The paper is based on the archival records of the Rajasthan State Archives, Bikaner, published INA papers and also poems which reveal the popularity of Subhas Chandra Bose and INA among the people in Princely Rajputana.

Emergence of INA as Saviour of *Praja Mandals* in Rajputana

The rise of Subhas Chandra Bose as a left wing leader in the Indian National Congress brought him closer to its prominent leader Jawaharlal Nehru and the young political activists of the Jodhpur Praja Mandal in the Jodhpur State in Rajputana. Under the directions of Jawaharlal Nehru, the President of Indian National Congress, the *Jodhpur Praja Mandal* observed 'Subhas Day', on 10 May, 1936, and passed a resolution in a public meeting protesting against the "repressive policy of the British Government" for arresting "the great Subhas Chandra Bose for an indefinite period without assigning any reason, and demanded his immediate release."[5] This avowal support of the *Jodhpur Praja Mandal* encourged Subhas Chandra Bose, the President elect of the Haripura Congress Session (February 1938) to visit Jodhpur to acquaint himself with the problems of the Indian States on 23 January, 1938. In his meeting with nearly 100 young *Jodhpur Praja Mandal* leaders outside the Aerodrome of Jodhpur State, he explained them that the aim of the Congress was "uniting India and achieving Independence," which could only be achieved by "great sacrifices." He assured them that their "difficulties are well known to the Congress," that due to its pre-occupations the Congress could not pay its attention to the problems of the Indian States and that "these bristling problems will now be considered at the ensuing session of the Congress at Haripura."[6] Enraged by the growing relations of *Jodhpur Praja Mandal* with Congress leaders, the autocratic State of Jodhpur rusticated Jugraj Bohra from the school for reading out the address of Subhas Chandra Bose, and banned the *Jodhpur Praja Mandal* as well as the Civil Liberties Union in 1937. Such incidents of repression in Princely States dissuaded Subhas Chandra Bose, the President of the Fifty-first Congress Session at Haripura in February 1938 to deviate from Mahatma Gandhi's policy of non-interference in the Princely States. The Haripura Congress Resolution pledged Congress support for social and political advancement of the people of the States. This assurance of the Congress support accelerated the political activities in the States. The *Marwar Lok Parishad* was formed at Jodhpur on 16 May, 1938 in place of the banned *Jodhpur Praja Mandal* (1937).

On his second visit to Jodhpur on 6 December, 1938,[7] Subhas Chandra Bose, the saviour of Princely States, addressed a public meeting of eight thousand people at Girdhi Kot in the centre of the Jodhpur city, organized under the auspices of the Town Congress Committee and the *Marwar Lok Parishad*. He expressed pain and anguish for the suppression of civil liberties in the State. In view of this, he stated; "Every subject of the State regardless of his religion or caste should make it a point to join *Lok Parishad*" so that it could approach the State with authority on behalf of the people to resolve their grievances. He assured the people of full support of the Indian National Congress to fulfil their legitimate aspirations and also alerted the Jodhpur State "to read the lessons of history" and "bow before the popular will." He directed the *Marwar Lok Parishad* to "launch a struggle for attainment of civil liberties and Responsible government," in the Jodhpur State on the principles and policy of non-violence of the Congress. He suggested that for the success of a movement against a powerful State three things were essential, "Organization, Unity and Readiness to suffer."[8]

Subhas Chandra Bose could do no more for the people of Princely States because of his resignation from the Presidentship of the Congress in 1939 and for his formation of the Forward Bloc which placed him opposite to Mahatma Gandhi's right wing camp and also made him an eyesore to the British government. Even after his disappearance secretly from India in January 1941 for organizing armed struggle against British Imperialism, he was remembered all over the Rajputana States as a leader of the Congress. For instance, the *Jaipur Rajya Praja Mandal* in its exhibition at Jaipur (the capital town of Jaipur State) on 7 June, 1941 displayed the photo of Subhas Chandra Bose alongwith that of Jawahar Lal Nehru and Mahatma Gandhi.[9] The broadcast of Subhas Chandra Bose about the formation of the Indian National Army and the Provisional Government of India at Singapore for the liberation of India created consternation among the people of Rajputana States as several of their relatives had also joined the INA to fight against British Imperialism. Even the defeat of the INA on the Indo-Burma border, and the news of untimely death of Subhas Chandra Bose could not create despondency among the people of Rajputana like the other parts of the country. The Praja Mandals and people of Rajputana joined the Congress in protesting against the trial of the INA officers in the Red Fort, and demanding the release of the INA prisoners. The people cheered the INA soldiers on their returning to their villages. In turn, the INA officers and soldiers created a political awakening among the students and Praja Mandal workers and affiliated themselves with the Praja Mandal movement for the attainment of responsible government in Rajputana States.

Growing Popularity of INA in Rajputana

1. INA germinated patriotism among British Indian Army

The military campaigns of the *Azad Hind Fauj* on the Indo-Burma border for the liberation of India not only created a thrill among the people of Rajputana States but also overwhelmed the British Indian Troops. The Fortnightly Intelligence Report for Rajputana States for the First half of August 1945 records that:[10]

> "On the 30th July , 1945 when two special trains carrying Indian troops passed Sawai Madhopur Railway Station (in Jaipur State) the troops shouted "*Inquilab Jindabad*", "*Hindustan Jindabad,* and *Subhas Chander Bose ki Jai.*" The terms "national army," "*Ajad Hind Fauj*" and "*Congress*" were also written in chalk on some of the carriages."

The pervading influence of Subhas Chandra Bose and the news of the military campaigns of the INA against the British Indian Army had also infused patriotic zeal among the latter. It was this glorification and popularity of the INA soldiers which created discontentment among the ranks and files of the British Indian Army and pressurized the British Government to grant freedom to India expeditiously.

2. Peoples' Response to INA : Press and Patriotic Songs

(a) Response of Press

Like the *Hindu* and other national newspapers in the British Provinces, the papers in Rajputana States such as, *Rajasthan Herald* (Jaipur),

Navyug Sandesh (Bharatpur), *Prabhat* (Jaipur) and *Praja Sevak* (Jodhpur) praised the adventures of the INA on the Indo-Burma border for the liberation of India.[11] The *Praja Sevak*, a pro-Congress weekly paper from Jodhpur opposed men and material support of the Jodhpur State to the British Government, during the Second World War, and paid tribute to the INA by publishing a special issue entitled, *Azad Hind Fauj* (1945).[12] Under the spell of the INA, the newly established *Samajwadi Party* at Jaipur started publication of a Hindi weekly, named *Azad Sainik* from December 1945. The paper stressed on the establishment of the socialistic pattern of society after the independence of India.[13]

(b) Patriotic songs laouded INA

The people of Rajputana States had high esteem for Subhas Chandra Bose and the INA for their engagement in the armed struggle for the Independence of India. It was revealed in the patriotic songs published in Rajputana in Hindi by the newspapers and by the individuals in their books.

i. A poet Captain Gopal of Jodhpur published a poem applauding the INA soldiers in the *Praja Sevak* (27 March, 1945), under the title *Azadi ke Sipahi*. As a mark of condemnation for British Imperialism, the poet warned the INA sepoys of Hind for not joining Japan in the venture of the enslavement of other countries but to fight only for the liberation of their motherland and appealed them to fight for the freedom of the country as India could brook no delay in attaining Independence. He called upon the progeny of Shivaji, Maharana Pratap, Guru Govind Singh and people of all the regions of India, such as, Punjab, Maharashtra, Bengal and Madras, and also all martial communities, Jats, Gurjars, Ahirs, Marathas, Rajputs and Gurkhas to unite for expelling the *Firangis* from India. In the last, he called on all the castes and communities of India to assemble under the tricolour flag to assist Netaji Subhas Chandra Bose in the armed struggle for the independence of India.[14] This song expressed the growing consciousness among the people of Rajputana for extending support to Subhas Chandra Bose in his armed struggle against the British Imperialism by foreign aid.

ii. Similarly, Vali Muhammad, a political activist of Pratapgarh Praja Mandal (in Pratapgarh State in southern Rajputana) composed a poem on 23 Janaury, 1946. He eulogized Subhas Chandra Bose for his flying the flag of *Azad Hind Fauj* in Singapore and spreading the glory of India abroad, alongwith striking communal harmony among the Hindus and Muslims, and as revealed the formation of the national liberation army to free India from the British yoke.[15]

iii. Pandit Banshidhar Sharma, Head Master of J.J.S. School, Kishangarh (capital town of Kishangarh State) composed patriotic songs during his tenure as President of *Kishangarh Rajya Praja Mandal*, and published them in a book, entitled: *Praja Mandal Gitanjali* in October 1946. He recited these patriotic songs in the public meetings and before the gatherings of people in towns and villages of Kishangarh State. These songs infused patriotic sentiments among the people. For instance, in a song (no.8), he stated about the domineering urge in Subhas Chandra Bose for the freedom of India and for its attainment he made sacrifices such as, going to jail several times, taking plunge to visit foreign countries and organizing the INA, infusing among its soldiers patriotic feelings, forming the *Azad Hind Sarkar*, and above all, instilled seeds of nationalistic sentiment among the people of India. The poet Bansidhar pointed out that because of the sacrifices of Subhas Chandra Bose for the freedom of his country, he even in the form of a man is worshiped like gods, and blessed are his parents who gave birth to such a brave patriot. This song appreciated his contribution for armed struggle for the Independence of India. Bansidhar pays homage to the INA by publishing *Jai Hind* at the top of cover page of his book.[16]

3. People Mourn the Death of Subhas

The students and the *Praja Mandal* members in Rajputana States were grieved to hear the news of the death of Subhas Chandra Bose in the air crash in Japan's territory at Hawai on 18 August, 1945. In the second half of August 1945, the *Praja Parishad* of Bharatpur State and the students and Praja Mandals of Alwar, Jaipur and Kota States and several others organized public meetings and *hartals* as a mark of their tribute to Subhas Chandra Bose, the leader of the second front of Indian

Independence Movement.[17] For instance, on hearing about his death the students of Maharaja's College, Jaipur observed *hartal* in the College, organized a condolence meeting and marched in a procession through the Jaipur city as a token of homage to the departed soul. So, also, on 25 August, 1945, the *Jaipur Rajya Praja Mandal* held a public meeting in this connection. Similarly, on 26 August, 1945, the *Kota Rajya Praja Mandal* observed a *hartal* and the students marched through the Kota city as a mark of mourning the death of their beloved freedom fighter Subhas Chandra Bose.[18]

4. INA Trials, INA Day and INA Defence Fund

The students of Rajputana States appreciated the sacrifices of INA for the liberation of India. They showed more enthusiasm than their elder leaders of Praja Mandals in showing unison with their counterparts and political parties in the British Provinces in demanding the release of INA men, raising INA Defence Fund and celebrating the INA Day. For instance, in the first half of December 1945, the students of the various local institutions celebrated the INA Day by taking a procession through the Bharatpur city, the capital of Bharatpur State. They also organized a public meeting at which the speakers demanded the release of the INA men and condemned the police firing and *lathi* charge on the students at Calcutta, Bombay and other places. The students collected about Rs.300 for the INA Defence Fund.[19] So also, the students of Bikaner State collected a sum of Rs.100 from the Sikh peasant dominated Ganganagar Colony,[20] and Rs.101 from Ganganagar District[21] and other places. They remitted this amount directly to the INA Defence Fund Committee. On 2 December, 1945 the Sikh community organized an *Akali Dewan* at Bikaner, the capital town of Bikaner State, and passed a resolution demanding the immediate release of INA men.[22] Likewise, the students observed INA Day in various towns of Jaipur State, and collected Rs.200 from the public for the INA Defence Fund.[23]

On 11 December, 1945, the *Marwar Students Federation* celebrated the INA Day at Jodhpur, the capital town of Jodhpur (Marwar) State by taking a procession of student strikers shouting INA slogans, '*Jai Hind*', and '*Quit India.*'[24] It also organized a public meeting in which Mathura

Dass Mathur, a stalwart leader of *Marwar Lok Parishad*, performed the flag hoisting ceremony, criticized the British Government for firing on students at Calcutta and assured support to the *Marwar Students Federation*. In reference to the INA trials, Hukum Raj Mehta, a student and a revolutionary, who was recently released from jail by the Jodhpur State in a Bomb explosion case, asserted in the public meeting that "if Indians could be tried for joining the INA, the Britishers deserved to be tried for cowardice in leaving Indians at the mercy of the Japanese at the time of the fall of Signapore". Resolutions were also passed at the public meeting for the release of the INA men.[25] Following the examples of the students of Jodhpur, on 14 December, 1945, the Dungar College Students Union, in Bikaner made efforts to pool subscriptions for the Defence of INA Fund. The Executive Committee Members under the Chairmanship of Laxmi Chand Goyal, President of Dungar College Students Union and a student of B.A. final class, adopted a resolution of raising funds for the INA Defence Fund.[26] He also lent a hand in the collection of funds as he was son of Sagarmal Goel, a businessman of Ganganagar.[27]

5. Adoption of the INA Slogan Jai Hind

The adventures of INA on Indo-Burma border, tidings of the death of Subhas Chandra Bose, the protests of the Court martial trial of INA officers at Red Fort spread a wave of nationalism among the students all-over Rajputana States like other parts of India. This change was perceptible among the students of Bikaner State who visualized a new perception of patriotic feelings by adopting *Jai Hind* style of salutation of INA, in greeting each other and their teachers with *Jai Hind* and even answering their roll call in the class with the same zeal. For instance, on 18 December, 1945, some students of Fourth Year class of Dungar College, Bikaner answered their roll call with '*Jai Hind*' instead of 'Present Sir' in the periods of their Principal and Professor Surrendar Singh.[28] Almost identical patriotic zeal seized the school students in other Rajputana States. In January 1947, the school students at Deeg in Bharatpur State responded to their roll-calls with *Jai Hind*.[29]

Imbued with the similar sentiments of nationalism, Inder Chand Sanchet, a student of First Year Arts in Benaras Hindu University and his friends studying in Pilani visited their home in Nohar during winter vacations in December 1945. They invariably greeted each other and teachers of Nohar School with *Jai Hind.* The students of the Nohar School followed them as they considered greeting each other with *Jai Hind* as a symbol of patriotism and freedom. Hence, they also began to use this form of greeting among themselves. In their zeal of patriotism, they also inscribed *Jai Hind* on their copies. On seeing this written on the copy of a student of 8th class, the Head Master, serving under the autocratic State of Bikaner, thrashed him. Thereupon, a large number of students retaliated by shouting *Jai Hind* frequently. They also wrote *Jai Hind* on the walls of school verandah and at several places in Nohar town as a symbol of their protest.[30] The efforts of the Bikaner State C.I.D. of Nohar to watch the movements of Inder Chand Sanchet to stop these activities of the students proved of no avail. [31]

The students of High School in Sujangarh, an urban town of Bikaner State, proved more vibrant than their counterparts in other towns of Bikaner State. On the morning of 18 March, 1946, Hem Raj, a student of 8th class and his friend Bajrang Lal, a student of 5th class alongwith 125 students of the school assembled at Chopra Bazaar with a tri-colour flag on which the word *Jai Hind* was inscribed. Instilled with nationalism and simmered with grievances against Bikaner State, about 400 Seths and Sahukars, Bajrang Lal, Secretary, Local Arya Samaj and other prominent residents of Sujangarh[32] also joined the students' procession. These processionists shouted slogans, such as, *Mahatma Gandhi ki Jai, Jawaharlal Nehru ki Jai, Subhas Chandra Bose ki Jai, Inqlab Jindabad*, etc. They raised their voice against the levy of grain and Income tax, and shouted the slogans, *Dhan* Committee *Murdabad*, Income tax *nahin lagne denge*. At the top of this, some of the processionists while passing through the Chopra Bazaar pasted Hindi written poster entitled, *Jai Hind* for wide publicity and for creating political awakening among the people.[33]

6. INA Martyrs from Rajputana

The INA records at National Archives of India and several other sources reveal that among the war prisoners of the British Indian Army under the custody of Japan in Singapore, several belonging to Rajputana States joined the Indian National Army (INA). They were residents of the States of Alwar, Bharatpur, Jaipur, Bikaner and Udaipur (Mewar) as well as Deoli, a town in the British territory of Ajmer-Merar in the *centrical* position of Rajputana States. These INA sepoys from Rajputana States fought alongwith the Japanese forces against the British Indian Army in the battles of Imphal and Arakan on the Indo-Burma border. In these battles, sixty-six INA soldiers of Rajputana States sacrificed their lives for their motherland in 1944-45. Among these martyrs, Lance-Naik Likhi Ram of 3rd Guerrilla Regiment, INA belonged to village Jaspura, Bharatpur State;[34] Sepoy Met Singh of 4th Guerrilla Regiment, INA was resident of village Bagana, Udaipur State;[35] Naik Sepoy Dip Singh of 4th Guerrilla Regiment, INA, hailed from village Kharsi, P.O. Borunda, Jodhpur State;[36] Lieutenant Shabrati Khan of 1st Bahadur Group, INA was linked with village Deoli, Ajmer District,[37] and Arjan Singh, Sub-officer in the 1st Bahadur Group of INA, was connected with village Bhadra, P.O. Chhair, Bikaner State.[38]

Reception of INA Sepoys of Alwar

The sacrifices of these martyrs for the liberation of India created political awakening and infused reverence for the INA among the people of Rajputana as reflected in their affiliation with nation-wide movement against the trial of the INA officers, in their patriotic songs and also in their cheering the INA soldiers on their returning to their villages. For instance, on 22 December, 1945, about 3000 people including students and Alwar Praja Mandal workers accorded reception at the Alwar Railway Station and marched with them in a procession round the Alwar town. Thereafter, they were felicitated in a mammoth public meeting wherein speeches were delivered in an anti-British ferment while the sacrifices and sufferings of the INA men for their motherland were appreciated.[39] In the wake of this, the *Alwar Praja Mandal* formed a committee at Alwar to collect funds for the relief of INA personnel of Alwar State.[40] Among the INA soldiers several of them belonged to Shekhawati (in Jaipur State), who sacrificed their lives in the battles in Arakan and Imphal and 125 of them returned to their villages.[41]

INA Soldiers Joined *Praja Mandals*

1. In view of the growing popularity of the INA all over India, the *Alwar Rajya Praja Mandal* also planned to invite and felicitate the INA officers Major General Shah Nawaz Khan, Lieut.Col. G.S. Dhillon and Lieut.Col. P.K. Sehgal at Alwar to boost the morale of people and to mobilize them to take part in political activity as the Congress leaders at that time were engaged in negotiations for Independence of India. The news of the visit of Shah Nawaz Khan to Alwar on 24 February, 1946 created a furore all over the *Nizamats* of Alwar State. A large number of people with excitement marched from all over the State with tri-colour flags in their hands and shouting the INA slogans and singing patriotic songs. They gathered in Alwar city to welcome their beloved INA Commander. The *Alwar Rajya Praja Mandal* leaders, such as, Mahavir Prasad Jain, Motilal Sharma and Rajendra Prasad, Praja Mandal workers and volunteers, students and women alongwith the INA soldiers of Alwar State walked in procession from the Alwar Railway Station through the city market with Shah Nawaz Khan standing in a open jeep, exchanged greetings with the spectators gathered on both sides of the road. In the front line of the procession, a jeep carried a life-size portrait of Subhas Chandra Bose, as a vanguard to the procession. On the route of the procession the workers of the *Khadi Bhandar*, *Praja Mandal* office and *Alwar Patrika* also gave Shah Nawaz Khan a standing ovation. The procession was converted into a public meeting at *Purana Katla* (later on named as Subhas Chowk). Babu Shobha Ram, a stalwart leader of *Alwar Rajya Praja Mandal* presided over the public meeting. In his long speech, Shah Nawaz Khan commended the contribution of the INA soldiers like Major Man Singh, who was at this time languishing in internment in Bhopal. Quoting the example of Rani Lakshmi Bai Regiment of the INA, he impressed upon the women in the audience to join

the *Praja Mandal* Movement for the establishment of responsible government in the Alwar State. He raised his voice against the British government for creating communal divide for weakening the Indian freedom struggle.[42]

Master Harinarain Saini, a prominent leader of *Alwar Rajya Praja Mandal* has recorded in his reminiscences that the visit of Shah Nawaz Khan motivated the residents of Alwar State to take part in the responsible government movement under the auspices of the *Alwar Praja Mandal* on 26 August, 1946.[43] He was right in his observation as along with the civil population and students, a group of INA soldiers of Alwar State also associated themselves with the 1946 August Movement for responsible government under *Alwar Praja Mandal*. For instance, several INA soldiers of Alwar State, such as, Gugan Singh (village Jamalpur), Bhanwar Singh (village Shanoli), Dalip Singh Yadav (village Gandala), Ram Yadav (village Shanoli), Sohan Ram (village Bahror), Murali (village Darbarpur) and Kunwar Balwant Singh (village Majara Kanhawas) after returning to their villages joined the main-stream of political life in Alwar State according to the directions of their commander Shah Nawaz Khan. They whole-heartedly participated in the *satyagraha* for the formation of responsible government under the auspices of *Alwar Rajya Praja Mandal* in August 1946.[44] So also, in the neighbouring State of Bharatpur, Thakur Daryab Singh of INA, organized a branch of *Azad Hind Dal* at Kaman (in Bharatpur State) on 15 July, 1946 with the co-operation of INA soldiers.[45] This *Azad Hind Mandal* assisted the *Bharatpur Praja Parishad* in organizing a Political Conference of Workers at Kaman on 17-18 December, 1946. At this occasion, the volunteers of the *Azad Hind Dal* under the command of Sanwal Prasad Chaturvedi presented a Guard of Honour to Krishna Dutt Paliwal, a member of the Legislative Assembly of Bharatpur State. Daryab Singh was arrested for his participation in the *satyagraha* movement of the *Bharatpur Praja Parishad* for the responsible government in Bharatpur in July 1947.[46] Thus, the INA soldiers not only moved into the main-stream of national movement by associating themselves with the Praja

Mandals in Rajputana States but they also transformed themselves into votaries of non-violent *satyagrahis*.

2. Like Shah Nawaz Khan, Raja Mahendra Pratap Singh spurred the people to political activity in Alwar State. On the invitation of Mahavir Prasad Jain, a revolutionary and President of the Students Congress, Raja Mahendra Pratap Singh, a revolutionary and a close associate of INA Supreme Commander Subhas Chandra Bose in Burma visited Alwar on 23 August, 1946. He was taken in a one-mile long procession alongwith thousands of students and people from Nangoli Chohraya (near Alwar Railway Station) through the Alwar city in defiance of 144 Article and in the presence of Alwar State Army deployed all over the city to overawe the political activists. The procession changed into a public meeting at the Purana Katla.[47] Raja Mahendra Pratap Singh in his speech appealed the audience to join *Alwar Rajya Praja Mandal* movement for the establishment of responsible government in Alwar State. His speech galvanized thousands of people in the meeting to take a pledge to participate in this movement on 26 August 1946.[48]

In this way the visits of Maj. General Shah Nawaz Khan and Raja Mahendra Pratap Singh encouraged the INA soldiers and people to join the Praja Mandal in Alwar State. This resulted in their transformation into *satyagrahis* and strengthened the *Alwar Rajya Praja Mandal* in the struggle for responsible government. This marked the fulfilment of the objectives of the *Alwar Rajya Praja Mandal* in inviting the INA leaders to Alwar State.[49]

Endnote

References

1. Speech of Subhas Chandra Bose as Chairman of All India Youth Congress, Calcutta, 25 December, 1928. See for details, J.B.S., *Speeches and Writings of Subhash Bose*, the Indian Printing Works, Lahore, 1946, pp. 81-82.
2. *Ibid.*
3. S.C. Bose's Broadcast message to Mahatma Gandhi, 6 July, 1944. See, T.R. Sarin (ed.), *Indian National Army : A Documentary Study*, Gyan Publishing House, New Delhi, 2004, Vol.III, Document No.38, pp. 153-160.

4. K.K. Ghosh, *The Indian National Army: Second Front of the Indian Independence Movement*, Meenaksi Prakashan, Meerut, 1969, p. 224.
5. Letter of Abhaimal Jain, Secretary, Jodhpur Praja Mandal to Jawaharlal Nehru,12 May, 1936. Quoted from Sobhag Mathur, "Netaji Subhas Bose's Visit to Jodhpur (1938)," *Proceedings of Rajasthan History Congress*, Vol.X, Udaipur Session, 1977, p.104.
6. F.No.4-A, Political Department, Confidential Records, Jodhpur, 1938, pp.25-28, *Rajasthan State Archives, Bikaner* (hereafter abbreviated as *RSAB*). Quoted from Girija Shankar Sharma, *Sources on Social and Economic History of Rajasthan, 17th – 20th Century A.D.*, Vikas Prakashan, Bikaner, 2005, pp.92-93.
7. *Ibid.*, pp. 94-96.
8. Sobhag Mathur, *op.cit.*, pp.105-107.
9. Translation of Confidential Report about *Jaipur Rajya Praja Mandal* Volunteer Corps. Jalsa, dated 7 June, 1941, submitted by C.I.D. Branch City Kotwali. File No.490/130A, Mehakama Khas, Jaipur, Confidential Records, *RSAB*.
10. Fortnightly Intelligence Report for Rajputana States for the First half of August 1945. File no.10 (4 of 1945), Mehakama Khas, Udaipur, Confidential Records, *RSAB*.
11. L.P. Mathur, *Role of Press in the Growth of Representative Institutions in Rajasthan*, Book Treasure, Jodhpur 1994, pp. 26-27, 151-152.
12. *Ibid.*, p. 27.
13. Mahendra Madhup, *Jaipur Ki Patra Patrikaon ka Swadhinta Andolan main Yogdan*, Jaipur 1970, pp.47-48. See also, L.P. Mathur, *op.cit.*, p.29.
14. *Praja Sevak*, 27 March,1946, cf., J.K. Jain (ed.), *Swadhinta ke Geet*, Rajsthan State Archives, Bikaner, 1987, pp. 51-52,
15. Pratapgarh Praja Mandal, Document, no.2, cf., Jain, *op.cit.*, p. 25.
16. Pandit Bansidhar Sharma, *Praja Mandal Gijtanjali*, Part I, Bansidhar Pustakalaya, Dindwada, V.S. 2003, Song No.8, pp. 12-13.
17. Fortnightly Intelligence Report for Rajputana States for the Second Half of August 1945, S.No.10, File no.4 of 1944, Mehakama Khas, Confidential Records, Udaipur, *RSAB*.
18. *Ibid.*

19. Fortnightly Intelligence Report for Rajputana States for the first half of December 1945. S.no.10, File no.4 of 1944, Mehakama Khas, Confidential Records, Udaipur, *RSAB*.
20. *Ibid.*
21. *Ibid.*
22. *Ibid.*
23. *Ibid.*
24. *Ibid.*
25. *Ibid.*
26. Notes and Order, Government of Bikaner State, F.no.XXVI of 1943, Confidential Records, Mehakama Khas Records, Bikaner, *RSAB*.
27. F.no.XVII of 1946, Mehakama Khas Records, Confidential Records, Bikaner, *RSAB*.
28. File no.XXXI of 1943, Mehakama Khas, Confidential Records, Bikaner State, *RSAB*.
29. Dwarkanath Kachru's Report on Bharatpur affairs of 17 January, 1947. F.no.15, Pt.I, AISPC Papers, NMML, New Delhi. Quoted from S.C. Mishra, *National Movement in a Princely State*, Pointer Publishers, Jaipur, 1993, p.226.
30. Notes and Order, 11 January 1946, Government of Bikaner, F.no.45 of 1945, Mehakama Khas, Confidential Records, Bikaner State, *RSAB*.
31. Copy of letter No.253, dated 19 December, 1945, from Head Master, Nohar to the Director of Education, F.no.45 of 1945, Mehakama Khas, Confidential Records, Bikaner State, *RSAB*.
32. Following eight prominent persons joined the students' procession through the Chopra Bazaar, Sujangarh – Panne Chand Chopra, Mangelal Vaid, Durgadutt Fatehpuria, Jai Chand Rampuria, Lalchand Mundra, Nemichand Bagaria, Bhanwar Lal Saraogi and Mohanlal Saraogi. cf. Notes and Orders, Government of Bikaner, 21 March, 1946. F.no.XVII of 1946, Mehkama Khas, Confidential Records, Bikaner State, *RSAB*.
33. *Ibid.*
34. *INA Papers*, F.no.498-INA (1945), Quoted from Basudev Chatterji (ed.), *Dictionary of Martyrs; India's Freedom Struggle(1845-1947)*, Vol.2, Pt.II (L-Z), Indian Council of Historical Research, New Delhi, 2013, p.17.
35. *INA Papers*, F.no.379, INA (1946), NAI. Quoted from Basudev Chatterji, *op.cit.*, Pt.II, p.64.

36. *INA Papers*, F.nos. 1, 2, 5, 12, INA, NAI (1945). Quoted from Basudev Chatterji, *op.cit.*, p.195.
37. *INA Papers*, F.no.498, INA, NAI (1945). Quoted from Basudev Chatterji, *op.cit.*, pp.283-84.
38. *INA Papers*, F.no.460, INA, 12, INA, 464, INA, NAI (1945). Quoted from Basudev Chatterji, *op.cit.*, Vol.2, Pt.I, p.35.
39. Fortnightly Intelligence Report for Rajputana States for the Second Half of December 1945. S.no.10, File no.4 of 1944, Mehakama Khas, Confidential Records, Udaipur, *RSAB*.
40. *Ibid.*
41. For the list of 125 INA soldiers of Shekhawati, See, Raghunath Singh Shekhawat, *Shekhawati Pradesh ka Rajnitik Itihas*, Jhunjhunu, VS 2055, pp.177-78.; Mohan Singh, *Shekhawati ke Svatantrata Andolan ka Itihas*, 1990, pp.164-65.
42. *Alwar Patrika*, 23 February, 1946; F.no.98/102, Basta No.3, Alwar Praja Mandal Records, *RSAB*. Kamal Yadav, *Deshi Riyasaton men Rajnaitik Chetana aur Jana-andolana (Alwar ke Vishesha Sandarabha men*), Ritu Publication, Jaipur, 1998, pp.155-56;. See also, Hari Narayan Saini, *et. al.* (*ed.*), *Azadi ka Andolana aur Alwar*, Alwar Zila Svadhinata Svarna Jayanti Samaroh Samiti, Alwar, August, 1998, pp.124-125;
43. Harinarain Saini, *op. cit.*, p.125.
44. Saini, *op.cit.*, pp.194, 197, 199, 200, 204, 211 and 214.
45. F.no.48, Basta no.18, Bharatpur Praja Mandal Records, *RSAB*; S.C. Misra, *op.cit.*, p.211.
46. Kashinath Gupta (ed.), *Bharatpur ka Swatantra Sangram*, Bharatpur, 1987, pp. 119, 139; S.C. Misra, *op.cit.*, pp.214, 222.
47. Saini, *op.cit.*, p.175.
48. *Ibid.*, pp.182-183; Kamal Yadav, *op.cit.*, p.161.
49. Saini, *op.cit.*, pp. 124-125.

Appendix-I

आजादी के सिपाही से

कप्तान गोपाल

वतन से दूर जाकर, औरों को गुलाम करने।
जाना न गैरों के संग, किसी की आजादी हरने।।
अय हिन्दी सिपाही!

खूब है बहकाया तुझको, चिकनी-चुपड़ी बातों में।
इज्जत तेरी रुलती देखी, गुलामी की लातों में।।
अय हिन्दी सिपाही!

तेरे ही तो भाई वो, सहगल, ढिल्लन, शाहनवाज।
भाई-भाई ने मिलकर लगाई है आजादी की आवाज।।
अय हिन्दी सिपाही!

आज तू भी ललकार उठ, कहै मौलाना आजाद।
अब ना कर तू दूर, भारत हो रहा बरबाद।।
अय हिन्दी सिपाही!

जाग, जाग रे मराठा, शिवाजी के लाल।
मजा दे जंग आजादी की, खून से कर दे धरती लाल।।
अय हिन्दी सिपाही!

क्यों सोता है तू, ऐ रे मर्द बालक वीर पठान।
फिरंगी ना टिक सके, जब तू मचाए युद्ध घमसान।।
अय हिन्दी सिपाही!

अय राजपूत वीर, महाराणा प्रताप की सन्तान।
आजादी लेने को फिर, उठा ले तीर-ओ-कमान।।
अय हिन्दी सिपाही!

गुरु गोविन्दसिंह के बन्दे, ओ पंजाब के जट।
ललकार तू फिरंगी को, कि जाए हिन्द से हट।।
अय हिन्दी सिपाही!

गूंजे स्वर में इनकलाब, तिरंगा हो तेरे हाथ।
आजादी के खातिर बढ़ा, गुरखा अब हमारे साथ।।
अय हिन्दी सिपाही!

वतन की लाल बचावे, बंगाली, मद्रासी, डोगरा।
बढ़ जायें चालीस करोड़, औरत, मर्द, बालक, बुढ़ डोकरा।।
अय हिन्दी सिपाही!

अमन-खेती जंग-ऊधम मचाने वाले, गूजर विशनोई, अहीर, वो लाट।
'तिरंगे नीचे आ' हुकम दे रहे नेताजी, ओ भगवान कृष्ण की सन्तान।।
अय हिन्दी सिपाही!

Source: Praja Sevak (Jodhpur), 27 March, 1946. J.K. Jain (ed.), Swadhinta ke Geet, Rajasthan State Archives, Bikaner 1987, pp. 51-52.

Appendix-II

गीत

वली मुहम्मद

आजाद हिन्द का तू फरैरा उड़ाये जा।
हिन्दोस्तां के नाम का डंका बजाये जा।।

हिन्दू जो शीर हो तो मुसलमान हो शंकर।
आपास में इतफाक का रिश्ता बढ़ाये जा।
हिन्दोस्तां के नाम का डंका बजाये जा।।

अब नेताजी की है मिसाल तेरे सामने।
तू किस्मते फिरंगी को चक्कर में लाये जा।
हिन्दोस्तां के नाम का डंका बजाये जा।।

गुलामी और रुसवाइयों से भर चुकी तारीख।
इज्जत के चार चांद तू उसमें लगाये जा।
हिन्दोस्तां के नाम का डंका बजाये जा।।

Source: The song was composed on 23 Jaunuary, 1946. F.No. 2, Pratapgarh Prajamandal Records, RSAB. J.K. Jain (ed.), Swadhinta ke Geet, Rajasthan State Archives, Bikaner, 1987, p.25.

Appendix-III

गीत

पंडित बंसीधर शर्मा

श्री प्यारे सुभाष ने कुछ से कुछ कर दिखलाया।
श्री प्यारे सुभाष ने सोतों से हमें जगाया। टेर।।

वह आजादी का था भूखा, आजादी पर बौराया।
कितनी बार गया जेलों में, कभी नहीं घबराया।।श्री.।।

छोड़ा भारत लखकर मौका, देश-विदेश सिंधाया।
जहाँ-जहाँ पर गया बुद्धि से लोगों को चकराया।।श्री.।।

आजाद हिन्द सरकार बनाकर, दल निज एक बनाया।
देश-प्रेम का शर्बत जिनको, छका छका कर पाया।।श्री.।।

वीर गर्जना की कुछ ऐसी, सारा जग थर्राया।
देश-प्रेम का बीज हृदय में, हम सकबे पनपाया।।श्री.।।

'वंशी' नर होकर के भी वह, देवों सा पुजवाया।
धन्य धन्य वे मात-पिता, जिनने उनको उपजाया।।श्री.।।

Source: The Pandit Banshdar Sharma, Prajamandal Gitanjali, Part I, Banshidhar Pustakalaya, Dindawada, V.S. 2003, Song No.8, pp.12-13.

The 'Springing Tiger' on the Eastern Frontier: Two Narratives

Abhijit Choudhury

This paper is based on two brief narratives about the roles of Subhas Chandra Bose and the Indian National Army (INA) on the eastern frontier of India during World War II. One is an unpublished memoir of a late Indian military officer of the British Indian army, written in Bengali in the late nineteen seventies. In translation it may read: *Reminiscing the War and Netaji, Post-War Frontier and Naga Disturbance.*[1] The writer is Late Sudhir Kumar Chaudhury (1913-1989). The other is an account of discovery of the last war headquarters of Bose at a village in Nagaland and the experiences of Naga Villagers, written by a Naga Engineer, Er. Vekho Swuro. Its title is: *Discovery of Netaji Subhas Chandra Bose Delhi Chalo Last Camp in Nagaland.* It has been translated into Bengali by Smt Uma Bhaumik.[2] Incidentally, the title of this paper has borrowed the words within quote from the banner of the INA, which have also been used by Hugh Toye and Gerard H. Corr.[3] This paper is based on content analysis of these works.

The memoir narrates Late Chaudhury's experiences in the War extending from Kohima-Imphal sector to Burma, Malay and Singapore till his repatriation from South East Asia after it was over. These include what he learnt about Bose and the INA as well as the Japanese. The title of the Smriticharane suggests the memoir goes beyond the War to the decades after India was granted Independence in 1947. The Smriticharane contains four chapters. But only the first chapter is relevant for this paper. The second book has ten chapters with a chronology of military actions from March 21 to June 27 1944 in Manipur and Naga Hills. There are a number of interesting sketch maps and photographs given at the end. The emphasis is on Bose's arrival at Chesezu village near Kohima in April 1944 (pp.37-55). It begins with brief sketches on Netaji's life and mission, the INA and Indian Independence League. Brief descriptions of Nagaland and Chesezu Village follow (pp.12-26).

To start with it would be relevant to present brief biographical sketches of the authors. Late Chaudhury was born in Shillong. After completing school education he did his B.Sc in Industrial Chemistry from Benares Hindu University. Thereafter, he joined the Accountant General's Office in Shillong.[4] Later he left it to join the Assam Police Department as Police Inspector. With the outbreak of the War he joined the British Indian army, completed course at the Officers' Training School in Bangalore and was commissioned as 'Lieutenant' in Signals Branch (p.01). On his release from the army, he rejoined the Assam Police Service as Assistant Commandant of a battalion.[5] He also served in Nagaland. After retirement in 1968, he again served two terms on contract in Nagaland from 1969 to 1975. It was during this period that he began writing his memoir, which ends with 1971.[6]

Shri Swuro is from Ruzazho village of Phek District, Nagaland. He graduated in Civil Engineering from North Eastern Institute of Science and Technology, Itanagar (Arunachal Pradesh). He has worked with various departments of Nagaland Government and won Governor's award for meritorious service. Now he is with the Nagaland Vigilance Commission.[7] Learning from friends that the last war head quarters of Netaji was at Chesezu village he went there with a few of them and a photographer on 12 June, 2004 (p. 37). He took interviews of a few Naga associates of Netaji. At present he is engaged in preserving material evidence of the presence of Netaji, the INA and the Japanese at Chesezu, as also the collective memories about them through the interviews of those who either actively assisted them or saw and heard about them from their elders. The Dak Bungalow at Chesezu where Bose sojourned[8] and the stone slab on which he sat while interacting with the villagers or kept watch on enemy activities are preserved mainly with his initiatives.[9] The mountain peak near the village, where Bose established his HQ is now named, the 'Netaji Mount'.[10] Bose used to watch the military actions in and around Kohima from here.

Coming to the narratives, Chaudhury was posted at Barrackpore as "Cipher Officer' before moving to Assam. He was privy to many secrets and realized how different the ground realities were from media reports! Once, he came across a message about the British Government's interest in releasing Nehru, who was incarcerated during Quit India Movement, with the help of Chakravarty Raja Gopalachari so that the former could be sent to South East Asia to bolster the spirit of Indian soldiers there (p.07). He only mentions it, but does not say if it materialized[11]. But the writer observes that with the Japanese advance across South East Asia the Indian soldiers became aware of War situation. They were eager to get the news. However, the Government had banned listening to Berlin and Saigon Radio – to prevent the people from getting any information about Bose and the INA. Yet rumours spread with Indian soldiers and civilians escaping from South East Asia. Indian soldiers at every level of the British Indian Army secretly discussed the activities of the INA and admired their patriotism.[12] Government propaganda, on the other hand, was that some Indians in South East Asia had joined hands with the Japanese to form the *"Japanese Inspirited (sic) Force"* (JIF).[13] It was reported that Japanese planes had dropped some members of the JIF into the interiors of India. The Military Intelligence tried to collect information about it (pp.07-09). Chaudhury writes, "From around this time the practice of using the mutual greeting of '*Jai Hind*' came in vogue among the Indian soldiers" (p.08). However, he does not say whether they did it surreptitiously or otherwise!

There were widespread panic with the news of Japanese invasion of Manipur and Naga Hills. There were rumours about Netaji coming with the INA towards Bishenpur district of Manipur adjacent to Cachar (p.15). It generated excitement and inspiration among the people. Chaudhury writes that though the hill tribes of Manipur were initially indifferent towards the Allied and the Japanese forces soon they turned against the latter due to their highhanded and arrogant approach towards the villagers and their atrocities.[14] They faced stiff resistance and reprisals both in Manipur and Naga Hills. Chaudhury mentions only about the Japanese, but not the INA. It is known that Bose and the INA got the support of many hill tribals as well as the Manipuris.[15] The writer attributes the positive change in tribal attitudes towards the Allied authorities to the successful efforts of the Military Intelligence working among them and to the successful inroads made into Burma by the *Chindits*, the British guerrilla force commanded by General Wingate. They disrupted the line of communication of both the INA and the Japanese (pp.24-30). After the battles of Kohima and Mao were over, their unit moved to Imphal in October 1944. By March 1945 they proceeded towards Rangoon reaching there in July. After staying there for some time they moved to Singapore by sea in December 1945 (pp. 22-45).

On its way to Rangoon their unit had to halt at Minjan town. They came to know from local farmers that some members from the higher echelons of the INA were interned in the 'solitary cells' of the Central Jail. As various units of the British Indian army were stuck at Minjan for indefinite period, a 'Day Officer' was appointed for a week from among them. Every Sunday he used to take a walk and meet others at 'Pioneer Camps' of the road construction workers. On one occasion Chaudhury met two officers who wanted to know about the INA prisoners. On his reply in the negative they said that because he resembled the week's 'Day Officer', they committed this mistake. Chaudhury wanted to visit the Jail to see those prisoners. After carefully watching the ways of the concerned officer he decided to imitate him and succeeded in entering the Jail. The sentries did not suspect anything. The INA prisoners were thirty-four in number. There were persons from Bengal, Madras, Punjab and the UP. He noticed, they looked down upon the personnel of the British Indian army and were suspicious about them. They knew they would be hanged in near future, but were indifferent and spent their time reading religious books like the *Gita.* Chaudhury was aware of the great upsurge going on in India in support of the INA prisoners. Nehru and other leaders were determined to help them. Within that week rumour spread from the drivers of the *General Transport Company* that those prisoners at Minjan were taken by vehicle at night to the Indian border post on Arakan frontier. Later he learnt from the daily bulletin that some "bandits" tried to raid the border post but all of them were killed. Chaudhury was sure that those 'bandits' were none other than these INA prisoners and wondered how they were eliminated in a different manner (pp.35-37)!

After reaching Rangoon they encountered South Indian labourers of a Rubber Plantation where the 'Officers' Mess' was established. During conversations they not only praised the works of the INA, but expressed their love and respect for Netaji. It rekindled his hope to get more information about Netaji and the INA (p.37). But he was not ready for what he came to know! Reading an American magazine at the Mess he learnt about a British Citizen who visited Lhasa (Tibet) and became a Buddhist monk.[16] He was then residing in his *ashram* in Rangoon. He was known as U Prajnananda Swami and much revered. Chaudhury met him at the house of a former Burmese minister. In this he was also helped by a 'Madrassi' gentleman whom he met once on the road. U Prajnananda Swami was also a great yogi. He took him to his ashram. Commenting on the changing scenario after the War he told Chaudhury that a great change was coming to Bengal politics by August – September 1946 that final political settlement of the Indian question would be achieved with the visit of Lord Patrick (Pathwick-Lawrence?) Lawrence in1946. But a great surprise was awaiting him! The 'Swamiji' himself raised the issue of Netaji and said, "He is a great man, yet no one understood him"! He told him that when Netaji was in Rangoon he occasionally visited his ashram for discussions. He said further that towards the end of the War, the Japanese authorities were unfavourable to Netaji and virtually kept him under observation. Chaudhury could not believe himself when Swamiji told him that Netaji was still alive and that the Japanese had spread the rumour of his death in plane crash with dubious intentions. Chaudhury admits, "It never occurred to me that the shocking news of Netaji's death could be false!" he adds, "people from all communities in India received the news of Netaji's death in Taihoku plane crash with shock and mourning. There were no doubts expressed nor any question raised at that point of time".[17] Chaudhury did not doubt what Swamiji told him. Because U Prajnananda was a monk of very high order. How would he tell a lie? He firmly believes that the story of plane crash hides a mystery! (pp.38-42).

Chaudhury writes, "Why did I earnestly feel the urge for collecting facts about Bose and the INA, while I was in Burma? I would not perhaps be able to give satisfactory explanation then and now. For my own satisfaction I talked to many people I came across". He unexpectedly met one Bengali lady who used to broadcast the activities of the INA from Saigon Radio. When he asked her why did she join this work of propaganda leaving her family behind, she replied that one who sacrificed one's own well-being for a noble cause to jump into uncertainty, the joy would always be unbound ! He realized, perhaps many more persons did so silently for the cause of freedom. No one would know about their patriotism! (p.42).

But Chaudhury did not yet know that he would be in for the biggest surprise of his life! There was a Major who was in-charge of their unit in Singapore. He came from a very high aristocratic background and was of amiable disposition. Appreciating his sincerity towards duty he wanted to do a favour to him. After more than a week Chaudhury requested him to help him visit an office nearby, on the door of which were inscribed the words, "No entry for anyone other than the British"! The Major Sahib was red-faced, stopped talking to him. However, after around eight to ten days he arranged for his visit. Chaudhury was asked to reach there at 8 o'clock in the evening. He entered the compound through a special gate and passed three camps to reach the office. He saw surprise was writ large on the faces of the sentries. Exactly at eight the Major Sahib arrived. Hearing about his interest to see the *file* related to India, he gave it to him and told him he would come back at twelve midnight. However, going through this *special* file he could not comprehend anything since it contained comparative political analyses of the situation in Africa, Palestine and India. Other papers were also hard to understand. When the officer came at midnight Chaudhury told him, "With my limited learning I could not comprehend anything", and requested him if he could help with a file with papers written in "plain language". He gave him another file on India and told him that he would return by 5 o' clock in the morning.

It was a 'special' file containing many papers on India with important comments, which were easy to understand. Therein he came across reports on Netaji. He writes, "I was overwhelmed with excitement and read them. A report stated that Netaji *did not die* in Taihoku air crash. Rather the one who died was a different person. This information made me extremely happy! There was further information that the Allied powers had formed a 'United Search Party' to find out Netaji's whereabouts; that for this purpose teams were para dropped in *three* regions. One was dropped in an uninhabited area of Gujarat, another near Saigon and the third in mountainous areas of the North-Western frontier. Though these teams could not yet get any significant clue, there were descriptions of how these searches were being carried out. I was ecstatic and stunned at the same time. It was enough for me that Netaji was still alive! No Indian before me had entered this *special* office nor would any other after me. I felt I was lucky to have been privy to this amazing news! This news signified official confirmation of what U Prajnananda Swami told me in Rangoon. I spent next few days blissfully. I would never ever forget the help of my Major Sahib!"(p.51).

Chaudhury concludes his narrative with the following observation: "In the drama of the war my role as 'Cipher Officer' led me to many secrets, read reports of military policies and tactics. But I had to keep these to myself as there were no ways to share with anyone. However, this narrative regarding the 'plane crash' and the fate of Netaji would be incomplete if I do not divulge what I came to know. Because the people of India are trying hard to get at the truth, it would only be *natural* for the British and the Indian governments to co-operate in finding out what actually happened. A *third party* has been responsible for false propaganda. Unravelling the Netaji mystery is still far off. But from my personnel experiences I affirm that the secret operations of the 'United Search Party' were conducted since Netaji did not die in the plane crash" (pp.62-63). In fact, in his Prefatorial Submission (*Nivedan*) at the beginning of this memoir he states that what he learnt from U

Prajnananda Swami and later from the 'secret' file in Singapore were mutually corroborative. He also sounds clear in conscience stating that he is no longer bound by the 'Oath of Secrecy' on wartime or politically important facts, as no reliable witness from the Allied powers came forward to depose before the Enquiry Commissions on Netaji (p.ii).

Shri Swuro's narrative, though very brief, is particularly interesting in the sense that the writer interviewed some elderly as well as younger villagers from *Chesezu* and two other villages – *Ruzazho* (the writer's own village) and *Thenyizo*. Another interesting aspect of the narrative is the above-mentioned chronology covering the period of intense fighting in Arakan, Manipur and Kohima – Dimapur sectors from 21 March to 27 June 1944. We may begin with the Chronology (pp.63-65). After occupying an airbase on Arakan frontier in March 1944 the INA attacked Manipur. From 22 March there was heavy fighting in Kohima-Manipur sectors with the INA advancing rapidly. They defeated the British forces to take control of many areas. By 3 April they occupied Imphal-Kohima Road. Imphal was besieged. They had already occupied Mairang and hoisted the Tricolour. By early April Netaji arrived at Thenyizu village.[18] He established his HQ at Chesezu by early Apri.[19] However, the successes of the INA were short-lived as the British army in Kohima received reinforcements. With the onset of the monsoon they and the Japanese faced problems of supply. Imphal was relieved of the siege by June. The INA was on the defensive manoeuvres (p.65). Netaji had already left Chesezu towards the end of May after attack by the British troops. The INA and the Japanese soldiers fought the British at the Dak Bungalow. It appears from what the concerned elderly villagers told Shri Swuro that Netaji had moved away before the British arrived.[20] He might have had received advanced information.

What was the attitude of these villagers towards Netaji and the INA? When asked (Sarvashri) Puracho (of Thenyizu village), Vezo Swuro, Vepratlu and Poswunyi (all of Chesezu village) talked about the gentle and charming personality of Netaji, who had never been harsh or arrogant in his dealings. Vezo mentioned that only once they saw his anger when the villagers devised a stratagem to avoid weekly supply of rice to the soldiers as they were unable to meet their demands in spite of Netaji's request.[21] Incidentally, Chesezu was a prosperous village. However, its economy was adversely affected due to the problems of supplying the soldiers.[22] All the interviewees were unanimous that the villagers loved Netaji as he never differentiated between them and himself. They tried their best to help him. They were impressed with his courage and leadership qualities. The Japanese soldiers never dared to disobey his orders. Puracho and N.Theyo narrated one incidence when Netaji was informed by one Naga Villager L. Pukropra about the Japanese soldiers forcing the villagers of Thenyizu to part with food grains; he immediately mounted his horse and went there. He felled two Japanese soldiers to the ground with his slaps; they stood up and saluted him (as he was their commander in that area). He warned them never to repeat this mischief and returned to his camp. They did not disturb again (pp.39, 55). Poswunyi told the writer that once Netaji was informed of the Japanese soldiers collecting excess supplies, than they required, from Chesezu. Immediately he put up a 'note' on the main entrance of the village, in Japanese, warning the soldiers not to do so. Thereafter they no longer harassed them (p.46). Almost all the interviewees from these villages told the writer, they had never seen a leader like him who maintained equanimity in all situations. They lamented that had he won his struggle for freedom they would have seen developments in their area. Because Netaji would have kept his promises! Puracho considered Netaji a "great man". He would always feel proud that he was a companion of Netaji who treated him as a 'brother'. He said, "as far as I know Chesezu was the last war camp in his anti-British struggle for liberation" (pp.39-40). Vezo Swuro preserved a poster with Netaji's portrait. An emotional (like Puracho) Vezo told the writer, "I talked about Netaji with many, but no one had shown interests. Many of our elders are no more. Had they been around you could have got many more historical evidence. I am very happy that you are recording my statements. Thank God, my experiences with Netaji are being recorded before I pass away!" (p.44). He said, he saw Netaji when he was just six years old. "But every incidence is live in my memory"(*ibid).* His last message to the writer was, "Naga people and Netaji are bound by intimate friendship. No one in this world can severe this bond. Had he won in the war our village could have prospered again. His memory would always linger!"(p.45).

At the end of the day it may be said that the two narratives, under our consideration, are important additions to the literature extant on Subhas Chandra Bose and the INA. While the first is in the form of a memoir the second is a typical instance of how *orality* may be used to reconstruct the collective memory of a people about a historical actor and events. Late Chaudhury had twin advantages during the war. As a 'Cipher Officer' he came across many secrets which he could not divulge. Secondly, he moved with the British Indian army into South East Asia and in the process saw military situations, observed and met people from whom he could get information. He was particularly interested in Netaji and the INA. *Why*? Though a member of the British Indian army, at the core of his heart he was a *nationalist* in sentiment. He grew up in the era of freedom struggle, knew about the activities of Bose. Then, like many other Indian servicemen in the colonial armed forces he faced insult and racial slur from the British superiors.[23] One such instance of suffering is narrated, which he had to face (while posted in Silchar) from war volunteers consisting of officers from 'Tea Planters-Padre-Rail Colony' class (pp. 18-22).[24] However, he also appreciated the British 'cadet officers', who were from England and never discriminated between the British and the non-British *(ibid),* as also the qualities of some British commanders like General Wingate, Admiral Mountbatten and obviously his own 'Major Sahib' in Singapore. He admired the British attitude to duty too. This memoir is unique in one sense that the present writer does not know if any other Indian military officer of the British Indian army had written his reminiscences with reference to Netaji and the INA. Chaudhury mentions the presence of (then) Brig. J.N. Chowdhury in Singapore at the HQ of the South East Asia Command. But we are not sure if he has left any memoir.

Shri Swuro has done a highly commendable job in recovering the *lost* history of the role of Netaji and the INA from a remote rural area of Nagaland. He has gone to the field, inter-faced a cross section of the people who in their youth had either seen him or collaborated. Perhaps Swuro's interests in Netaji and the INA were generated by his

76 years old father, one Shri Poswuyi of Ruzazho village who narrated his experiences of Netaji when he came to their village after the battle of Jessami. Netaji was known to them as the 'Japanese Durga'.[25] According to Poswuyi the villagers believed that such a great and humane leader could never die in war. They had unbound love and sympathy for him. Others from Ruzazho, who claimed to have seen Netaji, shared the views of Poswuyi. They informed the writer that the INA and the Japanese forces advanced along the Jessami-Phek-Ruzazho-Yoruba-Chesezu route (pp.53-54). Shri Muleyi Khusoh too heard about Netaji from his late father who was close to Bose. At present he is taking care in preserving the stone slab where Netaji used to sit. He wants to honour the wish of his father (p.45). Shri Puracho requested the writer to convey his blessings to the daughter of Netaji (p.40). Everyone knows that the Nagas are a 'warrior' people. They would naturally appreciate a courageous, self-less and humane leader like Bose who was straight forward in his approach – precisely the reasons for which the colonial masters feared him!

References

1. Original Bengali Title: *Smritichārane Juddha O Netaji, Juddhattor Simānta ebong Upadruta Nagabhumi.*
2. Residing at Lumding, Central Assam, she is a retired college principal. The second edition of her translation has been published from Guwahati by Vicky Publishers in 2013 (first published in 2012). We have used the translated version.
3. Hugh Toye, 1959/2001. *Subhas Chandra Bose (The Springing Tiger). A Study of a Revolution.* Bombay : Jaico Publishing House; Corr, 1974. *The War of the Springing Tigers.* Bombay: Jaico Publishing House. Actually Bose "added a springing Bengal to the tricolour flag" which became the symbol of the INA.
4. Interview with his daughter, Dr. Sumita Chaudhury, retd.Head of the Department of Physics, Lady Keane College, Shillong, 12 January 2017.
5. Page 64 of the Smriticharane. Also the interview with Dr. Chaudhury.
6. Interview with Dr. Chaudhury. The Smriticharane ends with 1971, when he returned to Shillong after completion of the first term. He began writing the memoir during the second term after 1971. He finally retired from

Nagaland in 1975 (Telephonic conversation with Dr. Chaudhury on 27 January, 2017).

7. The *blurb* in the front inside cover.
8. Photo in p.81.
9. Photo in p.77.
10. Photo in pp.79-80
11. As far as we know it did not materialize due to prevailing circumstances. Chaudhury could not have known it.
12. Corr, *op.cit.*, points out, it is impossible to estimate "how many of the first" twenty thousand volunteers from the Indian PoWs were genuinely patriot. According to him their patriotism was consequent of their grievances against the British including racism and discriminations. In some cases coercion of various types were employed to persuade the reluctant ones. However, rejecting the legend that "all the Gurkhas remained loyal", he says that quite a few "volunteered" (pp.118-124 for details). In course of his interface with the present writer in 2011, late Nor Bahadur Gurung of Shillong, an ex-INA man, told him that at-least five hundred Gurkha PoWS in Germany volunteered to join the *Indian Legion*, after Bose addressed them. They were inspired by him. See Abhijit Choudhury, 'what Do We Owe Them? Three non-Tribal fighters against the Raj', in Sanjay Hazarika, *ed. Little known Fighters Against the Raj: Figures from Meghalaya'*. New Delhi: CNES&PR, Jamia Milia Islamia, 2013, pp.74-88. He does not deny that patriotic sensibilities were totally absent.
13. *Ibid.* Corr says it was "Japanese Indian Forces", and occasionally called, "Japanese Inspired Fifth-columnists" (p.91). Its code name was 'BAT' – (Chaudhury, Smriticharane. pp. 07-09).
14. Some of the interviewees of Shri Vekho Swuro too mention their highhanded and coercive approach in collecting essential supplies from the Naga Villages. However, while Vezo Swuro told the writer that neither the INA nor the Japanese soldiers ill-treated the villagers, in reply to another question he said that the Japanese soldiers often killed the domestic animals without taking permission of their owners (pp. 49-51). Corr, *ibid*, points out that one of the reasons of reluctance of some Indian PoWS was that they were aware of the Japanese atrocities even on the Indian PoWs in Malay.
15. See Dr. J.B. Bhattacharjee's *Presidential Address* to the Golden Jubilee Session of the Indian History Congress in Gorakhpur (1989-90), under title,

'World War II & India : a fifty years perspective'. It was later published also in *The Cause* (Netaji Subhash Chandra Bose Birth Centenary Souvenir 1897-1997) brought out from Shillong (pp. 36-53). See also 'Introducing the theme' in *The Cause* (pp.III-IV).

16. Chaudhury, Smriticharane. The Swamiji fought in the Great War (1914-1918) and won the Victoria Cross. After the war he grew inclined towards spiritualism. This background story may remind one, of Somerset Maugham's fiction, *The Razor's Edge*, albeit in a different context !
17. However, Gandhi sent a telegram to Sarat Bose asking him not to perform the last rites for Subhas.
18. Interface with Shri N. Theyo (p.55).
19. Interface with (Sarvashri) Puracho, Vezo Swuro and others (pp.37-52).
20. *Ibid.* (Sarvashri) Puracho, Vezo Swuro and Poswunyi.
21. *Ibid.* Vezo Swuro, pp. 40-45.
22. *Ibid.* Also Shri Muleyi Khusoh, then chairman of the Village Council of Chesezu. He heard about Netaji from his late father (p. 45).
23. In course of his interface with the present writer in 1997, late Dharanidhar Mahanta, who participated in the Royal Indian Navy Mutiny in 1946, told him that the Indian naval ratings were often ill-treated. There were discriminations against them. In such a situation they were inspired by the news of exploits of Bose and the INA. See *The Cause*, pp. 59-61. Also see Abhijit Choudhury, *op.cit.*, in Sanjay Hazarika 2013.
24. He suffered because he retorted back when a 'padre' officer made an insulting comment on Indian food in the Officers' Mess, and resisted his attempt to assault him. Later he and his associates brought false charges against him and he was court martialled. However, he was acquitted by British Military judges of the Tribunal.
25. (Sarvashri) Vepratlu and Poswunyi of Chesezu Village told the writer that the villagers knew Netaji as the 'Raja of Japan' (pp.45-46).

The Nature and Extent of INA's Freedom Offensive: British Intelligence Assessment

Tapan Chattopadhyay

Introduction

Prior to and during the World War II, British Intelligence in India was keeping an avid eye on the activities of Indian revolutionaries in East and South-east Asia. This was due to the fact that since the first decade of the twentieth century a fair number of Indian revolutionaries were settling down and organizing their political activities in Japan, Malaya, Thailand, Hong Kong, Singapore and Shanghai. As far back as in 1905 the Indians had observed the Shivaji festival in Tokyo with pomp and pride with active local support.[1] Japan's spectacular victory over Russia in the war of 1904-1905 had enthused the Indian revolutionaries and freedom-seekers all over the globe with a new hope of throwing off the British yoke as an Asian nation. The sympathy of Japanese populace and government for Indian aspirations for Independence and their anti-British feelings were particularly evident when in 1905 the speaker of the Japanese House of Peers declared that the sacred duty of Japan was to stretch a helping hand to India to win freedom.[2]

A branch of the revolutionary organization 'Free Hindustan' was started at Aoyama in Tokyo in 1906 under the name of 'India House', recalling Shyamji Krishnavarma's organization of the same name in London;[3] and the anti-British propaganda took a virulent form at the behest of Maulavi Mehmood Barkatullah, a teacher of Urdu originally from Bhopal, in 1909 so much so that the Viceroy of India sought Japan's intervention to make him leave Japan for the USA *via* Thailand and Java.[4] Anti-British activity again took a boost in Japan after the arrival of Rash Behari Bose incognito in June 1916, under the pen-name of 'P.N. Tagore'. Anti-British propaganda and activities spread similarly in Malaya, Thailand, Java, Hong Kong, Shanghai, and Singapore at the initiative of Indian revolutionaries who took refuge in those countries. A sizeable section of these revolutionaries were Ghadarites having experience of organizing their activities in India, Europe or the USA. These fragmented groups of revolutionaries were unanimous on one point: they believed in the military means to oust the enemy.

The British Intelligence was keeping abreast of these activities through their contacts and sources as best as they could. In Myanmar and Malaya they had left behind some sources at the time of retreat that helped them during the War. Some of them even acted as spies and agent provocateurs in the Japanese-conquered territories including the Andaman & Nicobar Islands.[5]The fraternal OSS (Overseas Strategic Services) – the precursor of the CIA - under William J. Donovan also developed a good access in Japan and Southeast Asia and helped the British Intelligence with useful inputs. In Thailand, the British had a viable information infrastructure that had helped them compete with the French in influence-peddling in the past. A number of Indian activists arrested in Singapore, Hong Kong and other places, moreover, yielded a plethora of useful information on the revolutionary moves, methodology and personalities. So, immediately after the start of the War when the movements were gathering momentum around the idea of forming a revolutionary army to attain independence in Tokyo (under Rash Behari Bose, Anand Mohan Sahay and Debnath Das); Malaya (under Amar Singh and Pritam Singh); Thailand (under Swami Satyananda Puri alias Prafulla Kumar Sen of Faridpur, now Bangladesh); and in Shanghai and Malaya (under Baba Hari Singh *alias* Osman Khan), the British Intelligence kept a tab on them.

When two most important leaders of the Indian Independence movement – Swami Satyananda Puri and Pritam Singh – died in an air crash in a Japanese plane with two other colleagues near Nagoya Bay on their way to attend the crucial Tokyo Conference (March 28-30, 1942), the British propagated that they had been purposely got rid of by the Japanese. They interpreted it as Japanese ploy to facilitate Rash Behari Bose who was a Japanese citizen to have the control of the Indian Independence League (IIL) and the Indian National Army (INA) instead of Satyananda Puri, a revered, influential revolutionary and a scholar, who was wary of Japan.[6] This propaganda had then created a serious misgivings about Japanese intentions among the delegates and common Indians in Southeast Asia. The anti-Japanese propaganda thus engineered in the INA and Mohan Singh's anti-Japanese and anti-Rash Behari Bose mindset continued to plague the organizations and led to the arrest of Singh and the dismantling of the first INA in December 1942, *i.e.* within a year of its formation.

Information on INA Activities

Before this happened, the British Intelligence had come to know about the INA in depth for the first time in October 1942 when Captain Mahabir Singh Dhillon of the INA's intelligence outfit stationed at Kalewa in Myanmar, close to the Manipur border, surrendered to the British with vital documents on the INA. Lt.-Col. Niranjan Singh Gill whom Mohan Singh had put in charge of cross-border intelligence operations in India only two months back and to whom Dhillon was close was assessed to have instigated this defection and was arrested from Mohan Singh's residence on December 8, 1942, twenty-one days before Singh's own arrest. From all indications, Gill had acted as a British 'mole' in the INA.[7] Mahabir Singh Dhillon's statement before the British, which is available now, makes it clear that he betrayed the INA and gave them the first detailed information about the organization, for which he was awarded a medal by the British Indian government soon after his defection. He was later conferred the prestigious title of the 'Member of the Most Excellent Order of the British Empire' (announced in London Gazette on 30 March 1943). His admission also reveals that Niranjan Singh Gill was fully implicated in this betrayal.

In the case of Gill, his incarceration by the Japanese seemed strangely to be a factor in his favour in Nehru's government after Independence; and he was made India's ambassador in many countries till old age overtook him. According to a British Intelligence report, Mohan Singh himself received a letter of congratulations from Lieutenant-General A.E. Percival, GOC of the Malaya Command then detained in the Changi Camp at the eastern extremity of Singapore.[8] When Subhas Chandra Bose requested him soon after arriving in Singapore to be a part of the team in a cozy discussion at the place of his detention, Mohan Singh was avowedly and exceedingly impressed by Bose and his purpose, but he declined the offer.[9] Some have averred that he had developed cold feet about the movement for fear of British retribution.[10]

The betrayal of Gill and Dhillon prompted the government to set up "a fully developed organisation on the land frontier between Burma and India by which all arrivals were organized and, if found in any way suspicious, sent to other centres for further interrogation."[11] The border intelligence posts that were now created or strengthened enabled the government to keep track of the INA infiltrations for the purpose of espionage and subversion in India, as also secure inside information about the organisation's formations, activities, plans and programmes. In the same vein, the Intelligence Bureau which had regional headquarters then at Shillong and a proactive office at Kohima along with units at several forward places like Mokokchung, Zuneboto, Melauri, Tuensang, Ukhrul and Silchar etc. and the provincial Special Branches were alerted about the INA. The British Intelligence termed the INA's land-based operatives as 'JIFCS' (Japanese inspired fifth-columnist spies) and the trained paratroopers who were dropped by parachutes in India for carrying out espionage and subversive operations as 'BATS' (Burmese area trained spies).

INA's Apparatus for Propaganda and Subversion

In reality, a number of intelligence training centres were organized by the first INA in 1942 in Thailand, Malaya, and Myanmar at the behest of the Japanese. Operatives trained in these institutes commenced their liberation war much before the joint military offensive in the Arakans and the Kohima-Imphal sector. In most cases Mohan Singh had no clue to what was happening, as the long-existing Indian revolutionary outfits in far-flung regions used for this purpose were accustomed to operating independently. These outfits and the INA's training centres were subsequently reshaped, coordinated, and brought under his firm control- without any Japanese interference whatsoever – by Subhas Chandra Bose; and some of them became top-class intelligence units dreaded by the British.

A 'strictly secret' intelligence report to be handled in close confidence despatched from Bangkok on August 23, 1942, by OKW, OKH and the Attach Section of the German Wehrmacht bearing No. 499 V.20.8 under the heading: 'Indian National Army' stated, among other things, that General Terauchi's headquarters at Shonanto (Thailand) was evincing keen interest in the training of Indian agents at Shonanto. The training facility at Shonanto was particularly preparing Indian political agents for contacting Indians and spreading propaganda for causing disaffection especially inside the police and the defence sectors in India. Military agents were also being trained for providing secret information separately for the defence forces.[12]

It is also known from the contemporary British intelligence assessment that a number of spy schools were loosely run by the INA in 1942 and early 1943 with the help of the Japanese at Penang in Malaya. Among them were: Penang Propaganda School, Tehjong Bungah School (also known as Muslim Spy School) and Singhalese Party School headed by Lieutenant-Colonel S.N. Chopra under the general direction of Baba Hari Singh alias Osman Khan.[13] Apart from these institutes, Dr. Sudhinanda Roy ran the Bengali Spy School quite effectively since May 1943 at Port Dickson; and the famous Sandycroft School,[14] whose courses were specially designed by Subhas Chandra Bose with the help of N.G. Swamy soon after taking over the charge of the INA, launched several successful operations. In Rangoon too, the Swaraj Young Men's Training Institute (SYMTI) was started by Baba Hari Singh alias Osman Khan at Thingangyun towards the end of 1942 with about ninety volunteers.[15] The SYMTI had its branches at Kanbe and Maymyo in Myanmar, of which the Kanbe branch acquired increasing importance in course of time. Bose set the recruitment target of the SYMTI, Kanbe, at 5000, of which 800 were to be drafted from the INA and the remaining cadres were to be recruited from among civilian volunteers.[16]

A report of 5 F.I.C., Security Corps, of 18 Advance Base of the British Indian army mentioned that in December 1943 there were 600-700 'JIFCS' undergoing training at Kanbe. It was stated in the report that a number of minor spy training centres were closed down in Burma and that the trainees of these centres were brought to Kanbe.[17]Like Sandycroft in Malaya, Bose chose the spy training centre at Kanbe in Myanmar for strategic-tactical reasons to perform the multi-faceted intelligence tasks. It was used as a springboard for launching spies across the land and the sea into India. Most importantly, this institute trained paratroopers to be dropped behind the enemy lines in north-eastern India. The paratroopers and land-based spies of the Thingangyun and Kanbe institutes – often known to the locals as 'Congresswalas' - infiltrated north-eastern India in a large number in late 1943 and early 1944 and prepared the ground for the INA's combined offensive. One frontier intelligence outfit named 'Nishi Kikan' employed Chins, Kumis, Kukis etc. and worked in close tandem with the Indian counterparts since December 1943.[18] The British administration often used harsh methods, as the intelligence inputs and the reports of the senior officers indicated, to keep the local tribes away from their influence.

British Counter-measures

The INA's freedom offensive was threatening the British most since the 1857 uprisings. They had already taken the gradualist Congress politics and approach in their stride and created enough assets and fissures in the party and the over-all Indian politics to steady the boat rocking from time to time. They had worked on Jawaharlal Nehru and secured his support for British war efforts, as the recently released British archival records indicate, with the help of Marshal Chiang Kai-shek and also of Madame Chiang's charm.[19] The suave, affluent, Cambridge-educated Bose and his mindset were an enigma to them; and they hated and feared, as was their wont, what they did not understand. They assessed the potential of the INA's subversive activities and took several counter-measures to neutralize them, apart from taking military measures to frustrate the combined Japanese-INA military assaults.

Special care was taken to obstruct all kinds of propaganda made by the INA and the Japanese government from reaching Indian masses. A three-pronged operation called 'Operation Denial' was launched in this regard with the following tasks: jamming of frequencies of the Azad Hind Radio Stations of Tokyo, Rangoon, Bangkok, Kuala Lumpur and other places to frustrate propaganda aimed at stirring a rebellion in India; throttling of the Indian media about the INA and Bose; and ensuring strict vigil and taking into preventive custody all those who were sympathetic to Bose and his cause.[20] The operation succeeded greatly; and very few in India knew about the extent of the INA's preparations and deeds before the disclosures during the famous Red Fort trials after the War, which literally shook the country. The top British bureaucrats gloated over the unprecedented success of 'Operation Denial' in their official deliberations.[21] When Pabitra Mohan Roy, leader of the Secret Service group, was sent by submarine to Calcutta to form a communication set-up, he was surprised to see that common people had little idea of the activities of the INA and its Netaji.[22]

The DMI (Directorate of Military Intelligence), the DPR (Director of Public Relation) and the DIB (Director of Intelligence Bureau), Home department and the Southeast Asia Command (SEAC) took a conscious decision during their exhaustive deliberations between November 1943 and 1 March 1944 to disclose nothing officially, but to rely on the 'spill-over' information from channels like army intelligence broadcasts, verbal propaganda of the army recruiting staff and the central liaison officers and, of course, the 'JOSH Group system' to counter Japanese and INA propaganda, some of which was inevitably finding its way to India.[23] It was felt that anything published now "whether 'debunking' the JIFS or otherwise, would be seized upon by the Nationalist Press and splashed" and "would cause something of a sensation throughout the country and would become the subject of heated controversy in the public prints, with flaring tendentious headlines." Little of what would be said would reflect well on the Indian Army either in the public eye or, more important still, in the eyes of the British and Allied troops. "It might also adversely affect JOSH".[24]

The 'JOSH Group system' referred to the systemic pro-British and anti-Bose political propaganda and virulent vilification-cum-disinformation campaign organized by the civil and army units and certain political elements, including the communists.[25] The word 'josh' meant 'pep' as given out in an army circular of May 15, 1944 and the group referred to the communists headed by P.C. Joshi, who actively supported British war efforts and was a useful contact of the Intelligence Bureau.

Impact of the Offensive

Never before the British had faced such an organized onslaught in an adverse political milieu as the INA's. The legendary deputy commissioner of the Naga Hill District, Charles R. Pawsey, who had considerable hold in the tribal *hohos* (local parliaments) and was knighted after the War for his contribution to the British victory, has given a graphic eye-witness account of the situation then prevailing. He wrote in his official file: "The siege of Kohima will go down in history as the siege that failed, but only just. The Japanese boasted on April 9th that they had captured Kohima – a boast that was absolutely justified in view of the fact that by that time they held Kohima Bazar, Kohima town, Kohima village and every building of importance including the Deputy Commissioner's bungalow. Only the hill above the DC's bungalow was held (by the British), and the Japanese had completely surrounded and cut off the small garrison that was left to defend it. If the garrison had fallen, the Japanese would very likely have overrun Dimapur, where there was no force strong enough to oppose them, nor natural feature strong enough to defend. Ever expert at fighting in the jungle the Japanese would have found it easy to penetrate to the railway, and advance along the line until eventually all Assam would have been in their hands. No trained fighting troops were there to oppose them, nor would their advance have been stemmed until they were held up by the Brahmaputra. After this it would be unprofitable to attempt to predict what might have taken place".[26]

There was a plethora of intelligence reports confirming what Pawsey described. In one such account, the army intelligence officer Arthur Campbell, who was then posted to Dimapur and was in Kohima just before the battle, has written: "The people of Dimapur were frightened people, men and women alike. The women were leaving in a hurry, and the men were ruled by the rumour, both the civilians in the small bazaar and the base troops handling the stores in the depots. Rumour infected everyone so that it was difficult to find a true picture even from the intelligence people in the military headquarters.[27]

The commander of the Allied forces, Lt.-Gen. W.J. Slim, has described the situation thus: "We were not prepared for so heavy a thrust; Kohima with its rather scratch garrison and, what was worse, Dimapur with no garrison at all, were in deadly peril. The loss of Kohima we could endure, but that of Dimapur, our only base and rail-head, would have been crippling to an almost fatal degree. It would have pushed into far distance our hopes of relieving Imphal, laid bare to the enemy the Brahmaputra valley with its spring of airfields, cut off Stilwell's Ledo Chinese, and stopped all supply to China."[28]

This was precisely what Bose had wanted the combined forces of Japan and the INA to do. It was a blunder on the part of Field Marshal Terauchi, supreme commander of the Japanese forces in Southeast Asia, Lt.-Gen. Kawabe, chief of the Burmese Area Army (BAA), and Lt.-Gen. Renya Mutaguchi, commander of the 15th Army, as admitted by some Japanese officers after the War, not to attack Dimapur and take the battle to the Assam plains as desired by Bose instead of wasting time at Kohima when indeed their intention was to make a way for INA troops to pass through into India.[29] Had Bose obtained the necessary military support to lead his 30,000 men (plus, 20,000 men under training), instead of having 10,000 soldiers in all used at different stages in the offensive, the result might have been different.

Conclusion

According to the government estimate, 19,500 INA soldiers were taken prisoner in the war, of which 1,500 had taken part in the Imphal campaign.[30] Many of them entered India during the operation taking advantage of the border, as found in the accounts of some of them. As the report of the Director, Military Intelligence (DMI), indicated, many of them when arrested were subjected to ruthless physical torture and were even summarily executed.[31] Britain was desperate to besmear the activities of the INA and hide them from the public view for fear of losing her empire.

For one thing, the INA movement exhibited for the first time, the capacity of the Indians to stride together, irrespective of religion, caste and creed, as a nation. The British intelligence reports were immensely more respectful of the INA than the British public posture. One assessment just after the War reads thus: "Many thousands of civilians, after training, were drafted into INA units (in 1 Div there were only 5% civilians: in 2 Div there were 40% civilians and in 3 Div there were 70% civilians) and any civilian showing ability or leadership was sent for OTS training. Mohan Singh thought of the INA as a military movement only. It required the wider vision of S. C. Bose to mobilize Indian manpower resources in S. E. Asia and to weld the military and trained civilian resources at his disposal into what he fondly conceived as an irresistible army of liberation. The civilians in the INA fought few battles and won little glory; they deserted in thousands when the Japanese capitulated. But it is beyond doubt that the influences of communal training, living and fighting will continue to affect the thoughts and outlooks of all these civilians for many years to come. The present level of political consciousness amongst Indian civilians in Malaya/Burma is but one certain aspect of the aftermath of S. C. Bose's mobilization of civilian manpower. S. C. Bose may be dead but much that he did lives still".[32]

The secret assessment of the chief of the Indian Army, General Sir Claude Auchinleck, and the home office was that the liberation efforts of the INA and the consequent disaffection among the Indian soldiers in the British Army and Navy had advanced the prospect of India's independence by about twenty years.

References

1. Lancelot Lawton, *Empire of the East, Part II* (London, 1912), p. 805. See also A.C. Bose, Indian Revolutionaries Abroad, 1905-1922: In the Background of International Developments (Bharati Bhawan, Patna, 1971), p. 67.
2. *Ibid.*
3. *Ibid.*
4. Roger Beaumont (ed.), *In the Footsteps of the Monsoon – A History of India's Influence in Thailand* (City Media, Bangkok, 1996), p. 138.
5. Photographs of some such spies who acted against the INA are now displayed as patriots in the museum of the erstwhile Cellular Jail along with those of the revolutionaries jailed by the British.
6. Stephen C. Cohen, *The Indian Army – Its Contribution to the Development of a Nation* (Oxford University Press, Delhi, 1990), p. 153.
7. Tapan Chattopadhyay, *The INA's Secret Service in Southeast Asia – Its Background, Infrastructure, Resources and Activities During World War II* (Readers Service, Kolkata, 2011, third reprint 2014), pp. 107-108.
8. Memo No. SC/INT-A/2/514 dated 23 November, 1943 of the Commanding Security Corps, Hq. Eastern Army, 12 Adv. Base, P.O. India, addressed to the officers in charge of Nos. 2 and 5 F.I.Os.
9. General Mohan Singh, Soldiers' Contribution to Indian Independence – The Epic of the Indian National Army (Army Education Store, New Delhi, second edition, 1974), p. 270.
10. Maj. Gen. G.D. Bakshi, Bose – An Indian Samurai – Netaji and the INA – A Military Assessment (K. W. Publishers Pvt Ltd., New Delhi, 2016), p. 89.
11. Statement made by the Home Member at the National Defence Council in July 1943.
12. National Archives File No. 433/INA containing an assessment of the Government of India.
13. *Ibid.*
14. National Archives File No. 985/INA (Part–I) containing British Intelligence reports under heading: "Part III I J.I.F.C. Training Schools", pp. 54-56.
15. Ibid.

16. Most Secret Memo No. 4086/13/G/2 of 5 F.I.C., Security Corps, 18 Adv. Base, P.O. India, dated 2 December 1943.
17. Part III – JIFS Organisations and Activities – E. Part III: Connected with "I" Offensive against India, paragraph 2, p. 60.
18. Maulana Abul Kalam Azad, *India Wins Freedom* (Orient Longman, Bombay, reprint 1959), pp. 56 and 66. Nehru was also deeply influenced by Louis Mountbatten and his wife Edwina. See Alex Von Tunzelmann, *Indian Summer – The Secret History of the End of the Empire* (Pocket Books, London, 2007) for a detailed account.
19. Most Secret Memo No. 483-95-C., Shillong, dated 4 February, 1944 of Inspector General of Police, Assam, forwarded to all Superintendents of Police including Hill districts (except Garo Hills), Political Agent, Manipur, and the Political Officer, Tirap Frontier Tract, enclosing copy of No. 34/60 dated 15 January, 1944 from the Deputy Chief Signal Officer, 202 L. of C. Area. Also, HQ. 202, L. of C. Letter No. D1 dated 8 December 1943 addressed to the Director of Civil Defence and Letter No. 24/60 of the Deputy Chief Signal Officer, HQ. 202, L & C Area, addressed to the same person.
20. UO No. DMI/5528 dated 21 August, 1944 of the Major General in charge of the DMI, New Delhi, National Archives File No. 432/INA.
21. Dr. Pabitra Mohan Roy, Netajir Secret Service (Agrani Book Club, Kolkata, 2003), pp. 62-66.
22. UO No. DMI/5528 dated 21 August, 1944 of the Major General in charge of the DMI, New Delhi, *vide* National Archives File No. 432/INA.
23. UO No. 1393 dated 28 February, 1944 of Deputy Director, Public Relation (DDPR), quoted by the Director, Military Intelligence (DMI).
24. Circular dated 15 May 1944 addressed to all commanding officers of Indian army units captioned: 'Activities of the "Josh Group" constituted by the Government of India to counteract the collaboration of INA with the Japanese' *vide* War Office Memo No. 208/804, Public Office, London. The circular has been reproduced in T. R. Sareen, Japan and the Indian National Army (Mounto Publishing House, New Delhi, 1996), pp. 260-263.
25. Arthur Campbell, M.C., *The Siege, A Story from Kohima* (George Allen & Unwin Ltd., London, 1956), pp. 37-38.
26. Field Marshal William J. Slim, *Defeat into Victory* (Cassell, London), pp. 261-262.

27. Maj. Gen. Mohammad Zaman Kiani, *India's Freedom Struggle and the Great INA* (Radiance Publishing House, New Delhi, 1994), p. 109.
28. K. K. Ghosh, *The Indian National Army* (Meenakshi Prakashan, Meerut, 1969), p. 298.
29. UO No. DMI/5528 dated 21 August 1944 of DMI, New Delhi, *vide* National Archives File No. 432/INA.
30. Monograph 6 captioned 'Guide to JIFC (Indian) Activities, Part II', paragraph 16, *vide* National Archives File No. 985/INA.

Japanese Invasions in Asia 1894–1942

Gautam Das

Introduction

This articls deals with Japan's military invasions and conquests in its neighbouring countries and in South-East Asia, till it reached its maximum extent in 1942. Japan's invasions of Asia have to be seen in the context of both its modernization - political, economic, and military– and the gradual militarization of Japanese society with the Samurai code of honour being transferred onto Japanese society as a whole.

As part of the new modern political system under the Meiji Restoration [1868-1912 C.E.], only policemen, regular soldiers and naval sailors were permitted to carry swords. Within the old Japanese traditional society, the warrior class known as the 'Samurai' enjoyed considerable privileges, and were the only ones allowed to carry arms. This dealt a severe social blow to the Samurai, because thereafter any humbly-born military conscript or policeman could carry a sword, while the Samurai could not. A Samurai rebellion grew, and in 1877, its leader, SaigoTakamori, led a force of 40,000 Samurai against a government army of conscripts in the bloody Battle of Kagashima. Their defeat proved to the Japanese society that any ordinary Japanese could fight as well as a Samurai. This belief gradually led to the belief that all Japanese could fight and defeat any other country in war, and thus started Japanese militarism.

Government-led industrialization also led to the creation of a modern military system based on western European models, under the slogan 'Enrich the country, strengthen the military'. Japan's expansionist policy of invasion and conquest began from 1894.

First Sino-Japanese War and the Rise of the Militarists

Without any formal declaration of war, Japan suddenly attacked China in July 1894, achieving surprise and a striking success. It was a lesson Japan did not forget. The First Sino-Japanese War 1894-95 ended with a Japanese victory, and the Japanese occupation of Korea, Manchuria, and Taiwan.

The sequence of events had begun before the first engagement of the war. With political unrest within Korea, creating tension between Korea, Japan and China, Japan sent a 8,000 strong force to the port of Inchon. This force moved to Seoul, taking control of the Korean government on July 20, 1894. On July 25, off the west coast of Korea a Chinese naval force base encountered a Japanese naval force, and lost the engagement.

The Japanese and the Chinese armies first clashed at Songhwan on July 29, 1894, the first overseas battle fought by a Japanese army in three hundred years. It was a Japanese victory. Japan declared war thereafter on August 1, 1894, and both China and Japan rushed additional forces to Korea. On September 16, the Chinese defence at Pyongyang, with a strength of 14,000 troops were attacked by the Japanese using a force of between 10,000 and 20,000. The Japanese captured the city, inflicting 7,000 casualties on the Chinese.

More Japanese troops landed on the Korean peninsula, while Chinese forces arrived at the Yalu River, the northern border between Korea and China, and fortified it. On September 17, 1894, the Japanese won a naval Battle on the Yalu River. The Japanese hereafter had control of the seas. On the night of October 24-25, 1894, the Japanese turned the Yalu River border fortifications and attacked from behind, winning the land battle. On October 19, 20, the Japanese forces attacked Port Arthur, while the Japanese Second Army was launched into the war, landing on the north-west coast of China on October 24, and advancing towards Port Arthur. The city was captured on October 24.

The Japanese First Army, advancing on Mukden, the capital of Manchuria, fought a series of hard-fought battles, often against larger but badly-led Chinese forces. The other Manchurian cities of Niuzhang and Liaoyang fell to Japanese attacks by March 4, 1895, and Manchuria was in Japanese hands.

The Japanese Navy opened another front in mid-January 1895, in China's Shandong Province, arriving outside the Chinese naval base of Weihaiwei on January 30, 1895. By the February 2, the Japanese had captured the port fortifications, and the port surrendered on February 12th.

The last phase of the war started onMarch 23, 1895, with an invasion of the Pescadores islands, an archipelago in the Formosa Strait. The planned capture of Beijing in a two-pronged attack, with one Japanese force from Shandong and the other from Manchuria was not needed, as the Chinese government sued for peace. The Treaty of Shimonoseki was signed on April 18, 1895, with large concessions made to Japan, including a large financial indemnity, the Liaotung Peninsula, Port Arthur, Taiwan and the Pescadores Islands.

This first Japanese war with China was a model for Japanese campaigns of conquest over the next half-century. Its success encouraged the militaristic factions of the Japanese society, with long-term implications for Japan.

Russo-Japanese War 1904-1905

Since, the end of the First Sino-Japanese War in 1895, Japan feared Russian encroachment on its sphere of influence. Russia's presence in northern Manchuria, and her development of a railway towards Port Arthur was seen as a potent menace. Russia wanted access to the ice-free Port Arthur, because her own port of Pacific-coast port of Vladivostok was operational only during the summer. Japan started talks with Russia, to pressurize her to leave Manchuria. Five months of negotiations achieved nothing, and on February 6, Japan broke off the talks. Within two days Japanese troops re-occupied Seoul, the Korean capital. A Japanese fleet arrived at Port Arthur on February 8, to find a Russian fleet at anchor in the harbour, and attacked it. The Japanese declared war three hours later. The eighteen-months long war February 8, 1904 –September 5, 1905 was the biggest modern war till then, with large, clearly-defined battles and many casualties. The major theatres of operations were the Liaodong Peninsula and Mukden in Southern Manchuria and the seas around Korea, Japan, and the Yellow Sea.

This war was fought on both land and sea, with the Japanese taking five months to win the battle of the siege of Port Arthur, which cost them 60,000 casualties. In February 1905, the Japanese attacked the strong Russian force at Mukden and overcame them after a three-weeks' long battle. There were three quarters of a million men engaged on both sides, but the decisive Japanese victory resulted in one-fifth of the total on both sides killed or wounded. The Japanese had, however, not catered for enough follow-up reserves, having concentrated on building up and training her front-line army, so were unable to consolidate their considerable gains.

This was the first time the tactics of entrenched positions for infantry defended with machine guns and artillery became vitally important, presaging the First World War. The number of Japanese Army dead in combat was around 47,000 with around 27,000 additional casualties from disease, and between 6,000 and 12,000 wounded. The Estimates of Russian soldiers killed range from around 40,000 to around 70,000 men. China suffered 20,000 civilian deaths.

Russia had despatched her remaining Baltic Fleet to join the campaign in the Far East. It sailed all the way around the Cape of Good Hope, the Indian Ocean and Malaya, taking over six months to arrive. The Japanese had estimated that the fleet would head for Vladivostok and a re-fit, *via* the Tsushima Strait between Kyushu and Korea, and the Japanese fleet met the Russian fleet there on May 27, 1905, in the Battle of the Tsushima Strait and destroyed it in two days. Japan had risen as a modern military power.

Though Japan had become a recognized international power by winning against a European power, politically Japan did not gain much. She had run out of money and resources to continue the war, and was forced to accept the terms of the Treaty of Portsmouth that followed, which was mediated by the USA's President Theodore Roosevelt. The Japanese felt that they had been cheated at the treaty by the USA.

The militarists were thus discontented, as they had believed at the start of the war that Japan could have elected herself leader of an all-Asian bloc, including China, India and smaller countries.

Japan's 1915 Demands and the 1929 'Tanaka Memorial'

In 1915, Japan presented her 'Twenty-One Demands' to China. These were intended to reduce China to a protectorate of Japan's, but the outright imperialism of the demands were opposed and prevented by the other world powers. Nevertheless, Japan gained major concessions in the Shandong peninsula and in southern Manchuria. Having joined the war on the Allied side, Japan gained the formerly German islands of the Marianas, the Caroline and the Marshall islands. Japan was now in control of the sea approaches to Japan and north-east Asia.

In 1929, came a declaration of Japan's intentions by Baron Tanaka, Japan's Prime Minister, stating:

> In Japan her food supply and raw materials decrease in proportion to her population. If we merely hope to develop trade, we shall eventually be defeated by England and America, who possess unsurpassed capitalistic power...
>
> "Our best policy lies in the direction of taking positive steps to secure rights and privileges in Manchuria and Mongolia. Having China's entire resources at our disposal, we shall proceed to conquer India, the Archipelago, Asia Minor, Central Asia and even Europe."

1930 Onwards

As per the April 22, 1930, London Naval Treaty the USA and Britain were to be limited to five major warship for every three held by Japan.

Since, the navies of Britain and the USA were much larger than that of Japan's, they were required to scrap many of their ships to bring their totals down to the agreed proportion, while Japan retained all of her warships. As the author Michael Hardwick has commented: 'Thus, in a paper battle, Japan sank several dozen ships without losing one of her own and emerged an even stronger naval power than before'.

On 18th September, 18, 1931, occurred "The Mukden Incident": A bomb exploded under a Japanese-owned express train in Manchuria, perhaps an excuse created for Japanese troops to occupy Manchuria. Japanese troops quickly captured the city of Mukden. While the Japanese government protested to its own army, a wave of enthusiasm and support for the army's operations became evident amongst the Japanese people. Relations between the army and the government had broken down in the name of 'patriotic' defiance. The militarists had gained virtual control of the country, and arrogant Japanese militarism had become a feature.

After the 'Mukden Incident', fighting broke out on the Sino-Manchurian frontier, which the Japanese government was unable to stop. China, as a result, boycotted Japanese goods, which caused the Japanese to retaliate with a naval force landing at Shanghai. The Chinese army defenders were pounded by aircraft from Japanese aircraft carriers.

Battle of Shanghai

On July 7, 1937, a Sino-Japanese skirmish occurred at the Marco Polo Bridge just outside Beijing, which sparked off a full-scale Japanese invasion of China. Japanese troops seized Beijing and Tientsin, and in August attacked Shanghai, where Chang Kai-shek's troops put up a fierce resistance, but were overcome. The Japanese bombers made the first trans-oceanic raids in history - from Taiwan and Kyushu to Nanking and Shanghai. In December 1937, Japanese forces attacked the Chinese Guomindang (Kuomintang) government's capital of Nanjing (Nanking) and captured it. After its capture, the Japanese commanders gave their men freedom to do as they wished with the city and its people, leading todays of looting, torture, murder and rape. Chiang Kai-shek however did not sue for peace, and shifted his capital far inland to Hankow, which took the Japanese almost a year to battle their way to Hankow fell to the Japanese, but the Chinese had shifted the capital further inland into mountainous country at Chungking and refused to surrender, leading to a long stubborn war of virtual stalemate with consolidated frontline positions.

The Second World War 1939-1945

In December 1938, Japan had proclaimed a "New Order in East Asia" with itself as its leader. In September 1940, Japan signed the Tripartite Axis Pact with Germany and Italy. Indo-China was attacked in September 1940, and the French force defending their colony was defeated. In July 1941, Japan moved more forces into southern Vietnam, and called on the USA to stop supporting the Chiang Kai-shek regime in China against her. Japan attacked the American base at Pearl Harbour in Hawaii by surprise on December 7, 1941, with an air attack from an aircraft carrier force, sinking a large part of the US Pacific Fleet. On the December 7th -8th, Japan invaded Thailand, Hong Kong, Burma, North Borneo, the Philippines and the Pacific Islands. Britain and United States declared war on Japan.

The Japanese had been preparing carefully for a *jungle* war in south-east Asia. From January 1941, a small military staff unit named the Taiwan Army Research Section had been functioning in Taiwan. It was tasked to examine the whole question of jungle warfare, and how it was to be waged in Malaya, and to solve the problems it presented. It was headed by Colonel Masanobu Tsuji, who later was the Chief of Operations and Planning Staff of the 25th Japanese Army which invaded Malaya. This research staff had undoubtedly become at the time the supreme authority on tropical warfare. The Japanese thus became well-organised and well-trained with the right equipment, including suitable tanks and bicycle-borne infantry.

To expand into Malaya and Burma, Japan had to subdue Thailand which was in the way. On December 8th, 1941, both Thailand and British-ruled Malaya were attacked by sea-borne landings. Breaking through the Allied defences on the Thai-Malaya border at the ill-prepared defences of the Jitra Line, the Japanese advanced down the Malayan peninsula. The British defence of her Singapore base had been based on seaward defence by the Royal Navy, but the battle-cruiser *Repulse* and the battleship *Prince of Wales* were easily sunk on December 10th by the Japanese torpedo-bombers. Unfortunately for Britain, she had neglected to cater for adequate fighter aircraft for the ships as well as for Singapore's defence, and the possibility of landward assault through Malaya had been discounted as impractical. Singapore was captured on February 15th, 1942.

The Japanese attack on Burma had started from January 20th, 1942, opposed only by a relatively small force of one Indian division and a weak Burmese division. By May 20th, 1942, conquered Burma, reaching the maximum expansion of Japanese military conquest in Asia. It is in this context of the Japanese victories in Malaya and Burma and the 'Greater East Asia Co-Prosperity Sphere' propounded by the Japanese that the Indian National Army (INA) comes into the political picture.

Michael Hardwick's comments on the Japanese military successes are worth noting:

> Capable of seemingly limitless endurance and indifferent by upbringing and training to discomfort or death, the Japanese soldier in jungle green pressed on against his ill-equipped, inexperienced enemies. Within six months of entering the war Japan had driven the Allies from Indo-China, Malaya, Burma, the East Indies, the Philippines and many key Pacific islands. . . All this had achieved by comparatively small forces – less than a quarter of a million soldiers – spearheaded by air and sea strikes of which the Allies, in their complacency, had never dreamed the Japanese might be capable.

It should be added that the Japanese soldiers were the bravest of soldiers of any nationality in the war, as attested by all senior Allied commanders. So brave, in fact, that the Japanese Army had instituted no gallantry awards, believing all soldiers to be equally brave.

Thereafter, the Japanese attempts to make the India-Burma border along the Patkai range of mountains the 'western wall' of their southeast Asian empire failed, because of serious miscalculations. They had not assessed the American capability for production of war material, especially aircraft. Their own logistics to support their forces in the field in Burma were over-stretched and inadequate, and the Americans and British controlled the skies. The Japanese no longer had sufficient fighter aircraft or even pilots. The Japanese forces in Burma and the INA thus starved or died of disease as they retreated before the Allied advance into Burma.

References

1. Abhyankar, M.G., *The War in Burma* 4th Ed., Dehradun, Natraj Publishers, 1974.
2. Connaughton, R. M. (1988), *The War of the Rising Sun and the Tumbling Bear—A Military History of the Russo-Japanese War 1904–5.* London, Cassell & Co., 2007.
3. Chapman, John and Ian Nish, (2004). *"On the Periphery of the Russo-Japanese War," Part I*, p. 53 n 42, Paper No. IS/2004/475, Suntory Toyota International Centre for Economics and Related Disciplines (STICERD), London School of Economics and Political Science (LSE) 2004.
4. Hardwick, Michael, *Discovery of Japan*, London, Hamlyn, 1970.
5. Mountbatten of Burma, Vice-Admiral, The Earl, Report to the Combined Chiefs of Staff by the Supreme Allied Commander South-East Asia, 1943-1945, London, His Majesty's Stationery Office, 1951.
6. Percival, Lt. Gen. A.E., Operations in Malaya 1941-42, London Gazette No: 38215, His Majesty's Stationery Office, 1948.
7. Rickard, J. (31 October 2013), *First Sino-Japanese War (1894-1895)*, http://www.historyofwar.org/articles/wars_first_sino_japanese.html
8. Republic of China, Dept. of Defense, Official Report, Chronology of Japanese Invasion of Asia 1894-1945http://humanum.arts.cuhk.edu.hk/NanjingMassacre/NMchron.html
9. Slim, Field Marshal Sir William, *Defeat into Victory*, London, Cassell & Co., 1956.
10. Swinson, Arthur, *Defeat in Malaya: The Fall of Singapore*, London, Macdonald & Co., 1970.
11. Tsuji, Col. Masanobu, *Singapore: The Japanese Version* [Translated: Margaret E. Lake], Sydney, H.V. Howe, 1960.

Subhas Chandra Bose and the Diplomatic Chessboard: Some Reflections on the Foreign Policy of the Provisional Government of Free India (Azad Hind Government).

Saradindu Mukherji

Much has been written all over the world about Netaji Subhas Chandra Bose, a man with unique global perspective, who moved valiantly from country to country and continent to continent.[1] As Ba Maw, the Burmese nationalist leader and the President during the war years, observes about Bose, "... pursued the Indian dream across half the world, through the Middle East, and then into Russia and Germany, then to the farthest end of East Asia, and back to South-east Asia, and finally to Burma, and for a few incredible weeks beyond the border into India itself".[2] In his grand mission to liberate India, he had the Indian National Army, while the Provisional Government of Free India (PGFI) or Azad Hind Government provided the crucial institutional bases. All this necessitated creating a sound mechanism for sustained diplomatic relationships with all the principal actors in the international arena at a very difficult phase of world history.

Objective and Scope of the Paper

This essay intends to examine how the Provisional Government of Free India (PGFI) had sought to navigate its way in the war-torn diplomatic arena in the early 1940s. This, however, is not meant to be an exhaustive account of the entire gamut of the foreign policy of the Provisional Government of Free India or its moving spirit, Bose's understanding and handling of international affairs. This paper merely seeks to provide a bird's eye-view of the international scenario that the Provisional Government of Free India had encountered, and how Bose had shaped and guided the PGFI at a tumultuous time. It seeks to reflect on some of the most audacious diplomatic initiatives by Bose, the background preparation that used to go behind this, and his ability to draw up and execute a plan of action based on the strength and weaknesses of various countries relevant in his scheme of things.

Bose's understanding of the fast- changing international scenario was grounded on a realistic assessment of the strategic importance of various major players in the diplomatic chessboard, and his expectation from them in the planned war of India's liberation. An Indian nationalist in the truest sense, every step that he took was for India's freedom, and dignity for its people. As neither self-projection nor personal gain ever entered his thoughts, as has been very common with many makers and shapers of foreign policy all over the world, including that of many in India, Bose's greatness becomes all the more striking.[3]

The amazing thing about Bose's handling of international affairs is his originality of approach, impeccable planning and unique capacity to deal with the world leaders, most of whom happened to be Heads of States of older and firmly established nation-states, his proven ability for swift adjustments in fast changing diplomatic/military scenarios, and that also without the usual apparatus of a State machinery for most of the time. One may remember that Bose's Provisional Government of Free India actually came to be recognised by nine nations.

His phenomenal grasp over the intricacies of international affairs, coupled with his instinctive capacity to opt for the most appropriate course of action may be explained by his unique ability to derive the right lessons from major international developments he had lived through.

Many of his eminent contemporaries in India had similar exposure to prevailing currents of international affairs and the advantage of academic training, both in India and abroad, yet, Bose had surpassed all of them in understanding of the issues which mattered most, and making the best use of the opportunities it offered to a revolutionary like him who strode like a Colossus in the international arena.

Convinced, as Bose was, about the ineffectiveness of non-violent means and passive resistance as a tactic in achieving India's independence, he remained confident, that the only way a genuine revolution was possible, at a time, when the "Sun never set on the British Empire" was to be achieved by forced expulsion or defeat of the British masters at an appropriate time. For him, there were two factors. Firstly, a European war, in which the British and its allies would be militarily defeated and, secondly, to subvert the loyalty of the Indian soldiers in the British Indian army.[4] Many of the revolutionaries in India had been planning the latter for quite some time-notably by Rash Behari Bose, Ghadarites and people like Jatin Mukherjee (Bagha Jatin) in the previous decades.

Bose's Education and Influence of Contemporary Issues and World Affairs

Bose's one and half year's stay in Cambridge, preparation for the Indian Civil Service examination, his resignation from the "heaven-born service" (1921) in the turbulent post-Versailles era, had exposed him to the main currents of British/European politics. The harsh treatment of a vanquished Germany, the rapacious behaviour of "liberal" victorious Powers in their extraction of reparations, and the irrelevance of Wilson's much vaunted 14(+4) Points must have taught him some practical lessons about the absence of morality and ethics in the conduct of international affairs, and the primacy of national interest as practiced by the Big Powers. Bose also watched the impotence of the League of Nations. As Leonard Gordon suggests, "Subhas's European experience and education and his continued reflections upon his own actions and maturation as a young nationalist led him to admire the passionate true-believers like Cromwell and Danton. The latters' call for "audacity, always audacity", according to Diip Roy, "was frequently on Subhas' lips."[5] He may have also learnt about the revolutionaries in Ireland, so highly regarded in India, particularly in Bengal during this period.

One of the earliest examples of Bose's forays in a major international affairs happened when the movement for Caliphate or *Khilafat*, which defying common-sense and sagacity, was thoughtlessly embraced by the Gandhian Non-Cooperation movement. Bose pointed out,

> *"The real mistake in my opinion did not lie in connecting the Khilafat issue with other national issues, but in allowing the Khilafat Committee to be set up as an independent organization throughout the country, quite apart from the Indian National Congress. The result of all this was that when later on Ghazi Mustafa Kemal Pasha, as the leader of the new Turkey, forced the Sultan to abdicate and abolished the office of Khalifa altogether, the Khilafat question lost all meaning and significance and the majority of the members of the Khilafat organizations were absorbed by sectarian, reactionary and pro-British Moslem organizations".*

He further observed,

> *"The introduction of the Khilafat question into Indian politics was unfortunate. As has already been pointed out, if the Khiafatist Moslems had not started a separate organization but had joined the Indian National Congress, the consequences would not have been so undesirable."*

While Bose had not said "that the Khilafat issue was an issue of extra-territorial loyalty, and had also desisted from saying that it had nothing to do with Indian nationalism, yet he could at least see that its consequences were quite unpleasant".[6]

His next important exposure to another non-Indian scenario (though Burma was part of British India till 1936) was more direct, though personally most unpleasant was his experiences as a prisoner in two Burmese jails-Mandalay and Insein (1925-1927), where he was incarcerated at the very young age of 28, whose significance has been missed out by scholars. There, he met Burmese political prisoners and "radical Buddhist monks". This gave him much idea about the Burmese society, politics and their freedom movement. Subsequently, Bose developed strong relationship with the Burmese nationalists like Aung San and Ba Maw spearheading the nationalist movement against the British colonialist.[7] Whether it was a coincidence or not, Sarat Chandra Chatterjee, the famous Bengali novelist lived in Burma at that time, and his famous novel in Bengali-"*Pather Dabi*" or "The Right of Way", woven around the story of a Burma-based Indian revolutionary Sabyasachi, came out in 1926, and was promptly banned by the British.

His European Visits in the 1930s

Bose faced all kinds of obstructions and impediments-starting from his passport being seized at Port Said, then being debarred from entering Britain and thereafter being put under British surveillance, wherever he travelled to -Berlin, Vienna, Rome, Prague, Belgrade, Sofia, Bucharest, Dublin and various other places. He met high officials, dignitaries, intellectuals, and of course the Indian community particularly the youth. Some of Bose's letters written from the Bhawali sanatorium (December 1932), found by police at a house search, had convinced the British that those were in support of the use of "Irish methods" in India. He visited Ireland, "in fulfilment of the request made to him by V.J. Patel before his death to maintain the contact between Indian national movement and Ireland". In Dublin, Bose met de Valera, Indian students and those running the Irish-India Independence League.[8]

Existing Organisations and People Abroad who were working for Indian Freedom

Much has been written about the various existing organisations, who were working abroad for India's liberation, and as Purabi Roy has done on Bose's contact with Indian revolutionaries like Abani Mukherjee of the Comintern and many people like Achar Singh Chena, formerly of the Ghadar Party, and some others who later came to be identified as the "Kirti" Communist Group. Bose had told Suniti Kumar Chatterjee, (later on India's one of the famous linguists) then based at Vienna in 1935, that he "was sure that there would be another war in five years and then we must create an opportunity for ourselves out of international jealousies when Western powers would become too exhausted and too disunited".[9]

Back home in Calcutta, after returning from Haripura Congress in 1938, Bose asked Sisir Bose, his nephew to "listen regularly to Moscow radio broadcasts, with particular reference to their reporting of Indian affairs and our national movement," and he himself listened regularly to all the radio broadcasts from Berlin, Rome and London, "and every discomfiture of the British in war or diplomacy gave him real satisfaction". In the meantime, Bose had met with some German officials in Bombay, and kept meeting the Japanese consular staff in the former's garden house on the outskirts of Calcutta, according to Bishwa Ranjan Sarbadhikary at whose house, Subhas Bose used to maintain an office. This is what Sarbadhikary had told this author in an extensive interview in Calcutta in June 1996.[10]

Bose in Europe: Hitler's Germany

Much has been written about Bose's high-risk, clandestine movements, sojourn in Peshawar and Kabul, and his desperate attempts to seek a safe passage to Europe. That also called for timely moves and a rare capacity to deal with the diplomatic staff, and read the minds of their bosses in Germany, Russia and Italy and Japan. By then, Bose's reputation had spread far and wide, and it was that iconic image of an uncompromising and selfless freedom fighter which facilitated his unprecedented success and subsequent activities in war-torn Europe.

Bose's arrival in Germany on an Italian passport, his experiences and and myriad achievements form one of the greatest true-life stories of all times. As R.C. Majumdar, put it, "Bose's journey from Calcutta to Berlin, full of thrilling details, was a historic one, and its nearest parallel is the escape of Shivaji from the clutches of Aurangzeb".[11]

Hitler's *Mein Kampf* had some very unpleasant observations about India, like this: "England will never lose India unless she gives way to racial confusion in her machinery of administration or unless she is forced to do so by the sword of a powerful enemy. Indian risings will never be successful. We Germans know well enough by experience how hard it is to force England's hand. Apart from all this, I, speaking as a

German, would far rather see India under British domination than that of any other nation". There were few more of such derogatory comments on Indians.[12] Bose wanted such portions to be excised, and protested when he learnt about the grievances of Indian students and particularly regarding the remarks made about Indians. A distressed Bose wrote to Dr Franz Thierfelder, Secretary General of the Indian Institute in Munich (25 March 1936):

> *"Today I regret that I have to return to India with the conviction that the new nationalism of Germany is not only narrow and selfish but arrogant. The recent speech of Herr Hitler in Munich gives the essence of Nazi philosophy--- there is another factor which affects us even more. Germany in her desire to curry favour with Great Britain finds it convenient to attack India and the Indian people".*[13]

Subsequently, Bose would have a markedly different and more meaningful encounters in Germany. The international situation was changing rapidly just as what he had anticipated. "The much expected crisis had at last come. This was India's golden opportunity", Bose observed on Sept 3, 1939. The war in Europe had just begun!

It goes to the eternal credit of Bose, that he maintained cordial relations with Hitler's government, was able to form the nucleus of a Planning Committee in Germany itself, secure from them all that he wanted a forum - Free India Centre, enjoying the status of a diplomatic mission, Indian Legion, Azad Hind Radio, and finally a crucial submarine to travel to South Asia, even when the Fuehrer was reportedly upset over the humiliating surrender of the British at Singapore, which for him was "destroying the position of the White race in East Asia", and was "not entirely enthusiastic over gigantic success of Japanese, and had reportedly said, he would gladly send the British twenty divisions to help throw back the yellow men".[14]

Captain Adalbert Seifriz, who was closely associated with the Indian Legion, observed that the "The agreement between the German Government and Subhas Chandra Bose, according to which the German partner was obliged to grant the technical assistance as well as the personnel for the establishment of a military unit, and according to which no interference was to be made with Bose's plans and efforts, directed towards India's independence by both sides."

To help grow perfect understanding between two nations, mutual give-and-take matters a lot. Seifriz gratefully acknowledged the fact: "The association with the Indian Legion was, for the German training staff, very profitable. They had the unique opportunity of coming in steady and intimate contact, and of being acquainted with a great nation and of entering into a world, unknown to them, and which had completely different thoughts and emotions and sentiments."

Seifreiz further says, that "German officers and NCOs engaged in this work had in the course of their duties got the chance to think on a wider scale, to enlarge their horizon and to perceive developments in the world which would not have become evident to them during any other military service. Each single day brought new problems, required new adaptability and mastering of new situation. The problem was to act with skill in a diplomatic way, to develop a pedagogic ability, to spread warmth in human relations and finally to act in a constructive way". Moreover, "The most rewarding fact was the real comradeship which grew between Indians and Germans, which proved true in dangerous hours, and exists still to-day in numerous cases. The Indian Legion was a precious instrument in strengthening and consolidating Indo-German friendship".[15]

Of course, it could not have been a hunky-dory affair for Bose and his team-mates all the time. Vyas, an Indian from East Africa, then a student in Germany, who was asked by Bose to join the Free India Centre in Berlin, had pointed out that, "Negotiations with the officials of the German Foreign Ministry was not smooth. While Herr von Ribbentrop had quickly gauged the firmness of Subhas Bose's mind, at the lower level, the spirit of superiority coupled with ignorance of India, held the upper hand", and many of the so-called India "experts" had "absorbed the British colonial mentality", who were "in their heart for continuation of the British colonial rule, or if not the least, 'white' domination".

Herr Woermann of the German Foreign Office, a "steadfast follower of the Fuehrer", a "friend as far as the requirements of our struggle against the British were concerned", and a neighbour of Vyas in Berlin, once told him that, "he had seldom seen the German Foreign Minister as courteous, other than to those of Japan and Italy". Anuj Dhar also drew a similar conclusion much later, "Apply the body language rules to the pictures which have recently been made public through Wikimedia Commons by the German Federal Archive and you will see Bose on the high table with Hitler's top brass, having them eating out of his hand."[16]

Girija K Mookerjee summing up the positive achievements of Bose's sojourn in Hitler's Germany, mentions that, he achieved two things there: to inform people at home (in India) about what he was doing and all that was happening in the world, and secondly, making an "intensive propaganda in Europe that India was not only fit for freedom but also that her freedom was long overdue". As these goals could not be achieved from a German base, he took the decision to "get out of Germany", and made "frantic efforts to go to East Asia after the fall of Rangoon".[17] It is obvious that Bose's unique position in the alien set-up was entirely because of his diplomatic finesse, sustained hard-work, deep insight, persuasive skill, tact and sincerity of the highest order.

By then, the British Foreign Office had an inkling of Bose's impending journey to South Asia. It informed the British mission in Moscow,

> notorious S C Bose of Calcutta is shortly planning to leave for the Far East. Route not known but likely to travel across Russia via Turkey/Afghanistan. It is of considerable importance to the Allied cause that Bose should not succeed in his plan. Take up urgently this with Soviet authorities, with M. Molotov - and request that all possible steps should be taken to watch for and detain Bose. Bose is an adept in disguise. It is of greatest importance that our knowledge of Bose's intentions should not reach enemy and more especially the Japanese.

And there was an instruction: "Please burn it after perusal". Fortunately for posterity, this Cypher telegram was not destroyed.[18]

Bose and Italy

From his experiences in Germany, we may move on to his Italian experiences. Though not as important as German and Japanese help in the most critical phase in his action plan, it was only with the passport issued in the name of an Italian that was provided to him by the Italian Embassy in Kabul and with that Bose set his foot in Berlin. Any prevarication by the authorities in Rome and the Italian Embassy in Kabul to help Bose in his daring mission would have put an end to his historic mission. To the critics of Bose, his interactions with Benito Mussolini, the Duce, and his Foreign Minister, Ciano, who was also his son-in-law, are just another flimsy opportunity for censoring him once more, just because Nehru had refused to meet Mussolini. Such admirers of Nehru cant hide the fact that Nehru maintained very cordial relations with both Mohammad Iqbal and Jinnah –the typical Islamo-fascists, a much older and persistent menace to human civilization than the short-lived Italian fascism. After all, both Gandhi and Tagore had cordial meetings with Mussolini in Rome.

Anthony Elenimittan describes Bose's meeting with Mussolini as cordial. On Mussolini's proposal to Bose for setting up a Provisional Government of India in Rome or in Berlin, the latter showed reluctance. Bose reiterated that, if ever such a thing was to be set up, it would not be in Europe and only after he returned to Asia. Further, when Mussolini conveyed his desire to have strong cultural relations with India, Bose told him that what mattered most then was freedom for India and find cure for its socio-economic problems. "First we are determined to live and then speculate and philosophize". Duce appeared to have appreciated and so did Ciano. That Bose used every opportunity to create a positive image of India, and the aura that he exuded wherever he left his foot-print helped greatly in his Herculean efforts. It is in this light, that we again look at what Bose told Duce, "The doors of cooperation are always open. India has all her portals wide open to the four corners of the world. Open mindedness has been one of the characteristic features of India, and India will grow on that national heritage". The British Embassy from Rome reported that Bose also gave him a copy of his "*Indian Struggle 1920-1934*", and Mussolini had felt that of all Indian politicians he had met, he admired Bose the most.[19] Later on, Bose had more interactions with Mussolini's government.

Bose and Japan

It was the relations of the Provisional Government of Free India with the Japanese that was the ultimate test of Bose's ingenunity and genius in the world of diplomacy and war. To cut a big story short, we would take up a few case-studies to illustrate his incredible mastery in the domain of international politics during those cataclysmic years.

The British Embassy in Rome had reported in February 1935, that, "In regard to Japanese "Pan Asiaticism, Mr. Bose is reported as saying that so far as Japanese policy is opposed to subjection of Europe it has India's support: but that Japan's aggressive designs against China offended Indian opinion." Bose remained fully conscious of the "... tremendous responsibility which Japan has undertaken by becoming the sponsor-nation in this task ... I hope and pray and trust that the youths and the students who are the future representatives of the nation will realize the tremendous moral responsibility which Japan has undertaken in initiating this new order". Bose had looked upon Japan as "British of the East".[20]

The British Foreign Office had duly noted: "The fanfare surrounding the arrival in Japan of Bose indicates the importance which Tokyo ascribes to the activities of the chief pro-Axis Indian nationalist leader" and fully conscious of "Bose's following in the populous and strategically located province of Bengal represents a potential menace".[21]

Col. Yamamoto, the Military Attaché in the Japanese Embassy in Berlin, who had received Bose when he came out of the submarine on May 6, 1943, and later the head of Hikari Kikan, remained in close contact with Bose for about 13 years. He felt that the German Foreign Office was reluctant to allow Bose to leave Germany and come over to Japan, as he was a "living encyclopaedia" for them on Indian affairs.

After arriving in Japan in May 1943, he kept meeting senior Japanese Ministers, including Prime Minister Tojo, senior military officials, and whenever he found time, he made it a point to "make inspection tours of industrial plants, military barracks and schools", and "improve ??????himself for the independence and the reconstruction of India", and it was then, that he gave the plan for the establishment of a provisional government of India and to fight for its independence with the "help of Axis powers and army in accordance with international law".[22]

When we talk of Bose's work and achievements in Japan, we need to keep in mind the unique role played by Rash Behari Bose, firstly, for having built a base for India's liberation movement, and then in shaping them up in the 1940s, and more particularly after Subhas Chandra Bose had arrived in Japan. Rash Behari Bose had founded the Indian Independence League in 1924 at Tokyo, and for seventeen long years he systematically worked to build the Indian Independence League ,"explaining the political condition of India before East Asians, "emphasising the supreme importance of Indian independence as a factor of Greater Asian freedom and unity. His slogan of "Asia for Asians" roused the East Asians from slumber and inspired them to rise to a man for expelling Western imperialism from Asia. It is not a little due to Rash Behari Bose that they began to look upon the political emancipation of India as a stepping-stone to Greater Asian liberation from bondage, and that they became sympathisers with the Indian cause in large numbers". p .147 "His new role was now in the capacity of the Supreme Advisor to the Provisional Government of Azad Hind the best of which was represented in him. Very truthfully Rash Behari has been described by Subhas Chandra Bose as "the Father of the Indian Independence movement in East Asia –".[23]

Rash Behari was considered very close to the Japanese and regarded as a "Japanese amongst Indians"; a close friend of Toyama, a elder statesman from the Black Dragon Society. 24.Much credit for founding the India Independence League and help setting up the INA and mobilising two million Indians in South Asia for Indian liberation goes to Rash Behari Bose.[24]

With a courtesy call at the Imperial Palace at Tokyo, and offering obeisance at the Yasukuni shrine, the national monument of Japan that commemorates their national heroes in early 1944, Bose had made the right diplomatic gestures, and thus taken the correct step in establishing a sentimental bonding with the Japanese people.[25]

Another important dimension of the Indo-Japanese relations of those years was the Japanese financial help given to Bose for the expenses incurred for running the Provisional Government, which was handed over by Yamamoto himself to Bose through cheques. Bose, in turn, gave him "I.O.U.S with his signatures in place of a receipt". Yamamoto also remembered, "I think he knew well that the Japanese Government had no intention of demanding payments for the aid given by them to the Indian Independence movement", but then, Bose was not the person to "be satisfied with receiving "charities", and further, that he "had reasons to be dissatisfied with Hikari Kikan".[26]

Just two days after Bose had met Tojo, the latter was so impressed that he announced in Diet, "Japan is firmly resolved to extend all means in order to help and expel and eliminate from India the Anglo-Saxon influence which are the enemy of the Indian people, and enable India to achieve full independence in the true sense of the term".[27]

Shah Nawaz Khan points out, "Japanese militarists wanted to help us but at the same time they wanted to influence our actions which were resented all along. After the arrival of Netaji, however, the position changed, and thereafter, the Japanese Militarists were influenced by Netaji to such an extent that no new move was made without consulting him and without his advice".[28]

S. A. Ayer shows the embarrassment to which Netaji was put in dealing with the Japanese Generals making some military demands immediately after a small group of INA field officers had "betrayed Netaji and went over to the enemy" and the question cropped up who would guarantee the loyalty of others. This called for tremendous tact to convince the Japanese about the capabilities of the INA. [29]

Bose expressed happiness at the decision of the Japanese government to establish diplomatic relations between the Imperial Japanese Government and the Provisional Government of Azad Hind that would help, "intensify our war-effort and thereby to play more active and substantial role in the common struggle for the defeat and overthrow of the Anglo-American Power and the liberation of my country".[30] As for this contentious issue - that Japan did not exchange an Ambassador with the PGI, even when it had played a key role in its formation, and had already accorded recognition. In the meantime, Tokyo had sent its Ambassador to Burma. Hence, a similar gesture was perhaps expected by Bose! Yamamoto's explanation was that the newly acquired southern area being under Japanese military control, Tokyo authorities did not consider it necessary. There is another facet of the story. Teruo Hachiya was sent by the Japanese government as their Ambassador to the PGFI but as he was without "proper credentials", Bose had refused to accept him.[31]

In Kunizuka Kazunari's account of his experiences with Bose, we learn that even when he was mostly dependent on Japanese help, he combined diplomatic finesse and tact with dignity in his meetings with Gen Dohihara, commanding the Seventh Area Army based at Singapore, and how their meeting was arranged, in which Bose's private courtesy call was reciprocated by Gen. Dohihara's official return call. Bose knew when and how to compromise in the larger national interest, and so did the all powerful Japanese General.[32]

After the British defeat and surrender in Burma, the INA had its Headquarters set up in Rangoon, but very soon, there was another problem for the British to worry about, having lost their Burmese empire. The C-in-C in India was apprehensive: "Bose's activities in Burma may have some harmful results. Offer by him on behalf of Japan to supply large quantities of rice for relief for the famine stricken people in Bengal" was considered a "clever move which may have inconvenient results, should it become widely known as food situation in this part of India remains most serious".[33]

When the Japanese, then controlling Burma, faced anti-Japanese hostilities, asked the INA to "attack' them, Bose refused to do it. But then, he had also refused to join the Anti-Fascist People's Freedom League (A.F.P.F.L). Being committed to the anti-British struggle, the INA remained neutral, and when there was no option left surrendered to the British.[34]

As Maw explained: "But whatever his relations with the local Japanese were Bose stood unwaveringly by the Japanese in the fight against the Western imperialist nations. He never allowed the main issue in the war to get lost among the far smaller personal ones", for him, what mattered was "whether the imperialism destroying the Asian nations should themselves be destroyed and who would destroy them. And he knew only Germany and Japan could do that".[35]

As early as April 1941, the Japanese Consul-General in Calcutta had informed the Foreign Minister Matsuoka about Bose, who was then in exile in Berlin, and wanted weapons etc to be supplied to the Forward Bloc so that it can "burgeon into a genuinely popular revolt", (and establish contact with Bose.) Maj Fujiwara also took notice of Bose soon thereafter. Subsequent history is better known. The Army Chief of General Staff Sugiyama, Prime Minister Tojo and Shigemitsu "developed a special sympathy for Bose". As Lebra puts it, when Bose requested the Japanese Government for recognition, for ceding Andaman and Nicobar Islands, and for an accredited diplomatic representative,

> In each instance the Japanese Government was willing to concede the form but not the substance of Bose's demands. The Azad Hind Government was recognized, the islands were ceded, and a minister was sent, but in every case the action was formal rather than substantive.

Even a critic like Lebra admits that despite Japan's deteriorating military situation, and "even in the midst of military fiasco men like Gen Kawabe hesitated when it came to disappointing Bose".[36] In a way Lebra has contradicted himself Kawabe's conduct that was less formal and more substantive. Even formality matters in tricky war-time situations.

For his critics in India like Nehru, who gave a call to fight the Jap/INA, one may heed to what Lebra had so unambiguously pointed out: "Japan at no time planned a major invasion of India or the incorporation of India into the Greater East Asia Co-Prosperity Sphere (contrary to the suspicions of Indians in the independence movement). "The Imperial Conference (Nov 15, 1941) had called for separation of Australia and India from Britain, and stimulation of the Indian independence movement.[37]

In his address to the Greater East Asia Conference on 6 November 1943, at Tokyo, Bose had observed, while surveying the history of Anglo-American domination in the 19th and 20th century, including the Washington Conference and Locarno Pact, "My thoughts also went back to the Assembly of the League of Nations, that League of Nations along whose corridors and lobbies I spent many a day, knocking at one door after another, in vain attempt to obtain a hearing for the cause of Indian freedom".[38]

Bose had totally ignored the line taken by Nehru that "any weakening of the British position in India would help the Axis to win the war, and that such a contingency would be bad for India". This line of thinking also influenced Gandhi. But Bose's counter logic was that, "Defeat of Britain could not automatically mean Axis domination of India. USA and the Soviet Union were still not at war and any Axis attempt at world domination would have met with their opposition", and also, "What if Britain lost, even without Indian mass movement, would India not be an easy prey to the Axis."[39]

As Bayly points out,

> "Up to the very last minute Subhas Bose had hoped that Japan would resist the Allies' resurgence long enough for his Azad Hind Government to secure something from the expected peace conference. If that did not succeed, he would approach the Soviet Union, which appeared increasingly antagonistic to Britain as the War ended. As their own nemesis approached in August 1945, the Japanese commander finally agreed to help him make contact with the advancing Soviet armies in Manchuria. The dropping of the atom bombs and the Japanese surrender forced him to move fast."[40]
>
> Yamamoto had something more to disclose- Bose's future plans regarding a possibility of seeking Soviet Russia's assistance. Bose had told Yamamoto, "As I have always told you I never refuse to get assistance from any countries as far as they are against Britain", and further, "And I am sure that

India will not turn 'red' if they have friendly relations with Russia".[41]

When in the last stage of the war, the Japanese army was evacuating Rangoon along with Dr Ba Maw's Government of independent Burma, an unique scenario was unfolding. As K.N. Kannampilly puts it: "The only Government left in the City was Netaji's Provisional Government of Azad Hind; the only organization still functioning, the Indian Independence League; the only Army still intact, the Indian National Army; and the only Head of State, Netaji Subhas Chandra Bose".[42]

Even at that hour of extreme crisis, with the British Army about to re-capture Rangoon, Netaji had that firmness to tell Lt. Gen. Ishoda, the chief of the Hikari Hokan, that he would leave Rangoon, only after the requisite transport for the Rani Jhansi Regiment was arranged, which had been diverted by the Japanese Army for the evacuation of its own retreating Army." In this case too, the transport was immediately arranged for the lady soldiers of the INA.[43] Netaji had a unique way of maintaining relations with countries at their highest levels, while not forgetting the paramount interest and safety of his soldiers.

An Assessment

Alexander Werth, who had worked with the German Foreign Office in the 1940s, and had dealt with Bose in Germany, opines that Bose

> *"will no doubt, be honoured some time in the future in Italy like the great Garibaldi who tried to liberate his country from Austria during the last century. In Communist China, Netaji will have in due time the dimension of Sun-yat-Sen who by operating from Japan succeeded in freeing China from the abuses of the Chinese Imperial Dynasty. Netaji will sooner or later surely also be recognized by the Irish people in a similar manner as a De Valera who started to liberate Ireland from the United Kingdom. And finally Netaji will probably be evaluated in most other European countries in the same manner as Masaryk who operated from Britain for the independence of Czechoslovakia."*[44]

Even a Euro-centric critic like Lebra acknowledges,

> *"Despite the military defeat of Japan and with it the INA, popular support for the INA ultimately helped precipitate British withdrawal from India. Japan's interest in the Indian independence movement, begun as a small-scale intelligence mission in Thailand and Malaya, developed into a complex propaganda and espionage network designed to foster anti-British sentiment, and finally burgeoned into limited support of and co-operation with a government-in-exile and revolutionary army".*[45]

R.C. Majumdar also suggests, "that but for the INA Britain would not have granted independence to India in 1947".[46]

To explain Bose's diplomatic moves and see him through the ideological prism is flawed on several counts. After all, following his ouster from the Indian National Congress, he had no other alternative left with, except going abroad and look for potential allies-both at diplomatic and military levels. An anguished Bose, wrote to Sarat Bose, that Gandhism, is "sickening to a degree" and wondered, which one among the "the British bureaucracy" or the "Gandhian hierarchy" hindered India's political future.[47] He did not expect much to come out of the efforts made by Krishna Menon running the India League in London, as it "only touched a fringe of the problem, and "Only military defeat or political exhaustion due to economic crisis, could force Britain to change the main character of her imperialist policies". According to Vyas, Bose felt that: "In spirit Jawahar is a part of the British Establishment. Had he been born earlier, he would have prided in being Lord Nehru". As for Gandhi's attitude, Bose's differences are better known, just not the former's non-violence methods and lack of will to "carry on the struggle uncompromisingly", but also his "inability to link-up India's case for struggle with the international situation".[48] Balachandran in his recent book cites Nambiar, to whom Bose, while acknowledging Nehru's "importance and influence in India's national struggle", felt that "Nehru's pro-British attitude could be a problem". As future events would show how prophetic Bose was in his assessment of

Nehru. may be recalled here that Nehru while going to China in August 1939, had received from Winston Churchill 'through a mutual friend his good wishes for my visit to that war-ravaged c country".[49] Hayes appears to be oblivious of the ground reality that prevailed in India in the late 1930s and early 1940s when he suggests that Bose should have stayed back in India, "like his more temperamental colleagues such as Azad and Nehru".[50] It is very well known that Azad, being more in the Deobandi mould was acceptable to both Gandhi and Nehru. Let's remember that Bose was "especially scathing about Abul Kalam Azad, who was taking action against the Bose brothers" in the name of "discipline",[51] while Nehru was not taken very seriously for his flexibile attitude on several issues as an anguished Bose had observed.

Those who see Bose as a "collaborator" of Nazi Germany, who had good relations with a Fascist Mussolini and a Fascist Japan, overlook the obvious, both from Indian and non-Indian experiences with the real-life diplomatic alliances and alignments in recent times. Contemporary nationalist Indian opinion was that, "Britain's record in Bengal was in every bit as bad as that of the Nazis at Belsen– 'will the UN have the courage and the fairness to hold trials in India?".[52]

In the 1940s, the top leadership of the Indian National Congress had repeatedly sought to engage in dialogues with Jinnah and other leaders of the Muslim League. In the morning of 16 August, 1946, the "Direct Action" day in Calcutta, Nehru had a meeting with Jinnah at his house in Bomay. Surely, Jinnah, who was responsible for the most gruesome genocide in our time, in an area bigger and scale than that of what happens in Palestine-Israeli areas– forced conversion of polytheists, violence against women–continued to be addressed as Quaid-e-Azam. Yet, the same Congress leadership had refused to reach an understanding with its democratically elected President for two consecutive terms. Subsequently, it is the same leadership which stood silently, when there went on a systematic ethno-religious cleansing of Hindu, Sikh, Buddhist and Christians in two wings of Pakistan, and no one ever thought of severing diplomatic relations with Pakistan, what to talk of categorizing it as a rogue state. Neither did any one come to the rescue of Kashmir's entire Hindu population who were victims of religious cleansing in the

1980s.[53] All these happened when India had not only refused to maintain diplomatic relations with Israel but also barred Indian citizens from even travelling to Israel. While India went on playing cricket and hockey with Pakistan but refused to play with South Africa, ostensibly, because of its policy of apartheid. By no stretch of imagination, theologically sanctioned persecution and inhuman treatment of the non-Muslims, who are also the original inhabitants of the soil in Islamic Pakistan and Bangladesh can be considered a lesser crime than apartheid. After all, both – religious persecution and apartheid are equally inhuman, barbaric, reprehensible and unacceptable.

As for the European neighbours of Germany, the fact remains that the latter's *Drang nach Osten* and the drive for colonies in Africa and elsewhere, short-lived though they had been, had merely followed the pattern set by the "liberal" and democratic Great Britain and France, who in turn had followed in the footsteps of the authoritarian and feudal European countries, like Spain and Portugal earlier. The worst had happened before, when the Arab imperialism had spread over Asia, Africa and Europe with the book, sword and fire in hand. It was a Christian Britain which had remained friendly towards the Ottomans, even when the latter had ruthlessly treated the Armenians, Greeks and other Christian nationalities, not withstanding a few honest observations from statesmen like Gladstone !

Even in the late 1930s, when the holocaust of the Jews was going on, the British and French had no hesitation in submitting to Hitler at Munich. Then came the Russo-German Pact. None of the Big European powers had any problem with the holocaust. This being the track record of others, for critics like Hayes, Bose alone should be held guilty of "ignoring the fate of European Jewry", for his "alliance with the most genocidal regime in history". In saying that, "History will not ultimately absolve Bose so easily for his alliance with Nazi Germany",[54] Hayes ignores some of the basic facts of history, especially certain policies taken by various nations in pursuit of their diplomatic goals. Both the USA and Britain have very often sided with an avowedly Islamic, non-democratic, military ruled Pakistan against a democratic and secular India. To illustrate this, we just refer to a few episodes from a long list of diplomatic wrong-doing by the two Big Powers and permanent members of the Security Council of the UNO.

In 1971, the American government encouraged and abetted Pakistan when the Bangladesh liberation war was going on, and three million people, mostly Hindus perished in the genocide orchestrated by the latter. Similarly, the Communist China continues to encourage and bolster Pakistan against India, which has a democratic polity and no history of aggressive expansionism. Even when Tibetan people are being mercilessly treated and being reduced into a minority, the world has no word of condemnation for the Communist China! On Kashmir related matters which is India's internal matter, United Kingdom and many European Union countries have consistently supported the Pakistani policy and thus abetted and encouraged various Islamic terrorist organisations. They have neither morality, nor history, nor logic in their attitude.

In recent times, India has given special importance to strengthen its relationship with Japan. Writing on Netaji's special ties with Japan and its importance for India, Taisuke Takaoka, who had once served the Japanese Commercial Mission in Calcutta, when Netaji was the Mayor of Calcutta Corporation, and used to meet him in various capacities, both in India and Japan, had observed, "I wish to write down that if Netaji was alive now, the relation of India and Japan would have been different".[55]

As Ba Maw sums up, "Netaji and I went through so much together. The fortunes of war were much alike for both of us, particularly the preposterous situations we got into, for both of us found ourselves fighting nearly all the time against two enemies: the open British enemy in the front, and the hidden enemy behind, and within and around".[56]

Conclusion

As Justice Radha Binode Pal, who gave the dissenting judgement in the Tokyo trial had thoughtfully observed,

> "Foreign Policy of no nation in the world indicates a conspiracy. Even when several nations form themselves into a group, and adopt a particular policy against any particular

ideology prevailing somewhere in the international society, we do not characterize this as a conspiracy. Whatever that be, circumstances certainly developed in such a way during relevant period as to lead Japan to adopt certain policies in her foreign relations, which as a matter of fact she did adopt from time to time."[57]

Much later, Yamamoto had told the Anglo-American interrogators after the Allied victory, that it was "wrong to call our part in aiding India to attain her independence, as a conspiracy", which "was a cooperative action taken by the provisional Indian government and the Japanese army".[58] Since Bose and the Provisional Government of Free India happened to get intimately connected with the Japanese government for liberation of India, we can firmly reiterate that their foreign policy was not only pragmatic but also ethically sound.

Whether one judges Bose by Kautilyaian or Machiavellian yardstick, depending on one's cultural- historical preferences, the fact remains, that very few nation-builders and statesmen had ever faced that enormity of challenge and in-built disadvantages that Bose had been saddled with. One may go on comparing him with Cardinal Wolsey, Oliver Cromwell–the "God's Englishman", Napoleon, Prince Metternich, Palmerstone, Gladstone, Garibaldi, Bismarck, Kossuth, Stalin, Churchill, De Gaulle, Ho Chi Minh, Kissinger and many such personalities and their diplomacy. But at the end, we would see, how, placed as Bose was in such a precarious situation, his handling of a multiplicity of factors–both human and logistical, in the chanceries, diplomatic high-tables and real-war situations, from Europe to Asia–was so refreshingly innovative. Far from geared to covet others' territories or aggrandizement of any sort, it actually helped many suppressed nationalities in their fight for national independence.[59]

In the famous address hailing Bose as a "Great leader of the nation" (*Deshanayak*), Tagore had seen in him the fulfilment of a promise held out in the holy *Gita* about the divinely ordained Man being sent out to rescue the suffering people from the clutches of the Devil.[60] Hugh Toye's overall assessment of Bose's life being characterised by " the magnitude and humanity of his dream, by the example of burning energy, tenacity and personal force, of the tradition he left of sacrificial patriotism",[61] is so graphically borne out by his deft handling of every situation including foreign affairs. As Gordon explains,

> "Bose wanted India to have a strong Central government after independence, but this did not make him a Hitler or a Mussolini or a Ribbentrop. He was not a quisling-i e someone who betrayed his own country- and not a fascist in the European mold of this period. Bose despised Nazi racism and brutality ---."[62]

Reams and reams of documentary evidence presented before the Justice Mukherjee Commission, and the recently declassified documents[63] testify to the regrettable perfidy on the part of India's post-independence ruling class to smother the true magnitude of Bose's Herculean efforts.

It is an established fact that there has been an orchestrated attempt from various quarters to prevent his unending legacy to reach not only the people in India but also the larger world. The ruling elite in India having succeeded so far in pushing him and the revolutionaries out of its official history text-books and public spaces,[64] except on certain ceremonial occasions, have thus created a big void in our national history

To end, we may suggest that India, as a self-respecting nation must make an intellectually honest effort to spread the message of Bose, just not his unparalleled commitment to the freedom of India, and his vision, but more specifically his impeccable planning for the future, conduct of foreign affairs, and then launching the military operations. The unique example of the Provisional Government of Free India and the Indian National Army needs to be told to the world. Bose's understanding and practice of diplomacy should ideally become a compulsory reading for not only our foreign and other civil service recruits but also for the members of the legislatures. India just cannot afford to put into oblivion any more, its greatest hero since Chhatrapati Shivaji Maharaj.

References

1 Saradindu Mukherji, "Behind the Spotlight", review of S. Balachandran, A Life in Shadow : The Secret Story of ACN Nambiar, A Secret Anti-Colonial Warrior,(Roli Books, Delhi 2016) in *The Hindu*, 9 April 2017. In recent times, there have been serious efforts to assess the role of Bose in India's freedom movement and the on-going controversy surrounding his fate after 18 August 1945 by Purabi Roy, *The Search for Netaji: New Findings* (Purple Peacock Kolkata, 2012), Anuj Dhar, *India's Biggest Coverup*, (Vitasta, Delhi, 2015) G.D, Bakshi, *Bose: An Indian Samurai.* Netaji and the INA. A Military Assessment. (KW Publishers, Delhi, 2017), Romain Hayes, *Bose in Nazi Germany* (Random House India, Noida, 2011) among many others. Earlier we had, Leonard Gordon, Brothers Against the Raj. (New York Columbia Press, 1990), Anton Pelinka, *Democracy Indian Style, Subhas Chandra Bose and the Creation of India's Political Culture* (New Brunswick, NJ (Transaction) 2003, Hugh Toye, *The Springing Tiger, The Indian National Army and Netaji Subhas Chandra Bose* (Allied Delhi, 2009) among many others. Sarat K Bose, Sugata Bose, ed., *Subhas Chandra Bose, An Indian Pilgrim. An Unfinished Autobiography.* (OUP, 2004). *The Indian Struggle 1920-1942.* Asia Publishing House, New Delhi, 1967). Mukherjee Commission's startling confirmation of no air-crash theory has greatly added to the scholarly interest in the subject. Even long before this, the doyen of Indian historians Romesh Chandra Majumdar ,ed, History and Culture of Indian People. Struggle for Freedom. Vol. Eleven. (Bharatiya Vidya Bhavan. Mumbai, 3rd Ed. Mumbai 2003,) p. 692, had also observed, that "—end of this valiant fighter for freedom is shrouded in mystery". In helping me to find a grip over the Bose papers and the Mukherji Commission Report at the National Archives of India, I am grateful to Shweta Singh.

2 Ba Maw, "Breakthrough in Burma. During the War". (New Haven, 1968) pp. 192-202 in, "Burmese Impressions of Subhas Chandra Bose" in T.R. Sareen, *Forgotten Images Reflections and Reminiscences of Subhas Chandra Bose.* (S. S. Publishers, Delhi. 1997. pp. 192-202). Hereafter Sareen

3 There have been major failures in the conduct of India's foreign relations since independence-in dealing with Pakistan, China, Bangladesh and other issues, especially regarding the safety and survival of Hindu, Sikh, Christian, Buddhist and Christian minorities there. Saradindu Mukherji,

The Pioneer, "The Impotency of Indian Diplomacy, 10 April 1992. "Blame the Pakistani Apologists in India", 26 June 1992. *The Pioneer*. "Subservience to Pan Islamism Must End", *The Pioneer,* 18 Sept 1992. "Jyoti Basus's Misguided Foreign Policy" 30 July 1993. "Stop Showing Bogus Diplomacy", 1 Dec 1995. *The Indian Express*, "Fanaticism at the Root of Dhaka Strife", 15 March 1996, "Bangla Policy is Out of Kilter" 15 Nov 2005, " "There is More to Dhaka Than Water", 11 Dec 1996. The Telegraph, Put Dhaka in its Place" 12 June 1992. *The Hindustan Times*, "The Unwritten Story of Partition", 7 July 1996: Saradindu Mukherji,"Status Quo or Big Leap Forward" :Domestic Constraints and Civil Society in Contemporary Asia" in M.Singh (ed), Building A New Asia (Delhi 2005).

4 H. N. Pandit, *Netaji Subhas Chandra Bose. From Kabul to Imphal* (Sterling Publishers, 1988 Delhi). Section.7, records some of the views of Bose: "The importance for India of Japanese Foreign Policy in the Far East." The overthrow of British power in India can, in its last stages be materially assisted by Japanese foreign policy in the Far East. If Japan decides on expansion southwards it will lead to an open clash with Great Britain. If war then breaks out, it appears more than certain that the East Indies and Far Eastern squadrons of the British navy will, under the present circumstances, be no match for the Japanese Navy. And even if America comes to the rescue of the British Navy a Japanese victory could still be hoped for. A defeat of the British navy in the Far East including the smashing up of the Singapore base, will automatically weaken British military strength and prestige in India. India is, therefore, intensely interested in the developments in the Far East. And since Japanese expansion southwards necessitates a prior agreement between the Soviet Union and Japan, India is greatly interested in a pact which will, on the one hand, expedite a settlement of the China Affair and will, on the other, enable Japan to move freely and confidently towards the South". In Appen dices, p.317. As for Bose's military planning see: Pandit,Secret Memorandum of Subhas Chandra Bose to the German government ,9 April 1941. Sec. 6 Only this comment " The Military position in India today". Among many other points, it mentions: "The British section of the army in India having a maximum strength of 70,000 is the only loyal force in India today on whom the British government can fully depend. The Indian section of the army has many anti-British elements and perhaps the only group that will be loyal to the British is composed of the Punjabi Muslims. The Punjabi Sikhs –the best fighters

in the Indian army-are the most anti-British at the present time. Since the war began, many regiments of Punjabi Sikhs have mutinied and they have been court-martialed. I know this from personal experience, because those who were not shot, were sentenced to long terms of imprisonment and then they were transported to the Andaman Islands; they passed through the same jail in which I was incarcerated from July to December 1940, viz, the Presidency Jail in Calcutta". "When the opportunity comes again and if its is properly utilized, revolts can be brought about in the Indian section of the army, in spite of the British personnel of the officers. In that revolutionary crisis, the British Government will have only the British soldiers to fall back on, if, at the juncture some military help is available from abroad(i.e, a small force of 50,000 men with modern equipment) British Power in India can be completely wiped out" pp. 315-317.

5 Leonard A Gordon, *Brothers Against the Raj: A Biography of Sarat & Subhas Chandra Bose* (Viking Penguin,1990), p. 65. Also Dilip Roy, *Netaji- The Man, Reminiscences*, (Bharatiya Vidya Bhavan, Bombay 1966. p.165, *Subhas I knew* (Bombay Nalanda, Year 1946) p.173, p. 191

A look at the British media-the big ones as well as the smaller ones- *The Times, Daily Express, Daily Mail, Monring Post* of the inter-war period, offers nothing for India's independence. Only the Machester Guradian and its celebrated liberal Editor C.P. Scott stood for a liberal attitude to India and so did the New Statesman. Decolonisation was never an item on their agenda. (British Library, Colindale, and Scott papers at John Rylands Library, Manchester University).

6 Saradindu Mukherji, "Netaji's Legacy", in B. S. Chhikara, ed, Ist Netaji Subhas Commemorative Lecture, *Souvenir*. (Netaji Azad Hind Fauz Smarak Nyas, Delhi, 2007), pp.38-41.

7 Jan Becka, "Subhas Chandra Bose and the Burmese Freedom Movement" in Sisir K Bose, *Netaji and India's Freedom*. Proceedings of the International seminar 1973 (Netaji Research Bureau, Calcutta, 1975), pp. 54-68. Sisir K Bose, In *Burmese Prisons.Subhas Chandra Bose, Correspondence* May 1923-July 1926. Netaji Collected Works Vol. 3. Sugata Bose, His *Majesty's Opponent. Subhas Chandra Bose and India's Struggle Against Empire*. (Allen Lane, 2011, p. 58) mentions 1924-1927 as Bose's prison term in Mandalay, but it should be 1925-1927.

8 From copy of the debate in Bengal Legislative Assembly on 23 March 1936 on Bose by Hallett, Home Secretary, refers to Bose as a "revolutionary left-

wing politician" and not merely a "left-wing politician" and for harbouring "definite ideas of a violent revolution" in File. P & J. Parliamentary Notice, 1935-36.M.A. Pratt to Secretary of State for India, dt 5 May 1936, conveying his feeling of being "so ashamed to read of the imprisonment of Bose and others in India" and wondered as to why they should "boast of our freedom", and how for the first time people were saying how ashamed they were "to be English". Also from British Consulate in Vienna to J.W. Taylor, Private Secretary to Secretary of State for Foreign affairs, dt 25 April 1936, "Bose complaining of surveillance to President of Police in Vienna on how his previous protest was ignored, made Bose feel that His Royal Highness the Prince of Wales does not know that "Austria is as yet not a British colony" , and demanded a satisfactory explanation for this. File. P & J, 2544/1936Confdl. Dt 22June 1936. Even Bose's passport was seized at Port Said. File. P & J. Parliamentary Notice, 1935-36. Question by Sorenson on 30. April 1936. From Eric Drummond, British Embassy, Rome dt. 29 jan 1935 to Sir John Simon; D. J. Cowan, Minister, British Embassy, Belgrade. No. 114(146/3/34) dt 9 June 1934 to Sir John Simon: C.H. Bentinck British Legation, Sofia, no. 145(139/4/34) to Sir John Simon: Also dispatch no. 145 dt 10 June 1945: from Bentinck, at Sofia no. 126/2/34 dt 26 May 1934: Joseph Anderson, British Legation, Prague. No –w 4905/2634/50 dt 15 May 1934 to O.G.Sargent, Foreign office; British Legation, Budapest.no. 126/153/1/34 dt. 18 May 1934 to Sir John Simon; Telegram from British Embassy, Roumania,dt 17 May 1934 R.H. Hadow, British Legation, Vienna dt 20 April 1934 to T.J. Kendrick, Passport Control, Vienna. British Embassy, Berlin no. W 3733/2634/50/ also 369/2/34 dt 18 April 1934.(India Office Librarty and Records, London). The Irish National Archives, Dublin- Taoiseach,has some records: D/ JUS F D27/36. S.C. Bose. Mayor of Calcutta. D/JUS 1943. S 243/40. Garda Siochana-Meterpolitan Division.Secret C.S. 252/40. Dublin. Also Saradindu Mukherji, "In Search of One's Roots" in The Pioneer, 17 June 1993. Saradindu Mukherji, Book Review on a related theme. Conor Mulvagh, Irish Days, Indian Memories, V. V. Giri and Indian Law Students at University College Dublin, 1913-16, (rish Academic Press Co., 2016 in Indian Historical Review. Vol.44. No.2, Dec 2017, pp.344-346.

9 N.G. Ganpuley, *Netaji in Germany. A Little Known Chapter*, (Bharatiya Vidya Bhavan, Bombay, 1959. Girija K Mookerjee, *Europe at War 1938-1946*. Impressions of war, *Netaji and Europe*, Meenakshi Prakashan, Meerut, 1968, pp192-197, N.K Barooah, Chatto, *Life and Times of an Indian*

anti-Imperialist in Europe, (OUP, Delhi, 2004) Balachandran, *op. cit.* R. C. Majumdar, op.cit. Ch. VIII, pp,198-235. Sisir K Bose & Sugata Bose, " Europe –Today and Tomorrow, Sept 1937, pp. 397-409. India's Spokeman Abroad. Subhas Chandra Bose. Letters, Articles, Speeches and Statements 1933-1937.Netaji Collected Works. Vol viii. (NRB, Permanent Black, Delhi, 1994, 2012), Roy, op.cit.,pp.xxii-xxiv. Bose rightfully accepts that ,"Indian revolutionaries have been exceedingly receptive to the influences exerted by revolutionary struggles abroad" in The Fundamental Problems of India, Tokyo 1944 in Subhas. C. Bose, Fundamental Questions of Indian Revolution (NRB, Calcutta,1970), p.69.Suniti Kumar Chatterjee, Subhas Chandra Bose, "Personal Reminiscences" in Sareen, *op cit*. p.53.

10 Sisir Bose, "The Great Escape ", pp. 111-149 in Sisir Bose, *op. cit.* All the while, Bose had remained fully involved in the freedom movement in the country. See among others, Saradindu Mukherji,"Unanticipated Catastrophe in Bengal in the 1940s " in Thierry Di Costanzo/Guillaume Ducoeur (eds), "Decolonization and the Struggle for National Liberation in India 1909-1971" (Frankfurt, 2013). pp. 169-184.

Romain Hayes, *op.cit*.p.11, Bose had refused German State hospitality and paid his hotel expenses from his own pocket.

11 Majumdar, *op. cit,* p. 683.

12 Adolf Hitler, *My Struggle (Mein Kamf,),* Paternoster Library(Hurst and Blackett Ltd. London, 1936.P.258, p.259. It is revealing to know that in the 1920s, Hitler had held the view that the Indian nationalists known to Europe, particularly the Germans were perhaps not ' a genuine "representative" of India, part of what he thought were "jabbering Orientalists". He had criticised those Germans, particularly those " Nationalists", "who never troubled to enquire, nor did they realize that these were people with nothing beyond them and without authority from anyone to conclude any sort of agreement; so that the result of dealing with such characters was just nil and mere waste of time"' p. 258 Obviously when Bose came to Berlin in 1941, Hitler had realised unlike the top leadership of the Indian national movement based in India, that he was indeed the real leader who had got the Indian people behind him and with whom he could conclude a substantive "agreement" .

13 Milner Hauner, *India in Axis Strategy, Germany, Japan, and Indian Nationalists in the Second World War* (Kletta-Cotta, Stuttgart, 1981).p. 62

14 Hauner, *op.cit.* p.31.Rudolf Hartog, *The Sign of the Tiger.Subhas Chandra Bose and his Indian Legion in Germany,* 1941-45,(Delhi, 2001).

15 Adalbert Seifrez, " Bose and Indian Legion" in Sareen, *op.cit,* pp.74-78 . Ganapulley.

16 It is quite revealing of Bose's style that he also managed to repay to Germany, after he had reached Japan, the first instalment for the cost ("regulated as loan") incurred by the former towards setting up the Indian Legion Hartog in Introduction. Vyas, *op.cit* " Rare Glimpses in Sareen, *op.cit,* pp. 79-86.) Dhar, *op.cit*, p.3.

17 Girija K Mookerjee, *Europe at War 1938-1946: Impressions of War, Netaji and Europe*, (Meenakshi Prakashan, Meerut, 1968), pp192-197. Alexander Werth," An Assessment of Netaji's Policy of Cooperation with the Axis powers during World war II". Bose "formed the nucleus of a Planning Committee" in Germany, and was concerned at the plight of Indians in South Africa, wanted to move them to other regions of Africa in Netaji Seminar Proceedings, Calcutta, *op.cit* 1973. P.253.

18 Foreign Office London to British Mission. Moscow, dt 22 June 1942. (Cypher(outward Telegram) Most Secret. In File.L/P & J/12 /217. F 115/24 (IOL R, London).

19 Eliminton, The Hero of Hindustan, Calcutta, pp.89-92. From Eric Drummond, British Embassy, Rome, dt 29 Jan 1935 to Sir John Simon on Bengal Detenus-S.C Bose and Sarat C Bose, L/PJ/7/793-1935.

20 From British Embassy Rome, no. w.1252/972/50 dt, 1 Feb 1935 to Northern Dept, Foreign Office in F. P & J. 1935-36. Subhas Chandra Bose, Fundamental Questions of Indian Revolution. pp.84-85 (NRB, Calcutta 1970, 1987.Sisir & Sugata Bose,ed,India's Spokesman Abroad, Subhas Bose to Kitty Kurta, letter of 1937 in .xvii.

21 Michael R Wright, Under Secretary of State, Foreign Office, 2209/1/43 dt 15 July 1943 in File. L/P/J/12/217 File 115/24.

Subhas C Bose, " Japan's Role in the Far East" pp.411-429. Written in Oct 1937, in Bose and Bose, India's Spokesman Abroad,Netajis'Collected Works. Vol.8 (Permanent Black, 2012, New Delhi)For a sympathetic account of Japanese foreign policy and its impact in India, see B.R. Nanda, ed The Collected works of LalaLajpatRai. Vol.6. Manohar, 2005, pp. 106-112.

22 Col. Yamatomo,"Bose as seen by the General of the Japanese Army" in Sareen, pp.95-104.

23 Uma Mukherjee, *Two Great Indian Revolutionaries: Rash Behari Bose and Jyotindranath Mukherjee* (Cal, 1966), p.142,162

24 Sareen, *op.cit.* Vol.5 Citing a report by Military Intelligence on Hikari Kikan, Japanese Laison Agency Dealing with INA citing war office Doc 203.808 (Public Record Office, London), PS Ramu, Rash Behari Bose. A Revolutionary Unwept, Unhonoured a Unsung, Delhi 1998

25 Sareen *op.cit* Vol.4, Citing Nippon Times, 4 Nov, 1944, P.15

26 Yamamoto, *op.cit.*

27 Hauner,*op.cit*, p.561. Also see, Mihir Bose, *The Lost Hero: A Biography of Subhas Bose*, Quartret Books, London, 1982, pp, 217-218. Bose's triumphant receptions by the highly placed people or commoners- Indian and non-Indian, important as they are in further helping his image or numerous anecdotes as to how he made the best use of the opportunities which were opening up before him like the one mentioned here, when Bose had ordered the Indian national tricolor on his eleven –seater aircraft that Prime Minister Tojo had gifted to him and similar details are not being mentioned here.

28 Shah Nawaz Khan, "Netaji As I saw Him", in Sareen, pp, 149-157.

29 Aiyar, "Netaji's Unique Courage" in Sareen, pp. 140-148.

30 Nippon Times, 27 Nov 1944 in DEF DOC 2760-D National Archives of Japan, Tokyo.

31 Yamatomo, *op.cit*, pp,95-104. Sugata Bose, p.285.

32 "Kunizuka Kazunari Account of Bose", in Sareen, pp.243-250. This extract was taken from his Memoirs in Japanese entitled, "Rainbow over the Indian Ocean". Tokyo, 1958.

33 Extract from Most Secret Cipher Telegram from C-in-C India to War Office .no. 69319/C cipher 3 Sep (Year not legible but should be 1942/43) in F 115/24. L/P/J/12/217.

34 Jan Becka, "Subhas Chnadra Bose and the Burmese Freedom Movement" *op.cit,* pp. 55-65. Netaji Proceedings 1973. As Aung San, as President of AFPFL pointed out later that whatever Bose and he did were the "correct steps" and no one could "challenge the patriotism of Netaji or ourselves". Speech delivered by Gen Aung San, as Chairman of a public reception given to Sarat Chandra Bose in the City Hall, Rangoon, on 24 July 1946. Appendix, Becka, *op.cit*, pp. 69-72.!

35 Maw, *op.cit,* pp.192-202.

36 Joyce Lebra, Jungle Alliance, Japan and the Indian National Army (Asia Pacific Press, Singapore, 1971) *op.cit*, p.21, 60-61,62-63.,214-215.

37 Lebra, pp. 63-64.Selected Speeches of Subhas Chandra Bose, with a biographical introduction by S.A. Ayer Publication Division, Ministry of I & B, New Delhi, 1983. Broadcast from Azad Hind Radio Germany used from a Tamil version translated in Kuala Lumpur 23 April 1942. Which had stated that Japan has no designs on India and Gen Tojo, the Japanese PM has "repeatedly asserted the slogan of "India for Indians" .p.130.

38 A. DEF. DOC 2760-D, See address of H.E. S.C.Bose, Head of the Provisional Government of Azad Hind on 6 Nov 1943. (National Archives of Japan, Tokyo).

39 Vyas, pp. 79-86.

40 Bayly & Harper, p.21.

41 Yamamoto *op.cit*

42 Kannampilly, "Jai Hind ! We'll meet Again" in Sareen, pp, 274-275. There was more: As Bayly and Harper, op.cit.point out, that "in Rangoon the INA men had helped administer the city before the British returned in force, saving it from further despoliation".p.20.

43 Ibid, also Mihir Bose, The Lost Hero. A Biography of Subhas Bose Quartret Books, London, 1982, pp, 217-218. Bose's triumphant receptions by the highly placed people or commoners- Indian and non-Indian, important as they are in further helping his image or numerous anecdotes how he made the best use of opportunites like the one Mihir Bose mentions, whenNetaji Bose had ordered the Indian national tricolor on his eleven–seater aircraft that Prime Minister Tojo had gifted to him and many such details are not being mentioned here.

44 Alexander Wreth, *Netaji in Germany*, Netaji Research Bureau, Calcutta, 1970.pp,6-7.

45 Lebra, *op.cit*. p.21.

46 R.C. Majumdar, in "Foreword" to K.K. Ghosh, *The Indian National Army*. Second Frontof the Indian Independence Movement (Meenakshi Prakashan, Meerut, 1969).

47 Hayes, *op.cit*, p22-23 citing Sisir and Sugata Bose, ed, Netaji Collected Works. Vo.8, p.256.

48 Vyas, op.cit in Sareen, pp. 79-86.

49 Balachandran, *op.cit*, pp 261-262.

50 Hayes, *op.cit.* pp.164-165.

51 Saradindu Mukherji,"Maulana Abul Kalam Azad: His Mission and Political Legacy" in M.Singh, ed, *Maulana Abul Kalam Azad: Profile of A Nationalist* (Delhi 2003).Sugata Bose, His Majesty's *op. cit,* p.178.

52 Christopher Bayly & Tim Harper, Forgotten War. The End of Britian's Asian Empire. (Penguin Books, 2008), provides some coverage to Bose and the INA.*op.cit*, p. 83, citing Amrita Bazar Patrika, 22 Nov 1945.

53 Saradindu Mukherji, The Pioneer, "Genocide of Hindus Must Stop" 27 Dec 1991, "Blame the Pakistani Apologists in India", 26 June 1992, "Tin Bigha and International Communalism", 31 July 1992. "Time for Ties with South Africa", 11 Dec 1992 , "Are the Minorities in Bangladesh Endangered, 22 Oct, 1993. "Do Something about Chakmas, 21 Oct 1994. 11 Dec 1992, "Anatomy of Pakistan's Flawed Inheritance",14 July 1995, "Pakistan Must Apologise for War Crimes", 22 Sept 1995: The Indian Express, "Minorities Trauma in Bangladesh", 15 June 1994, "The Plight of Minorities in Pakistan" 8 June 1995: The Hindustan Times, "Chakmas –A Sad Story" 10 Aug 1995, "The Unwritten Story of Pakistan" 7 July 1996: The Times of India, " Harassed Minorities of Bangladesh", 15 Nov 1994, " The Horror Stories of Pakistan's Minorities" 14 March 1995, "Chakma Conflict" 24 May 1995, "Kashmir Migrants are Refugees" 24 Dec 1994: "The Hidden Story of Kashmir's Refugees" (OHA, Philadelphia, 1996) Subjects, Citizens and Refugees. Tragedy in the Chitagong Hill Tracts, 1947-1998. (Voice of India, New Delhi, 2000). Hindus Betrayed: Religious Cleansing in Bangladesh(IPF, Delhi 2013). Also see "Pakistan and India Can Not be Equated". *The Pioneer,* 14 Aug 1992. Pakistan is Not a Modern State 31 March 1995.

54 Hayes,*op.cit*, pp,164-165.

55 Takaoka, "In Memory of Netaji" in Sareenop.*op.cit*.pp, 268-269.

56 Ba Maw, *op.cit*, p.202 in Sareen.

57 Preface by R. N. Sanyal, (ed,) International Military Tribunal For The Far East. DissentientJudgement of Justice R.B.Pal (Sanyal& Co, Calcutta, 1953), p.558.

58 Yamamolo *op.cit*

59 R. F Holland, *European Decolonisation 1918-1981: An Introductory Survey* (Macmillan, London,1985), while acknowledging how the Asian societies had "Japanese influences implanted upon them; the ideology of a 'Greater Co-Prosperity Sphere,was rooted into the local environment and

this bundle of ideas(with its material emphasis implied in the title) played a vital historical role in generating an Asian consciousness which, after 1945, could not be forced back into colonial encounters", p.40, yet desists from mentioning Bose and the INA, though he has an entire chapter on " Japanese revolution in East Asia" pp,38-51. Saradindu Mukherji, 'Nehru's tryst with Edwina: Mountbatten Snared Him", The Pioneer, 22 July 2007.

60 Rabindra Nath Tagore Rachanabali. Vol. xiii,"Deshanayak", (West Bengal Govt, Calcutta, B.E. 1368), pp, 387-390.

61 Hugh Toye, *op. cit.* p.285.

62 Gordon, *op.cit.* p.454.

63 Mukherjee Commission Related Documents and Netaji Declassified Papers at Kolkata and New Delhi. I had located three files on Bose/INA at the Arkib Negara-National Archives of Malaysia, Kuala lumpur few years back, when they were not open to scholars. Whether they have been accessed since then I have no idea. While, European/American history text books completely smother such major episodes, the ground reality in India is no better!

64 Saradindu Mukherji, "Blinkered Vision of Indian Academics", *Sunday Observer*, 22 Sept 1991, "Are we consigning Netaji to oblivion ?", *The Hindustan Times*, 23 January 1995. "Beware of Academic Fascists", *The Hindustan Times*, 23 January 2002.

NCERT history text books barely take note of Bose. See "Class XII Text Book. A Case Study of Progressive History Writing, 19 June 2015 "Progressive Distortions in NCERT Class XII Text Book." 22 July 2015, in India Facts. For some historians, Syed Ahmad of Aligarh fame and Jinnah are makers of modern India, and Bose just does not matter.

G. Barraclough, *An Introduction to Contemporary History*, (Penguin, London, 1967), writes about the non-European developments without mentioning Bose or the INA. He does refer to Patel's role in the Kheda movement and how the national movement had a "Bengali imprint". P.36, p.180. E Hobsbawm, "Nation and Nationalism since 1780. Programme, myth, reality" (Cambridge University Press, 1990), p. 149. Bose is funnily described as a "hero of the Bengali masses", while the INA gets just one line!

One may note how Bose is marginalised by Nehru, and how glowingly Nehru writes about Babar and Mohammad Iqbal in his Discovery of India. Also see how C.A. Bayly, Origins of Nationality in South Asia. Patriotism and Ethical Government in the Making of Modern India (OUP, Delhi, 1998, p.317), narrates his experiences after he had hanged a picture of "Subhas Chandra Bose, hero of the Indian National Army in the last room of the National Portrait Gallery, London at an exhibition on "The Raj: India and the British 1600-1947. 1990".

Netaji Subhas Chandra Bose's Perception of the Soviet Union, its Ideology and Role in International Affairs

Nirmala Joshi

By the second decade of the twentieth century the Indian National Movement was gathering a new momentum and a new phase in its history. The nationalist fervor was spreading engulfing the entire nation. Netaji Subhas Chandra Bose had just returned from Cambridge after successfully qualifying for the Indian Civil Service. But Subhas Chandra Bose could not insulate himself from the on-going national ferment. Being a true patriot he joined the Indian National Congress (INC) and plunged into the national movement. His aim was to serve the motherland and work for the social upliftment of the masses. An equally historic development occurred around this time – "the October Revolution of 1917 in Russia – that shook the world. An underground organization had defeated the mighty Tsarist Empire. Consequently the October Revolution impacted on several liberation movements in Asia reeling under colonial yoke. The October Revolution stirred the imagination of several Indian leaders of the national movement, who drew inspiration from the revolutionary changes in Russia and Subhas Chandra Bose was no exception. There is no doubt that the October Revolution instilled hope and confidence in the leaders of the Indian freedom movement. Several write ups in national weeklies and journals such as *Kesari*, a popular Marathi daily, *Prabha,* a monthly and *Sansar* from Kanpur published articles about the October Revolution. What is commendable is that, these write ups appeared in difficult times in times of strict censorship.

Like his contemporaries Subhas Chandra Bose was also impressed with the developments in Russia. His sharp intellect began to explore and study the Marxist ideology; the fundamental basis of the new state. At the same time the prevailing international environment also came in for closer scrutiny and examination. He paid special attention to the Soviet foreign policy and its diplomatic moves.

However, it must be made clear at the outset that Subhas Chandra Bose was not a Marxist. He had two primary goals; the freedom of the country and the social and economic welfare of the people by striving to bring about the requisite changes. If the October Revolution fired his imagination, it was only to learn from that experiment and possibly to adapt the relevant features to Indian conditions. It was not a direct transplant of that experiment into India as the Communist Party of India attempted.

Views on Marxist Ideology

In his understanding of the Marxist ideology Subhas Chandra Bose was in agreement with some of its postulates, while disagreeing with some. For instance he accepted the dialectical principle in analyzing societal change in history. According to the dialectical methodology in every society from an historical perspective there is conflict between 'haves' and 'have nots'. From an ideological perspective there is a conflict between 'thesis' represented by the masses who did not have the means of production and hence were exploited, while 'anti thesis' was represented by the capitalist exploiters who had the means of production, and hence were able to exploit and subjugate the masses. In short the crux of the ideology was the class approach.

Subhas Chandra Bose's acceptance of the dialectical method was, however, not unqualified. He did question some of the basic tenets. In his view "The materialistic interpretation of history which seems to be a cardinal point in Communist theory will not find unqualified acceptance in India, even among those who would be disposed to accept the economic contents of communism".[1] Elucidating further in his peech at Tokyo Subhas Chandra Bose believed that the class approach over emphasized the role of the working class in bringing about the revolutionary changes. In a developing and a backward country the peasantry constitutes a huge majority and ignoring this critical mass was not the right approach. Hence, in Subhas Chandra Bose's view India being predominantly a country of peasants the problem of peasants will have to be accorded greater importance. In India industrial development was in a nascent stage and so the working class was a minuscule minority. In this regard Subhas Chandra Bose's understanding was absolutely correct. In the Indian context an inclusive approach had to be adopted, which included the peasants, the working class and other sections of the Indian society. A collective approach had to be factored in any future strategy for social and economic development.

Subsequent developments in the Soviet Union proved the correctness of Subhas Chandra Bose's understanding. The Soviet Union being an underdeveloped and a backward country at the time of the October Revolution, the leadership subsequently (around 1920) realized that the overwhelming mass of the peasantry was getting sullen and that this mass could not be ignored. The success of the Revolution required that an alliance with the peasantry was essential. Incidentally from the ideological perspective the peasantry was considered as reactionary, the least brutal animal in the farmyard. Consequently, the *New Economic Policy* (1921) had to be launched that included incentives for the peasantry.

Importantly, Subhas Chandra Bose was of the view that "Where communism is deficient is that it does not appreciate the value of national sentiment what we in India would, which will fulfil the social needs of the whole people".[2] In his thinking the struggle for socialism the importance of economic motive and material needs stand foremost. However, apart from economic motive there are other elements in man, that is, physical, ethical, aesthetics etc. which guide the course of history.[3] Moreover, history has shown that the materialistic needs of a human being keep not only changing, but growing as well. Subhas

Chandra Bose's aim was a progressive government based on national sentiment (a point often emphasized in his speeches and writings) which would focus on the well-being of the whole people and the prosperity of the nation.

A second cardinal principle of Marxism that appealed to Subhas Chandra Bose was the goal of building a socialist pattern of society. This very significant step was taken under the influence of the Soviet example. Subhas Chandra Bose opted for a socialist pattern of society as it focuses on bridging the social and economic gap. As mentioned the quality among people was a very dear cause to Subhas Chandra Bose. Thus in his Presidential address to the fifty first session of the INC at Haripura in 1938 he said "I have no doubt in my mind that our chief national problems relating to the eradication of poverty, illiteracy and disease and the scientific production and distribution can be effectively tackled only among socialistic lines".[4] The Soviet Union's rapid industrialization, the establishment of the Planning Commission to chalk out the future road map were highly appreciated. As the president of the INC Subhas Chandra Bose formed the Planning Commission with Jawaharlal Nehru as its first Chairman. He also believed that although socialist reconstruction is not possible before political liberation, nevertheless the struggle for socialism and the struggle for Independence could go on simultaneously and need not necessarily follow the Russian precedent.[5] However, Subhas Chandra Bose's ideal of social reconstruction had to be based on 'national sentiment', a point often reiterated in his speeches and writings.

Given his sharp intellect Subhas Chandra Bose wrote in his book *The Indian Struggle:* "Gandhism and Communism were not mutually incompatible. While Gandhi had given the country the method of *Satyagraha*, he had not offered a programme for social reconstruction, and that such a programme was available in Communism".[6] This passage was quoted by the soviet writer K. Mikhailov and drew his ire for this comparison by Subhas Chandra Bose, for after the Sixth Congress of the Comintern in 1928, the line towards national liberation movements had undergone a radical change. Consequently, the bourgeoisie was now (

after 1928) regarded as reactionary. Subhas Chandra Bose was called "a politically reactionary stupid man".

Despite his fascination for the socialist experiment and the eagerness to learn from it, Subhas Chandra Bose did not attend the Fourth Congress of the Third International or the Comintern held in Moscow in 1922, though he was personally invited. The Comintern was established in Moscow in 1919 for the promotion and support of national liberation movements in Asia and elsewhere.

Some of Subhas Chandra Bose's ideals such as freedom of religion, a secular model of governance, emancipation of women, universal education were derived from the teachings of Indian thinkers such as Swami Vivekananda, Ramakrishna Paramahamsa etc. These values were to an extent compatible with what the Soviet Union also espoused. The major difference lay in approaches; it was force versus persuasion.

Views on Foreign Policy

Being an internationalist Subhas Chandra Bose was also keenly following developments on the international scene. In the thirties the liberation movements in Asia were entering a new phase, a phase marked by activeness and aggressiveness, while developments in Europe were worsening and heading towards a conflict. Though the Nazi-Soviet Pact of 1939 stunned the developed world, Subhas Chandra Bose blamed the intransigence on the part of Great Britain and France and their refusal to respond to the Soviet overtures for an understanding of the developments in Germany and the rise of Hitler. It was basically a policy of appeasement. The following write up demonstrated Subhas Chandra Bose's sympathy for the Soviet Union. In an editorial in *Foreward* on 2 December Subhas Chandra Bose wrote "Russia had consistently and tenaciously endeavoured to secure an understanding with Great Britain and France and also with Poland. It was only after she was convinced of utter hopelessness of this effort that she decided to enter into a non-aggression Pact with Germany".[7]

In the late thirties the international situation deteriorated further and was heading towards a conflict. In 1939 the Second World War began and the radical freedom fighter in Subhas Chandra Bose compelled him to leave India in search of international support for the freedom struggle, which was entering a decisive stage. In 1941 Subhas Chandra Bose left India. Subhas Chandra Bose firmly believed that in these turbulent times, pacifism would not lead to freedom. It had to be snatched possibly by military means. Although he did not support either Communism or Nazism, he still sought help from both Germany and the Soviet Union. This was because he felt that the British colonial yoke had to be thrown off by any means including military means. The goal of Independence was much higher than any 'ism'. Hence ,the Indian National Army (INA) was formed.

In October, 1943 in Singapore Subhas Chandra Bose announced the formation of a Provisional Government of Azad Hind (Free India). He had observed that such a move was in accordance with the prevailing practice. For instance the Irish people had set up a Provisional Government in 1916, the Czechs and the Turks had also set up their Provisional Governments. Subhas Chandra Bose was keen that the Soviet Union also accord recognition to the Provisional Government of Azad Hind. Although by that time nine countries had already accorded recognition to it. In a letter to the then Foreign Minister of the Soviet Union V.M. Molotov he wrote "… I avail myself of this opportunity to express my sincere desire that there should exist between our two governments and our two nations the most cordial relations of amity and friendship".[8] The Soviet Union did accord recognition but indirectly to the Japanese Embassy.

After 1945

It is not clear what Subhas Chandra Bose thought about the Soviet Union's entry into the Second World War on the side of the Allies or the disbandment of the Communist International in 1943 in order to facilitate better cooperation with Britain and France. He was convinced that this was a tactical agreement as the commonalities between them were limited and the area of schism was deep and wide. The ideological divide between the Soviet Union and its partners was fundamental and hence an alliance could not be permanent. In a broadcast from Singapore on 25 May, 1945 Subhas Chandra Bose said "I firmly adhere to what I have consistently said in the past, namely, that the collapse of Germany will be the signal for the outbreak of an acute conflict between the Soviets and Anglo-Americans. The whole world knows that the war aims of Soviet Russia are quite different from those of the Anglo-Americans".[9] This prediction proved correct for we find that at the San Francisco Conference in 1945 the differences surfaced signaling the onset of the Cold War.

Earlier Subhas Chandra Bose had led the Indian National Army's (INA) march towards India *via* Burma and North East, but his attempt failed. An unfortunate turn of events led the British Indian Army to gain an upper hand and Subhas Chandra Bose's attempts were thwarted. Besides the Second World War was drawing to a close and the defeat of Japan was imminent. Given the unfavourable situation in South East Asia for Japan, Subhas Chandra Bose expressed a desire to go to the Soviet Union. In his perception the Soviet Union was still a "friendly and a safe" country. Perhaps the Soviet Union could promote the cause of Indian freedom struggle.

The year 1945 is extremely critical in the annals of Indian history. As the Japanese Army was retreating from South East Asia the preparations were made for Subhas Chandra Bose and some of his cabinet colleagues to fly to Japan, possibly *en route* to the Soviet Union. In August 1945, when Subhas Chandra Bose alongwith a lone member Habibur Rahman were on their way to Japan, the news came that the plane carrying Subhas Chandra Bose and Habibur Rahman had crashed at Taihoku in Formosa, today's Taiwan. Within no time the Japanese government announced on 18 August 1945 that Subhas Chandra Bose had died in the plane crash.

Since, then conflicting news/reports appeared at regular intervals questioning the Japanese version of the air crash theory. A plethora of circumstantial evidence suggests that the air crash theory was fabricated, and Subhas Chandra Bose had reached the Manchurian air base then under the Soviet occupation. Both the British Foreign Office and the people of India did not believe that Subhas Chandra Bose was dead.

The British Foreign Office was of the view that the death of Subhas Chandra Bose was a deception plan on the part of the Japanese government, and that he was alive in the Soviet Union. The British apprehensions were on two accounts firstly the Cold War had begun and therefore attempts to seek the soviet cooperation would be futile, and Secondly, Subhas Chandra Bose's presence in the Soviet Union was equally worrisome. Negotiations with the Indian leaders regarding the future arrangements were at a delicate stage. An extremist view in Britain forecast that Subhas Chandra Bose with the support of the Soviet Union could advance into India; this time *via* the North West. Hence, every news/information about India in the soviet writings was examined carefully particularly the British Intelligence. For instance the request of the Soviet Embassy in Kabul for subscription of Indian newspapers threw the Foreign Office in a tizzy. The start of the Cold War and the presence of Subhas Chandra Bose fuelled fears in British thinking.

On the other hand a strong conviction prevailed in India that Subhas Chandra Bose was alive. What lent credence to this point of view was even Mahatma Gandhi believed that Subhas Chandra Bose was alive. In this context the following observation by the British *Fortnightly Intelligence Weekly* noted that "The statement of Gandhiji in India that he believes Subhas Chandra Bose to be still alive was received with great joy by the General Indian Public and the INA. There is a rumour also that he (Bose) is still doing some useful work for the freedom of India".[10]

Soviet Writings on India

Before proceeding further it is essential to evaluate the soviet writings on India. Prior to India's Independence the soviet articles were of a general descriptive nature. This was the period when neither India nor other Asian countries had gained Independence. In fact, they were on the threshold of independence. The pioneers of Indology in the Soviet Union were A.M. Dyakov and V. Balabushevich. Dyakov in his article *Contemporary India* observed that India had not only furthered the interests of British capitalism by providing economic resources, but also served as a base for furtherance of British imperialistic designs.[11] V. Balabushevich in his comprehensive article titled *The Struggle for Indian Independence* gave a detailed account of the on-going political development in India.[12] The comparatively soft line on Indian developments underwent a drastic change after India became independent. E. Zhukov the most authoritative Soviet scholar on Asia came out with a strident criticism of Indian leaders and development in his article "*The Situation in India*". In his view Nehru had abandoned his anti-British posture in order to collaborate with the British Imperialists, while Gandhi in Zhukov's opinion was the apostle of India's backwardness, the opponent of industrialization. Importantly on India's option of non-alignment in world politics was viewed with distrust. Zhukov wrote "In reality the theory of neutrality only emphasized India's closeness to British imperialism". Zhukov found it absurd to compare America with the USSR.[13] Several factors such as the acceptance of the plan for partition, India's decision to remain within the Commonwealth etc. were misperceived and hence drew harsh criticism.

In reality on Indian independence as well as on other countries' the Soviet Union was not well posted with information on India's socio-economic conditions and political developments. The Soviet approach towards India was hence based on certain Marxist theoretical generalizations on colonialism rather than on empirical evidence. Hence only to the extent that India's struggle to achieve independence weakened British Imperialism did the Soviet Union encourage it; and whenever it was in desperate need of capital and industrial goods from the West, it played down the struggle in India.

This strident line towards India was abandoned in 1955. From then onwards India was considered as the most progressive country. However, throughout the Soviet period no mention was made in newspapers or journals about Subhas Chandra Bose or the possibility of his presence in the Soviet Union. Some reports in India did mention that the Indian ambassador to the Soviet Union Dr. S. Radhakrishnan met Subhas Chandra Bose in a prison near Moscow in 1949. However, till his death Dr. Radhakrishnan maintained a studied silence and refused to either confirm or deny such reports. The veracity of this report needs to be probed. It was during the period of *Perestroika* and *Glassnost* initiated by Mikhail Gorbachev, the Secretary General of the Communist Party of the Soviet Union, that the first article on the controversy surrounding Subhas Chandra Bose's death probably in the Soviet Union appeared. T.F. Deviyatkina, a well-known Indologist observed that the mystery of Subhas Chandra Bose's death has neither been confirmed nor disproved. After many controversies his relatives officially confirmed it. However, "this does not remove the shroud of mystery".[14] There is no doubt that the whereabouts of Subhas Chandra Bose after 1945 still remain shrouded in mystery. There is the imperative need by historians and others to unravel this mystery.

In conclusion it can be said that Subhas Chandra Bose was undoubtedly impressed with the socialist experiment. At the same time his approach to the freedom struggle and commitment to socialist reconstruction were of paramount importance. His unwavering ideals were firmly rooted in Indian realities and milieu. Subhas Chandra Bose's ideology and socialist reconstruction had to be based on national sentiment.

References

1. Subhas Chandra Bose, *The Indian Struggle*, Bombay 1964.
2. Speech at Tokyo.
3. *Ibid.*
4. *Report of the Fifty-First Session of the Indian National Congress, Haripura*, 1938 (Allahabad, n.d), p. 174.
5. Ideology of Netaji, *Thesis of the All India Foreward Bloc* (Published in 1949 from Calcutta for Leftist Book Club accessed on 25 January, 2017.
6. K. Mikhailov, "About Developments in the Indian National Congress", in *Revolutionary East* (in Russian) (1935, no. 2), p. 140. [Is it К. Михайлов, 'О сдвигах в Индийском национальном конгрессе'. Революционный Восток, Issues 29-34 ??].
7. S.C. Bose, *Crossroads 1938-1940* (Calcutta, 1962), p. 222.
8. Purabi Roy, *The Search for Netaji: New Findings,* Purple Peacock Publications (Kolkata, 2012), p. 103.
9. *Ibid.*, p. 140.
10. *Ibid.*, p. 182.
11. A. Dyakov, "Contemporary India", in *Bolshevik* (Moscow), no. 4, 1946, pp. 38-42 in Russian. Quoted in Nirmala Joshi, Foundations of Indo-Soviet Relations (New Delhi, Radiant Publishers, 1975), pp. 154-55.

12. V. Balabushevich, "The Struggle for Indian Independence", in *World Economy and World Politics* (Moscow), no. 9, 1946, pp. 39-52 in Russian, ibid., pp. 156-158.
13. E. Zhukov, "The Situation in India", *ibid.*, no. 23 (1947), pp. 3-14, in Nirmala Joshi, *ibid.*, pp. 158-59.
14. Purabi Roy, no. 8 *op.cit.*, p. 260.

Netaji and Empowerment of Indian Women The Role of the Rani Jhansi Regiment to India's Independence

Monmayee Basu

The participation of Indian women in the nation's struggle for freedom is well-known. Their entry into the National Independence Movement is inextricably intertwined with the name of Gandhiji, who, it is believed, for the first time brought the women out of the precincts of their homes into public forum, and gave them the opportunity to take part in the movement at par with men. While agreeing with this notion, I wish to put forth the fact that Netaji, too, in his revolutionary way, has ensured that women fought on a completely equal footing and went to the extent of creating a full all-women regiment that would fight for the liberation of the motherland. It was in those days, an unimaginable, unmatched action, the first of its kind in the world after the Women's Battalions, the all female combat units formed after the February Revolution in 1917. At one stroke Netaji proved that he was not only an intensely patriotic revolutionary leader, but at the same time a great liberator of women, - a 'feminist' in the true sense of the term. This is because he whole-heartedly believed that no nation could progress by keeping half of its population in chains. Netaji re-iterated this innumerable times on several occasions. He had immense faith in the capabilities and potentials of Indian women. He said, "Not only in the history of the Passive Resistance Movement but in the history of the Revolutionary Party also, we have the examples of our brave sisters who have played a noble part. I know of many sisters who became daring revolutionaries. If one type of courage was necessary for passive resistance, another and more active courage is necessary for revolutionary efforts, and in this too, I found that our sisters were not wanting. In 1931, an English Magistrate was shot dead by two girls: the age of one was 16, the age of the other was 17...You can easily imagine what wonderful courage those young sisters might have had. Such courage does not descend from the skies; it comes from the soil of India; it has its roots in the age-old traditions of India's past."[1]

In his early years Netaji Subhas Chandra Bose was deeply inclined towards spiritualism. In fact, as Dr. Lakshmi Sehgal observed in her interview to Teen Murti Oral transcript section, that Netaji had once told her that it was a rather hard decision for him to choose between spirituality and full-fledged revolution. [2] In fact, he was a great follower of Swami Vivekananda whom he looked upon as his spiritual *guru,* while his political mentor was Deshbandhu Chittaranjan Das. The goddess he revered most was Mahakali who was also the central deity in the mind of Vivekananda. Dr. Karan Singh recalled of having seen a "beautiful photograph" of Mahakali in his room at Netaji Bhawan at Elgin Road in Kolkata. [3] At the same time he was a worshipper of Durga also who was annually worshipped with pomp and splendour at Netaji's ancestral house in Subhasgram (Kodalia) near Kolkata. Both these deities, apart from having boundless grace, were also known to be symbols of prowess and fearlessness. Netaji wanted to see these qualities in women. Netaji, therefore, visualised women to be the great repositories of energy, strength and courage.

The women who moulded him and left an indelible impression on his heart and soul were his mother Smt. Prabhavati Devi, Deshbandhu C.R. Das's wife Basanti Devi (whom Netaji used to call 'mother'), Sister Nivedita whose unflinching devotion, patriotism and sacrifice moulded his character. And of course the great Indian Queen Rani of Jhansi. Rani Jhansi was the ideal character whom, Netaji believed, every Indian woman should emulate. "The same India, which produced great women in the past also produced the Rani of Jhansi at a grave hour in India's history and today while we are facing the gravest hour in India's history, I have confidence that Indian womanhood will not fail to rise to the occasion...for the Independence of the whole of India to liberate 38 crores of Indians, India has to produce and shall produce thousands of Ranis of Jhansi".[4] He was an ardent admirer of the great women of India's past". - the women who excelled in different fields. He said, "our past has been a great and glorious one...The history of the great women in India is as ancient as the Vedic Period..." we have figures like Maitrayee in India's ancient days, we have the inspiring examples of Ahalyabai of Maharashtra, Rani Bhawani of Bengal, Razeya Begum and Noor Jehan, who were shining administrators, in recent times prior to British rule in India. I have every confidence in the fertility of the Indian soil..." [5]

Netaji therefore, took immense interest in uplifting the status of Indian women. In his different capacities he took measures to empower them because although he had tremendous faith in their potentials, he was aware at the same time of the several handicaps from which Indian womanhood suffered. It did not elude his attention that despite tremendous odds the women formed their own organisations, even combat forces. The Mahila Rashtriya Sangha of Bengal deserves special mention in this connection. As the Chief Executive Officer of the Calcutta Corporation he set up for the first time in 1924 an Education Department which would aim at providing a comprehensive education system to girls and boys alike. In 1928 he organised a 300 strong women's section of Bengali volunteers who would parade in the streets of Calcutta on the occasions of the meetings and rallies of the Congress in the city. [6] They were all immaculately dressed in green sarees with red border and left an amazing impact. Latika Ghosh, the organiser of the Mahila Rashtriya Sangha who was the niece of the great revolutionary and Saint Sri Aurobindo and daughter of Manmohan Ghosh led the parade. She was greatly inspired by Subhas Chandra Bose. He was also the role model for two sisters Bina and Kalyani Das, who were the daughters of his respected teacher Beni Madhav Das who had profound influence on Subhas Chandra. They also had joined the parade. Bina attempted to shoot the Governor of Bengal, and in this act, according to her, she had the full support of Subhas Chandra Bose. Two girls, Shanti Ghosh and Suniti Chaudhury of Comilla who shot to death the Magistrate there in 1931 were closely associated with him and received his constant guidance in their revolutionary activities.[7] Netaji Subhas Chandra, was the father of national planning which he first initiated in India through the National Planning Committee in 1938 when he was the Congress President. It was drafted by Meghnad Saha. It had a complete vision of all-round national education for all and had a detailed plan for it,including night schools for the youth. He was immensely fascinated by the education system set up by Rabindranath Tagore at Shanti Niketan. Education alone, he believed, could deliver a country and its men and women alike from deep inertia and despondency.

Netaji always wanted to bring out women from the precincts of the four walls of their houses and to engage them in important activities of society and nation. In his Presidential address at the Maharashtra Provincial Conference at Poona on 3rd May 1928 he clearly said, "The Status of women should be raised and women should be trained to take a larger and a more intelligent interest in public affairs." With this broad mission in view, he persuaded Basanti Devi, the wife of C.R. Das, to take up some of the unfinished work of her husband after his death. He had tremendous reverence for her. Even Emilie Schenkle in her interview to historian B.R. Nanda, emphasised how much Bose respected her.[8] Basanti Devi was always by the side of her husband in his political activities, and warmly welcomed all young men who visited her husband in their house, and even had courted arrest while trying to sell khadi. Although Basanti Devi kept on refusing, Subhas Chandra Bose was not deterred from entreating her again and again. This is clear from his several correspondences with her. In one such letter he wrote that the youth of Bengal were eagerly waiting for her to come forward and take up their leadership. He refuted her argument that a Hindu woman's duty was within the limits of her family – behind the scenes and not on the public platform. He wrote, "Mother, today our house is on fire. When the house is on fire, even a woman observing *purdah* has to take courage in both hands and come out on the street. She has to work as hard as a man to save her child, to protect valuable property from fire"[9] (translated from original Bengali).

Another interesting anecdote is worth mentioning here in this connection. Subhas Chandra in his over-enthusiasm to see women shouldering important and serious public work had once craved to make Emilie Schenkle a journalist – a special correspondent of *The Hindu*, one of India's leading daily newspapers. He corresponded with *The Hindu* on her behalf that they would accept two articles from her every month for 2 pounds. And he wanted her to write on issues of Balkans and Near East, and sent her several letters on the history of those places. But it was very difficult for Emilie to cope and as a result the first draft turned out to be disastrous. Subhas Chandra first wanted to read it before being sent off to *The Hindu*. He was extremely disappointed and furious. He wrote back a list of Emilie's mistakes, the first of which was Bad English. He also sent a copy to A.C.N Nambiar who in the light of his journalistic background suggested that Emilie should rather start with articles on films etc. But Subhas Chandra did not agree at all, as he wanted Emilie to start first with serious stuff like the Balkans.[10] Such was the passion of Netaji to bring women at par in public life with men, such were his radical ideas about the emancipation of women. He even wanted women specially girl students to act as secret messengers and underground workers and provide shelter for the men who fight.[11]

These concepts of Netaji were reflected in his organisation of the Rani of Jhansi Regiment when he took over the charge of the Indian Independence League (IIL) and INA in 1943 from Rash Behari Bose, the great revolutionary from Bengal and the first President of IIL. Till that time in East Asia the concept of women's participation in public life was totally incomprehensible. However, Rash Behari Bose, had realised that no nation could progress with half of its population kept in the dark. Therefore, Rash Behari Bose took the initiative of involving women in works of the Indian Independence League. A women's section was set up by his efforts in the IIL in March 1943.[12] But that work was limited to that of nursing the injured soldiers in the INA hospitals and also relief work among the sick and the destitute. Women taking part in actual combat was still unthinkable. Everything, however, underwent a complete transformation with the coming of Netaji at Singapore on 2 July, 1943, because Netaji believed in complete equality of women in every field, including direct military action. Netaji always believed that women had the valour of the highest order and in the past also had proved to be excellent warriors and revolutionaries. He observed, "It will not be an exaggeration if I say that there are no public activities or departments of our national effort in which women are not participating. During the past many years of our national movement, women have been equal to men in undergoing suffering with joy and courage. The Indian women never lagged behind anybody in going from village to village, without food and water, addressing meeting after meeting, in carrying the message of freedom from house to house, in conducting election campaigns, in taking out processions in spite of Government's bans and in the face of *lathi* charge by the merciless British police ...Last but not the least, our heroic sisters also took an active part in the secret revolutionary activities."[13] So he announced, within a few days of his arrival that he would like to raise an all-women regiment, the second of its kind after the Women's Battalion of the Russian Revolution. Dr. Lakshmi Sahgal (then Lakshmi Swaminathan), who was practising in Singapore at that time, met Netaji when she heard of his intention to draft women and came out with a mandate to recruit as many women as possible. In this connection Dr. Sehgal observed in her interview that the very name of the regiment showed his profound faith in women's boundless energy of which Rani of Jhansi was the epitome. Manavati Arya, another soldier of the Rani of Jhansi Regiment also said in her interview with S.L. Manchanda of NMML on 4 February 1992 that Netaji had unflinching belief in "*stree-shakti*". Netaji himself observed on the occasion of the opening of the first camp for training at Singapore on 22 October, 1943, "When the Rani of Jhansi started her fight, her age was only twenty. You can easily imagine what it would have been for a girl of twenty, riding a horse, and wielding her sword in open battle. You can easily realise what courage and spirit she might have had; the

English Commander who fought against her said, 'She was the best and bravest of the rebels.' ....She died but her spirit can never die. India can once again produce Jhansi Ranis and march on to victory."[14] On another occasion while addressing the Rani of Jhansi Regiment from Burma on 14 May 1944 he said: "I feel confident that the Rani of Jhansi Regiment will prove to be a success and will achieve an abiding place on the history of our struggle for freedom. I have often lectured to you in the past that India needs today not one Rani of Jhansi but thousands of them...During the past twenty years, I have seen something of what our women are capable of. I have seen that there is no work and no sacrifice of which the women of India are not capable."[15] By his endeavour Discourses of Cultural and National Subjects was published by IIL in January 1944 which emphasised vehemently on the need of women's education and the inheritance of women to property in case of the death of her husband.[16]

Joyce C. Lebra of Colorado University has, in a very interesting way, drawn a parallel between Netaji and Rani Lakshmibai of Jhansi. There were innumerable common elements between the two. Firstly, both of them are legendary characters. "Each was the focus of popular aspirations in time of violent upheaval, a century apart. Both had a magnetism and charisma that inspired total devotion and faith in their followers. And from each of the two a legend grew and a myth infected nationalism."[17] Both had a common enemy in the Britishers; both were martyrs; both of them, despite their very limited military training, engaged in military operations in uniform; both died while in action, the Rani in the battle-field in Gwalior, and Netaji fatally wounded in a Japanese military plane while on his journey towards a destination that, he believed, would help to further his armed resistance. The valour, fixed determination and indefatigable spirit of both were unmatched, unparalleled. The kinship between the two was indeed unique and undeniable.

Raising an Indian army on a foreign land, especially accumulation of women for the Rani of Jhansi Regiment, seemed to be a herculian task. It was by no means easy. Lakshmi Sehgal in fact made a door-to-door campaign to recruit women. Even so, the response everywhere was overwhelming. Men and women in large numbers came forward to enrol their names. Netaji's magnetic personality and his speeches also made a great impact. One such prominent personality was Captain Janaki Davar (Puan Sri Datin Janaki Athinahappan) and her sister who lived in Malaya. Manavati Arya, an Indian of Burma left her job of teaching in Vishwa Bharati Academy in Rangoon and also her old parents to join the Regiment. According to her, on hearing the clarion call of Netaji, the Indian women living in Burma flocked in large numbers to join the Burma unit of the Rani of Jhansi Regiment.[18] Shanti Majumdar (Bhowmik) and her younger sister Anjali of Seremban in Malaya were 14 and 13 years old respectively. They joined the Regiment accompanied by their mother who handed them over to Lakshmi Swaminathan (Sehgal).[19] Captain Manoranjitha Sathyavathi Thaver, who later was in charge of recruitment has narrated some very interesting incidents in her reminiscences. At two in the morning a girl came running at the camp gate as she had fled from her home in the middle of the night to join the Regiment and came running all the way. She was injured by the rough rope by which she climbed down the window of her room and was bleeding badly from her hands and feet. [20] Such irresistible was the craving of the brave girls to join the movement staking everything they had,- their future, even their lives. Shanti Majumdar knew some families of which the husbands joined the Azad Hind Fauj, the wives and the daughters joined the Rani of Jhansi Regiment and the sons – Tokyo Cadet Corps.[21] Maya Banerjee and three of her siblings joined the Rani of Jhansi Regiment and the Azad Hind Fauj in Burma.[22] Large numbers of women stuck to their seats even under heavy downpour while Netaji addressed the women's section of the Indian Independence League, Singapore, on 12th July 1943.

As far as financial contribution is concerned, enormous funds came pouring in both in cash and jewellery. Many prosperous businessmen contributed lakhs of rupees, property, even houses, cattle, cars etc. Women in large numbers gave up their jewellery. In a personal interview with Bhagirath Mishra from Bengali Newspaper *Bartaman*, Commander Janaki Davar revealed that she herself gave up her diamond earrings and gold chain she was wearing when she went on her bicycle to hear Netaji speak at a rally in Kuala Lumpur. She was then only eighteen years old. Following her, innumerable people who were attending the rally, donated money and ornaments. Many young men voluntarily enrolled themselves in the Azad Hind Fauj.[23] Lt. Pratima Sen, an adjutant in the Rani of Jhansi Regiment, wrote about a day when Netaji was delivering a speech at the Town Hall of Rangoon. Hundreds of people went on to the stage to garland him after his mesmerising speech. These garlands and wreaths of flowers were getting plied up on a table beside Netaji. These were then auctioned one-by-one among the audience with the purpose of collecting funds for the war. Huge amounts, even lakhs of rupees were offered for each wreath.[24] Such was the impact of Netaji's clarion call.

Dr. Lakshmi Sehgal reminisced in her interview with S.L. Manchanda, "The other INA people used to say that the Rani of Jhansi Regiment was his specially pampered section of the INA, but this was not true. Netaji felt that the women being specially new to this sort of life, they should be well looked after; and I being a doctor, he would always tell me to see that their diet was properly balanced."[25] In fact, the training of the Rani of Jhansi Regiment was as rigorous and painstaking as that of any other military unit. This has been corroborated by all the members of the Regiment. A full account of their austere and tough regimented routine can be grasped from the writings and interviews of many of them. Training camps of Rani of Jhansi Regiment started formally on 23rd October, 1943 simultaneously in Singapore and Rangoon. The things were delayed partly due to the obstructive attitude of the Japanese. The concept of a women's regiment was totally incomprehensible to them. They employed their women as nurses, clerks, stenographers, typists etc. But women fighting enemies side by side with men was unthinkable! It was completely due to Netaji's intransigent and determined approach, and his discussions with the highest Japanese military authorities that the Japanese finally gave in. Perfect discipline was maintained in the Regiment. All the work of cooking, cleaning and washing were done by the volunteers themselves. The works were equally shared by everybody on a weekly basis. The training started at 6 in the morning with the hoisting of the Tri-colour national flag. Then the whole day they were occupied in various kinds of training processes like physical training, squad drill, training to handle and manoeuvre arms. Romanised *Hindustani* was the official language of the INA to avoid any kind of controversy over language. Roman script was adopted and proved to be most practicable. Out-door training consisted of Route Marches, chalking out and executing schemes of defences and attack, guerrilla tactics, night marches, jungle fighting etc. Training continued relentlessly for four months until they became a trained, competent combatant force by March 1944.

After training, they were ordered to proceed to the front at Burma. At that time bitter battle was going on between the INA and the British forces all over South Asia. The Rani of Jhansi Regiment was supposed to join them in Rangoon. The volunteers of the Regiment in Singapore, therefore, started for Rangoon under the leadership of Janaki Davar. She recounts in details to Bhagirath Mishra what an arduous and perilous journey it was. The arrangement of transport was another challenge for Netaji as the Japanese were not cooperating. However, in the end he got his way as always and the voyage began. They went first to Kuala Lumpur; from there to Penang and from Penang to Hajai on the borders of Thailand. They travelled in cattle trucks, but even so they consider this to be rather easier than the latter part of their expedition which started from Hajai. From Hajai they reached Pegu in Burma by station wagon which took them two weeks because of almost unapproachable roads. From Pegu they covered 200 miles to reach Moulmein through fast-flowing Sittaung river in rafts - an extremely dangerous journey. From Moulmein they reached Rangoon in a truck. The whole voyage took them almost a month. [26] A large part of the journey had to be covered in the dark hours of the night, especially the Thai-Burma border, as the area was the target of intermittent enemy bombings.

However, by then the retreat of the Azad Hind Fauj which had gone into action on the Indo-Burma Border had begun. They were fighting under desperate conditions and torrential monsoon had set in. Apprehending total annihilation Netaji had asked them to retreat. So, there was no question of the Rani of Jhansi Regiment to proceed any further. At this juncture many brave young women also volunteered for suicide squads hoping desperately that some fortunate turn would take place.[27]By the summer of 1945, however, the defeat of the Japanese was a foregone conclusion. In April 1945 Netaji ordered for the retreat of the Regiment. Their movement was generally during the night in the dark, as there was the fear of enemy bombardment. They could not light a torch, or even cook their food as the smoke might help the enemies to detect them. Even so, once a bomb had been dropped right on their truck. They escaped death providentially but their belongings were all destroyed. Furthermore, while crossing the jungles, they were attacked by the local tribes who assaulted them with "Ram Daos" in their hands. The members of the Regiment also opened fire on all sides and the attackers fled. [28] Two of Netaji's 'Ranis' died and three were injured while the train in which they were travelling was bombed. "It was difficult to imagine that these stalwart, upright, brisk women were once fragile, delicate, ill-nourished Indian women who had responded to the call of Netaji."[29] On occasions they had to cross rivers with neck-deep water balancing their arms upward, and sometimes they had to take shelter in hill caves to avoid enemy bombing. In this way they finally reached Bangkok on foot through enormous difficult circumstances. On their arrival they lost one of their members Mrs. Goorjal Kaur who succumbed to serious illnesses due to excessive strain and exhaustion.[30]

Such were the hardships that the Rani of Jhansi Regiment underwent. Why did they leave the protection and comforts of their homes and leap into such a life of uncertainty, stress and predicament? Netaji himself once said, "What can I give you now except fatigue, thirst and hunger?" They did everything for their extreme love and devotion for their nation (which many of these women living in East Asia had never seen) and for their charismatic leader Netaji. In the words of Janaki Davar, "There was the prospect of imprisonment once the British took over. This worried none of us. For were we not the daughters of India who were to lay down their lives for India's freedom? Prison, hardship, hunger these did not frighten us. The spirit of our beloved Netaji filled us with a courage and fortitude we ourselves never thought we were capable of."[31] Netaji's deep faith in the power of women and his ardent yearning to emancipate them from their shackles imbued them with an indomitable spirit and turned simple, peace-loving girls into spirited fighters ready to take upon the entire world, even to lay down their lives without batting an eyelid, for the sake of their motherland and their ever-dynamic leader. The enigma lay in the fact that even after such ordeal, all of them, without exception, felt that those days in the Regiment were the most glorious period of their lives. Their hearts were full of unflinching affection and dedication for their leader.

Although they retreated, it should not be perceived as their defeat. Nor was it surrender. They were winners in the sense that they set an unprecedented example before the whole world. Till the end all of them kept on hoping to have a chance to fight for their country. Thanks to their leader who was much ahead of his times, they showed what women's valour, tenacity and conviction were capable of doing. They left the Japanese awe-struck, they drove into British minds the fact that the INA was not a negligible force composed of P.O.Ws, but a real committed combatant army determined to take upon any power that stood in the way of the liberation of their nation. They will always remain a source of supreme inspiration for all generations to come. They are the epitome of patriotism and bravery and they fulfilled Netaji's life-long dream of empowerment and equality of women. These are the facts that have in recent years inspired a Danish scholar Vera Hildebrand to write a book on them entitled, *Women at War: Subhas Chandra Bose and the Rani of Jhansi Regiment*. Above all, the news of the gallant fightings of the INA in Arakan and Burma as well as the activities of the Rani of Jhansi Regiment spread among the Indian Navy through the ships that touched Malaya and enkindled in them strong emotions of patriotism and a sense of guilt for fighting the cause of the British. As a result mutiny among the naval ratings began in 1946 on the pretext of pay, food and racial discrimination. This ultimately forced the British to give up their control of India. On the second day of the mutiny, February 19, 1946, Cabinet Mission was sent to India. The British Prime Minister Attlee declared in the House of Commons on 20 February, 1947 that it would be impossible for the British to continue in India in the face of the bitter resistance of the Indian soldiers. In that sense, therefore, the Rani of

Jhansi Regiment and the INA rendered an invaluable service to India's Independence.

Regrettably enough, there are a few people who now remember them. They are forgotten heroines of the past. It is a pity that while foreign scholars like Vera Hildebrand and Tobias Rettig[32] were amazed by them, we the Indians, (except a very few) for whom they even laid down their lives, hardly acknowledge their contribution. We Indians make biographical films on so many people including gangsters like Veerappan, but not a single film on these heroic people! Almost all of them later married and settled down in life, but free India has done very little for these brave daughters who willingly staked everything for her liberation. As Dr. Lakshmi Sahgal related, many who came from Malaya were forced to take citizenship of that country as India had nothing to offer them. Some lived in penury, destitution and on charity, but their repeated pleas for some meagre pension enabling them to live in dignity fell on deaf ears.[33] Anyhow, they are not the least interested in whining about their tales of misery. They do not want any return from anybody. Rather they want to be remembered as being the parts of an unparalleled and unique example in the history of the globe, – an unmatched all-female regiment, – and as the adjutants of one of the greatest leaders of the world,' the king among men', Netaji Subhas Chandra Bose.

References

1. Speech delivered on the occasion of the birthday celebration of the Rani of Jhansi and opening of the first camp for the training of volunteers for the Rani of Jhansi Regiment at Singapore on 22nd October 1943. Taken from *Chalo Delhi: Writings and Speeches, 1943-45,* (edited by Sisir Kumar Bose and Sugata Bose), Permanent Black and Netaji Research Bureau, Delhi and Kolkata, 2007.
2. Oral Transcript of Dr. Lakshmi Sahgal interviewed by S.L. Manchanda of Nehru Memorial Museum and Library, Teen Murti House, New Delhi on 17th November, 1973.
3. Singh, Karan, *Three Decades of Indian Democracy: Triumph and Tragedy*, Memorial Address delivered by Karan Singh on the occasion of 95th Birth Anniversary of Sarat Chandra Bose at Sarat Bose Hall, Netaji Bhawan, Calcutta on 10th September, 1984.

4. Speech on the occasion of the birthday celebration of the Rani of Jhansi, *op.cit.*, p.1.
5. *Ibid.*
6. Rettig, Tobias Frederik, *Recruiting the All-Female Rani of Jhansi Regiment: Subhash Chandra Bose and Dr. Lakshmi Swaminathan*, South East Asia Research, 21(4), 2013, p. 629. Also. Sengupta, Nilanjana. *A Gentleman's Word: The Legacy of Subhas Chandra Bose in South East Asia*, ISEAS, Singapore, p.23.
7. Forbes, Geraldine, Mothers and Sisters: *Feminism and Nationalism in the Thought of Subhas Chandra Bose*, published in *Subhas Chandra Bose: Facets of a Great Patriot*, on the occasion of Netaji birth centenery, Netaji Institute for Asian Studies, Calcutta, 1996-97, pp. 31-34.
8. Oral Transcript of the interview of Emilie Schenkle Bose by B.R. Nanda, 11th November, 1971. Nehru Memorial Museum and Library, Manuscript Section, New Delhi.
9. Bose, Sisir Kumar (*ed.*), *Netaji : Collected Works,* Vol. 4, (correspondence), Netaji Research Bureau, Netaji Bhawan, Calcutta, 1982, p. 231-34.
10. Bose, Mihir, *The Lost Hero: A Biography of Subhash Bose*, Blue Leaf, Delhi, 2004, pp. 331-332.
11. Broadcast on Azad Hind Radio on 17 August, 1942 and printed in Bose, Sisir K. and Bose, Sugata, *Azad Hind: Writings and Speeches 1941-43*, Anthem Press, London, 2004.
12. INA Records, File No. 351/INA, Private Archives Section, National Archives of India, New Delhi.
13. Address to the Women's Section of the Indian Independence League, Singapore on 12th July, 1943, taken from *Selected Speeches of Subhash Chandra Bose*, Publications Division, Government of India, 1962, revised in 1974.
14. *Op.cit.*, Netaji's Speech on 22nd October, 1943, taken from *Chalo Delhi: Writings and Speeches*, 1943-45, pp. 126-27.
15. *True Daughters of Mother India*, Special message for the Rani of Jhansi Regiment from Headquarters, Burma on 14 May, 1944, taken from *Chalo Delhi*, *op.cit.*, p. 198-99.
16. *Discourses of Cultural and National Subjects*, published by IIL, East Asia, Syonan, January 1944, File No. 411/INA, India Independence League File, Private Archives Section, National Archives of India, pp. 71-74.

17. Lebra, Joyce C., *Myth and History in Indian Nationalism: Netaji and Lakshmibai,* a paper presented at the 4th International Netaji Seminar, Netaji Bhawan, 23-25 January 1982, published in *The Oracle*, Vol.V, No.2, October 1983, No.4.
18. Arya Manawati, *The Rani of Jhansi Regiment in Burma*, a paper presented at the Convention of Rani of Jhansi Regiment, Netaji Bhawan, Calcutta, 23-26 January, 1980, published in *The Oracle*, Vol. 2, April 1980, No.2.
19. Majumdar (nee Bhowmick) Shanti, *Netaji's Rani of Jhansi Regiment: Reminiscences*, published in *The Oracle,* Vol II, No.3. July 1980.
20. Thaver, Manoranjitha Sathyavathi, *The Rani of Jhansi Regiment*, INA Papers, File No. 339/INA, Private Archives Section, National Archives of India, New Delhi.
21. Majumdar, (nee Bhowmick) Shanti, *op.cit.*
22. Banerjee Maya, 'The Rani of Jhansi Regiment in Burma', published in *The Oracle*, Vol II, April 1980, No.2.
23. *Malaya Diary,* an interview of Janaki Athinahappan (Davar) by Bhagirath Mishra, published in Bengali newspaper Bartaman, Kolkata, Sunday, 3rd September 2000.
24. Sen, Pratima, 'A Memorable Period of My Life', published in *Jayashree*, journal founded by Leela Ray, No. 502, Chaitra 1408.
25. *Op.cit.*, oral transcript of Dr. Lakshmi Sahgal, NMML, Teen Murti House, New Delhi.
26. Malaya Diary, *op.cit.*
27. Swaminathan, Lakshmi, 'The Rani of Jhansi Regiment', an essay published in Sharma, Ram (ed.), *Netaji: His Life and Work*, Shiva Lal Agarwala & Co. Ltd., Agra, 1948, pp.199-205.
28. Majumdar (nee Bhowmick), Shanti, *op.cit.*
29. Swaminathan, Lakshmi, *op.cit.*, p.203.
30. Majumdar (nee Bhowmick), Shanti, *op.cit.*
31. Athinahappan,(Davar), Janaki, *The Rani of Jhansi Regiment*, published in The *Oracle*, Vol. II. No.1, January 1980, p. 32.
32. See above note 6.
33. Swaminathan, Lakshmi, *op.cit.*, p.205.

Rani Jhansi Regiment

Roshan Khanijo

Introduction

The first Women's Regiment of the Indian National Army (INA) was formed in 1942, during the Second World War, alongwith the other nationalist forces, in order to overthrow the British Raj. Most of the 1500 Indian women were very young volunteers from Indian families who were working at rubber plantations in Malaya. The Regiment was however raised in the Japan occupied Singapore and was assisted by the Japanese. Like their counterparts, they were organised into Officers/ Sepoys and were trained to use rifles, hand grenades and bayonet charges. They were extremely motivated women, and were led from the front by a highly educated woman named Captain Lakshmi Swaminathan. Some of the Ranis were also trained in the fields of medicine and jungle warfare, considering they were supposed to fight in the jungles of Burma. After the INA lost the battle of Imphal and were forced into a disastrous retreat, the Rani brigade also suffered losses from Allied air attacks during the retreat and were disbanded not long after.[1] Some of them were imprisoned and the fate of the most of them is not known, however, "Lakshmi Swaminathan returned to India, married a high-ranking INA member, Colonel Prem Kumar Sahgal, and resumed her practice as a doctor. In 1971, she embarked on a political career, joining the Communist Party of India (Marxist), which she would represent in the Upper House of Parliament".[2]

Genesis

Rani Jhansi Regiment was the brain child of the charismatic and revolutionary leader Netaji Subhas Chandra Bose. He was a man who encouraged, supported, and backed women's empowerment and women's movement in the late twenties. He wanted the women to break the shackles of drudgery and sought to emancipate them from all disabilities. He wanted them to become equal to their male counterparts. This was clearly a visionary and revolutionary idea of that time, considering women's function in those days were limited to managing the household chores and most of them did not have any rights or status. Thus, when most of the leaders were involved in planning the freedom of the country from British Raj, Bose did it both for the country as well as the women.

He became a towering leader of the Indian National Army (INA) and also helped the women by empowering them. Though Bose was a political thinker, but had an in-depth knowledge about the society, and the caste and class systems prevalent that time. As he was a fervent leader, he brought his passion to in all the activities he undertook. He wanted the women to be educated, and especially in the field of vocational education, as he believed that it would then make them financially independent in the true sense. He wanted to remove the evils of the society like system of *Purdah*, Caste biasness etc. His vision for the women was not only to take part in the Independence struggle, but also to organise "women's societies." In 1928, he organized a 300-strong women's section of the Bengali Volunteers who would parade in the streets of Calcutta on the occasion of the Indian Congress's gathering in the city. This was an early prototype of the Rani of Jhansi Regiment, as evident in the section leader being referred to as "Colonel Latika".[3] Thus, all this had an effect on the social milieu of India, particularly for the upper caste educated women, who started taking active part in the work for empowerment of women during the British Raj.

Bose emphasised that the women themselves should champion the cause of women's empowerment. Hence, when in 1943, during his speech in Singapore, Bose wished that a Women's Regiment with the name 'Rani of Jhansi' be raised, there was complete silence, as it was a novel concept. However, it was finally the work of Dr Lakshmi Swaminathan, a medical doctor, who, being inspired by Bose had come to Singapore from Madras, at the behest of Shri Yellappa took the leading role to organise this Regiment. Both of them together "devised a plan to create a guard of honour of armed women as a surprise for Netaji in the next planned rally. She quickly managed to locate twenty...women ... and they were drilled by INA Officers for several hours... using .303 rifles of the INA....[4] On 12 July, 1943, finally the first all–women Rani of Jhansi Regiment paraded in white saris before Netaji who took their guard of honour, and the women soldiers presented arms to Netaji. A surprised Bose commented, "There is no sphere of public activity, there is no department of national endeavour, in which Indian women have not gladly and bravely shared, alongwith our men, the burden of our national struggle.[5]"

The Rani of Jhansi Regiment

The Regiment's name was christened after the legendary figure– Lakshmi Bai, the Rani of the princely state of Jhansi (*c.* 1828–1858), who had revolted against the British, during the mutiny of 1857-58, and led her subjects from the front against them. The main aim for adopting this name was to indicate that women could undertake political and military leadership positions in spite of being supressed through societal evils like *purdah*, caste systems etc. Like Rani Lakshmi Bai, Bose found in Dr Lakshmi Swaminathan a born leader. She had "a" privileged background "and was politically engaged with the Indian Independence League (IIL)", which gave her the organisational skills, required to organise the Regiment. Further, "her position as a gynaecologist and obstetrician" whose client base included Indian migrants in Singapore, ..., and her tending to prisoners of war following the British debacle, made her a natural choice for a leadership position.... Bose made her the commander of the Regiment ... and appointed her as the Minister in Charge of Women's Organisation of the Provisional Government of Azad Hind (Free India). It was because of her network and dynamic leadership that she was able to mobilise "local born Indian women in Singapore and further up the Malaya peninsula." She personally would visit the families and convince the parents to allow their daughters to become the members of the Regiment. Starting from 20 the strength soon increased to a figure of 1500, which was a tremendous achievement that time and speaks volumes about the leadership skill of both Dr Lakshmi Swaminathan and her mentor Netaji. The best part was that the regiment had the women coming from diverse backgrounds some were well educated whereas others were plantation workers and other immigrant groups. However, the members were mostly overseas Indian, born in British Burma, British Malaya, and some volunteers even came from Shanghai, Hongkong, and Thailand "with diverse religious backgrounds like Hindus, Muslims, Sikhs, and Christians[6]. The Regiment fought in the jungles of Burma in 1944" alongside other INA forces and the Japanese army. 100 Rani troops are noted as forming a vanguard unit as part of the ongoing Battle of Imphal, while other Ranis gave support to the Nursing Corps there". In 1945, when the INA had failed at Imphal and were forced into a disastrous retreat", the Rani brigade also suffered losses from Allied air attacks during the retreat and were disbanded not long after".[7]

Military Training

The women were given basic military training and according to Dr Lakshmi, the women got "the same training as the men". "These included marches, parades, obstacle training, learning how to handle weapons, including the bayoneting of stuffed gunny sacks, and jungle warfare" and about "200 women were also trained as nurses[8]. Between 1944 and the first half of 1945 training camps were operating in Rangoon and Bangkok alongwith the original base camp in Singapore. Women were also trained as nurses and this was achieved in a short span of four months and they served in hospitals in Singapore.There was so much shortage of nurses that all the Ranis who were posted close to the hospitals also took the extra duty of nursing to help the hospitals. The cordial relationship which existed between the INA and the Ranis were often narrated by the women soldiers and they often commented that they found themselves much safer here, than at their villages where they were often treated badly by the Japanese soldiers in the absence of the menfolks. Once the war started, the Ranis travelled from Rangoon to Mandalay alongwith INA soldiers, often passing through rough terrains with backpacks and riffles. Their training included map reading, guerrilla warfare, camouflaging, ambushing, first aid, and digging trenches.[9] All this helpd them when the actual war started. However, initially there was reluctance to take the Ranis for active combat duties, as the Japanese soldiers were very sceptical and even Netaji was reluctant, but because of the persuasion of their leader Dr Lakshmi, they went to the field areas. Anyway, following the failure of the siege of Imphal and the INA's disastrous retreat, the Ranis also had to withdraw. Some of the Rani troops who were at the base camp coordinated the relief work and took care of the INA troops who arrived at Monywa and to Maymyo. Ultimately, the Rani Regiment was disbanded after the fall of Rangoon, and death of their charismatic leader Subhas Chandra Bose.

Post-War

The post-War life trajectories of these veterans went in two directions: the majority of them, who were from the rubber estates, returned there, got married and later on took active part in those businesses, and some of those who were sent back to India and were not educated, often died in obscurity and poverty. Though Lakshmi and Janaki worked tirelessly to obtain some pension for these INA soldiers, it was a struggle for them, nevertheless. However, the officer class and well- educated ladies continued with their professional careers and many of them joined politics and social development programmes.

Stalwarts of the Regiment

Dr Lakshmi Swaminathan was undoubtedly the shining star of the Rani of Jhansi Regiment. Her towering personality, dedication, commitment, and her appeal to motivate and lead the Regiment from the front brought her laurels and kept the Regiment going. Till the end, she was involved in the service of her INA comrades through her relentless work in looking after their needs. Janaki Athi Nahappan, the second in command of the Regiment, was one of the first officers, who were commissioned in Singapore and went to Rangoon in 1944. She was a fearless officer and often did not hesitate to speak her mind under adverse circumstances. She refused to salute the Japanese flag as the Japanese soldiers did not do the same when it came to saluting the Indian flag, and Netaji greatly appreciated her frankness, grit and bold demeanour. Though, she was just 17 when she joined, but her patriotism to her motherland, which ironically she had never seen, was admirable. The training in these adverse circumstances helped her in future, when post the disbanding of the Regiment, she helped John Thivy in establishing the Malayan Indian Congress. She was awarded the Padma Shri in 2000. Rasammah Bhupalanwas another prominent leader of the Regiment, who served in Burma during the World War II. Later on, she continued championing for the cause of women's right, education, and against drug abuse and other social injustices. The rcruitments in Burma was possible due to the efforts of another young woman named Manawati Arya, who was appointed as secretary to the women's department in FIPG, adorning the uniform she travelled villages after villages sometimes thirty miles per day to enrol civilian women[10]. She motivated the women who were mostly able to do household chores to cook for the troops.

There are innumerable stories where the officers and sepoys of this Regiment came out in open to fight against the British rule.

Conclusion

Netaji Bose was not only a revolutionary and a patriot but was also a social reformer. Much has been written about his role as a revolutionary leader and his contribution to the INA, which he raised in Singapore, (and the force's trajectory during the World War II), but his support and encouragement to women empowerment is equally significant and that needs to be highlighted. It was his vision to organise an all-women's regiment, because he believed in equality of genders, and wanted to emancipate them from all shackles and disabilities. It was his idea that women should actively participate in the nation building process hence, they should be included both in the army and the political process. Further, he wanted to have a political organization for women, which was ultimately realised in 1928, with the formation of theMahilaRastriyaSangha. His idea of: "Women should themselves champion the cause of women's empowerment" was the reason that many women came forward despite all odds to become a part of his vision. The Rani of Jhansi Regiment is one such endeavour where women like Dr Lakshmi Swaminathan took the lead in organising an all women regiment. Her dedication, commitment and inspiration made other women to break the shackles of '*purdah*' and caste system, and come forward to develop a chain where many suppressed women also could contribute to the Independence of India from the British rule. This Regiment thus will always shine in history as a bright star and will motivate women all over. We as Indian feel a sense of pride that the Indian women were the pioneers, when it came to the issues like equality of genders and women empowerment. Moreover, all the major stalwarts of the Regiment whether it was Dr. Lakshmi Swaminathan or Janaki Athi Nahappan or Rasammah Bhupalan, they all went on to shape the society later on through their work, by enlightening the society against the evils of drug abuse, dowry, women's right, education and women's emancipation. The Regiment might have lost the Indian Independence war, but the Ranis were able to win the bigger war for women's right to equality and social justice.

References

1. The Rani of Jhansi Regiment http://thefemalesoldier.com/blog/the-rani-of-jhansi-regiment, April 17 2015 "The Rani of Jhansi Regiment", http://thefemalesoldier.com/blog/the-rani-of-jhansi-regiment, dated April 17, 2015.
2. Tobias Rettig, School of Social Sciences, Singapore, Management University, "Warrior Queen : The Rani of Jhansi", IIAS Newsletter, 48 Summer 2008 Rettig Tobias, "Warrior Queen: The Rani of Jhansi", School of Social Sciences Singapore Management University, IIAS Newsletter, No.48, Summer 2008, p. 9.
3. Singh, Dr. Sukhbir, "Women's Organization of INA and Women Emancipation", *Journal for Studies in Management and Planning*, Vol. I, Issue 10, November 2015, p. 314.

4. Libra Lebra Chapman Joyce, *Women against the Raj: The Rani of Jhansi Regiment*, Institute of South East Asian Studies, 2008, p. 72.
5. *Ibid.*
6. *Ibid.*
7. The Rani of Jhansi Regiment http://thefemalesoldier.com/blog/the-rani-of-jhansi-regiment, April 17, 2015. "The Rani of Jhansi Regiment", http://thefemalesoldier.com/blog/the-rani-of-jhansi-regiment, dated April 17, 2015.
8. *Ibid*
9. Libra Lebra Chapman Joyce, Women Against the Raj: The Rani of Jhansi Regiment, *Women against the Raj: The Rani of Jhansi Regiment* Institute of South East Asian Studies, 2008.
10. *Ibid.*

INA Forced British out of India

Kingshuk Nag

One of the closely held secrets of India's freedom struggle is the role played by Netaji Subhas Chandra Bose's Indian National Army (INA) in making the colonial masters exit this country. The present wisdom that is based on the narrative built by he scholars close to the first rulers of Independent India gives almost the entire credit of attaining freedom to the Congress party and its programme of non-violence and *satyagraha* They argue that the 'soul force' generated by the non-violent civil disobedience coupled with war fatigue experienced by the British after the World War II made them quit India. But this is largely a faulty narrative which fails to give credit where it is due.

The fact of the matter is that the colonial masters exited India only because of the fear in them instilled by the INA. They apprehended that the British Indian Army inspired by the fight put by the INA would break out in rebellion like in 1857 and kick the British out of India. Wanting the successor Indian government to be similar (as much as possible) to the British Indian government, the British quickly left India to prevent the possibility of being forcibly evicted.

Let us consider the following facts. Lt General Srinivas Kumar Sinha was one of the most celebrated soldiers of India who after retirement from the armed forces went on to become the Governor of Jammu & Kashmir and Assam. In August 1946, he was one of three Indian officers of the British Indian Army who were posted to the Military Operations Directorate (MOD). Sinha, who died last year, wrote in the Asian Age of 16 February. 2016 that his predecessor in MOD was a British officer who had been conscripted for war time duties. So, he was in a great hurry to leave India and get back home. He handed over the keys of a "top secret" almirah to Sinha and quickly left without actually handing over the files. On opening the almirah, Sinha found two files with a strange security classification. It said: "Top secret not for Indian eyes." Sinha wrote that the first file incorporated a paper written by Major General O'Brien, of the Directorate of Military Intelligence on the loyalty of the Indian officers of the British Indian Army. The main points were that the Indian army had expanded from 450 Indian officers to 12,000 Indian officers in the period 1939-45. This was in view of emergency recruitment for space. In the same period, Personnel below the officer rank had increased from 1.5 lakh to 2.2 million.

According to Sinha, the note grouped the Indian officers into three categories. The first category comprised the officers commissioned before 1933 and who had been trained in Sandhurst (in Great Britain). The second category consisted of the officers who had been commissioned in the period 1933-39. The third category comprised wartime commissioned officers. The note then suggested the officers in the first category were 'safe' from the British point of view and the officers in the second category had some grouses regarding pay parity with the White officers. The officers in the third category - who were the most numerous – were the 'most unreliable' and had been exposed to the ongoing movement for Independence. Unstated but implied was the fact that, these officers could change their loyalty and be a part of the forces to liberate India. Hence, a close watch should be kept on them.

The second file in the top secret almirah was related to 'Operation Gondola'. This was the code name for a plan for safe evacuation for the British civilians, who were located all cross the country, in case the need arose. In the first phase, these civilians would be escorted to the camps in select cities/ports of India like provincial capitals. In the second stage, these civilians would be taken away from the country. In total, there were about 43000 British citizens in the country.

The British Raj in India had been held together by the Indian soldiers and it is clear from a reading of these files that at the end of the War, British colonialists were no longer sure of the loyalty of the Indian officers and men of the army. Moreover, gearing up to such an eventuality, they drew up top security plans on how to evacuate the British from India.

The question is – why were the British establishment fearing acts of disloyalty and rebellion by Indian forces? Here is where the INA comes in.

Though the men of the British Indian Army and the Indian National Army were drawn from the same stock, there was a significant difference of outlook between the two. The British Indian Army had been raised to protect and perpetuate the British Raj in India. Therefore, the British raised an army that would work in consonance of their plans and this included internal security of the country. They did not want to touch the feudal social fabric of the country. The easiest way for them was to raise an army based on castes, religions and regions. Grouping soldiers on lines of castes and communities would keep their identity as a Rajput, Muslim or Gorkha intact and foster bonds based on community. In the ultimate analysis, this would prevent the rise of the feeling of nationalism among the soldiers – whose national consciousness would remain subservient to their caste or community identity. This would not allow them to rear their head against the British.

But Netaji Subhas Chandra Bose understood this clearly. For this reason, the endeavoured to set up a national army where the soldiers were first committed to the nation (which was then in British shackles). To foster this feeling of nationalism and aiding the breaking down feelings of caste and community, he raised mixed regiments of the INA. Thus, as an example the Sikhs, the Rajputs and the Muslims were all part of the same formation mixed down to the company level. Needless to add that all the men ate food cooked in the same kitchen. This further assisted breaking down caste and religious barriers. Unlike what was the case in the INA, the British Indian army that had separate kitchens for soldiers of different castes and communities? Further, the INA responded to the slogan of *Jai Hind*, while the regiments of the British Indian Army had their own battle cry based on their narrow identity. Much ahead of his time, Netaji also insisted upon the formation of a women's battalion– headed by a woman commandant - that was called the Rani of Jhansi Regiment. Netaji also wanted women in combat roles. To further foster nationalistic feelings among the men of the INA, Netaji insisted on military music and community singing. He also had an INA flag which had the Indian tricolour with the Royal Bengal tiger springing on a prey at the Centre. Major General G D Bakshi in his book, *Bose: An Indian Samurai- Netaji and the INA A Military Assessment* states that the INA at its peak had 60,000 men and 1500 officers who were organisd in three combat divisions. When the Allied Forces had surrendered to the Japanese at Singapore in 1943, 20,000 of the 60,000 Indian soldiers, who gave up to the Japanese, joined the INA.

Ultimately, some 26,000 of these 60,000 INA men died in their fight against the British and its aftermath. The INA men participated along with the Japanese combatants in two major battles of World War II. The battles of Imphal and Kohima, fought on the north east corner of the country, were two very important battles in the Second World War that tilted the balance in favour of the Allied Forces. When these battles were taking place, there was very strict military censorship of news in India. As a result, the Indians were totally ignorant of the fact that the INA was fighting alongside the Japanese in these battles. The aim of the supreme commander of the Indian forces Netaji Subhas Chandra Bose was to trigger a massive uprising in the country against the British which he hoped would be catalysed by the news of the INA fighting on the Indian borders. The existence of "Inner Line" restrictions that did not allow the Indians to travel to the interiors in the north east without official permission further curbed the flow of information by the way of word of mouth about the INA exploits. It is for this reason that Netaji was keen that the combined INA and Japanese army attack India through Chittagong. In that way the attack would be on the mainland of India and word would travel fast – the censorship notwithstanding. But that was not to be with the Japanese, afraid that the British intelligence network would gather this information beforehand and attack the forces the moment they landed.

The Allied Forces, which at one time looked vulnerable, were ultimately able to win the Second World War. After winning the War, the British thought that they would severely punish the men of the INA for their mutiny and make a lesson out of them for the future in the same manner as the rebels of the 1857 War of Independence had been. Reminiscent of the trial of the last Mughal King Bahadur Shah Zafar at Delhi's Red Fort, the British colonialists brought to public the trial of three officers of the INA. Red Fort was chosen not only to bring back the historical memories of the 1857 trial, but also because Subhas Chandra Bose had given out cries of "Delhi chalo." One officer was a Muslim (Lt. Colonel Shah Nawaz Khan), another officer was a Hindu (Colonel P. K. Sahgal) and the third was a Sikh (Colonel G. S. Dhillon). This was to convey the impression that the British Indian government was not discriminating against any religion. In the aftermath of 1857, the Muslims had felt that they had been specially punished.

The British Indian government had felt that with the end of the War, as censorship had been lifted, tales of the INA collaborating with the Japanese to raid their own motherland would provoke the Indians to hate them. The same hatred would be generated amongst the soldiers of the British Indian Army who had stood loyal to the colonial masters. They would see the INA collaboration with the Japanese forces of occupation negatively. But the reverse happened. As the tales began to be spread about the acts of bravery of the INA men, how they had waged war to free India and made the supreme sacrifice for the cause, the chests of ordinary Indians began to swell. There was unprecedented sympathy for the INA and pride for their bravado. A section of the personnel of the British Indian Army, who had not defected and joined the INA, started feeling 'sheepish' that they had fought on the wrong side. The Congress party (which had forced Netaji out of the party) and the Muslim League correctly read the mood of the nation and the enormous tide of support for the INA and came out in support of the INA men who had been put on trial. To cash in on the immense popularity of the arraigned INA officers, even Jawaharlal Nehru donned the lawyers' robes. The proceedings of the public trial only enhanced the image of the INA men. Geopolitical expert Stephen Cohen, in a study on 'Subhas Chandra Bose and the Indian National Army' that is a part of his anthology titled *The South* Asian Papers quotes from the autobiography of Colonel P. K. Sahgal, who wrote that he had inherited an extreme dislike for an alien rule from his father who had participated in the civil disobedience movement, and that his study of history and political science had taught him – 'it was the sacred duty of every Indian to fight for the liberation of the motherland'.

Cohen further notes that a 'significant reason for the attractiveness of the INA was the internal policy of the Indian army under the British, particularly regarding promotion policy, devolved authority, trust and personal treatment by British fellow officers'. By implication the Indians had joined the British Indian Army due to the pressures of building a career and were stifled there. They also fell for the nationalistic sentiments the moment it was fanned by Subhas Chandra Bose and the INA. Given the first opportunity many of them deserted the mercenary British Indian Army and joined the INA that did not even have a 'pay'.

What happened after the conclusion of the War bears eloquent testimony to the thesis that it was finally the fear of the INA that forced the British out of India. The major impact of the INA trials were seen in widespread rebellion in the ranks of the Royal Indian Navy (RIN) in February 1946, followed by that in the Royal Indian Air Force (RAF) and finally in the British Indian army units in Jabalpur in the same year. The RIN action saw 10,000 sailors in 66 naval ships and shore establishments from Karachi to Calcutta rise in rebellion. Ostensibly the demands were for better rations and service conditions but were actually against the British Raj. The action by men of the RAF were to express sympathy for the naval rebels but the army units in Jabalpur did not fail to raise the issue of treatment of the INA soldiers in the course of their strike. Though all these rebellions were successfully quelled by the British (with dollops of help coming from Congress stalwarts like Nehru and Patel) it was an eye opener for the British that it was time for them to leave before the situation turned more adverse.

Perhaps, the most telling statement describing the British imperatives for leaving India came from none other than Lord Clement Atlee who was the Prime Minister of Great Britain when India got independence. On a visit to Calcutta in 1956, Atlee (by then an ordinary citizen)was quizzed by the chief justice of Calcutta High Court (who was then the acting Governor of West Bengal) P V Chuckraborty about why the British left India. The acting Governor, prefacing his statement with the remark that the Quit India Movement had died out much before 1947 and there was nothing in the Indian situation that made it necessary for the British to leave India in a hurry, wondered why they had done so. Atlee in his reply cited several reasons the most important of which were the INA activities of Netaji Subhas Chandra Bose which weakened the foundation of the British Empire in India and the Royal Indian Navy mutiny that made the British realise that the Indian armed forces could no longer be trusted to prop up the British. When asked on whether the British decision to quit India was influenced by Mahatma Gandhi's 1942 movement, Atlees's lip widened in a smile of disdain and he uttered slowly, "minimal."

Thus, India got freedom in 1947 only because of the INA. Had it not been for Subhas Chandra Bose, India would have got freedom later – till another set of factors impelled the British to go out.

References

1. Lt. General Sinha (Retired), The INA and Independence in *Asian Age/ Deccan Chronicle*, 11 February, 2016.
2. Stephen Cohen, Subhas Chandra Bose and the Indian National Arm in The South Asian Papers (Harper Collins, 2016).
3. Major General G. D. Bakshi, *Bose: An Indian Samurai, Netaji And the INA, A Military Assessment* (K. W. Publishers, 2016.
4. Kingshuk Nag, *Netaji: Living Dangerously*, Rupa, 2016.
5. Jayanta Roy Chowdhury, Netaji's Contributions to India's Independence, yantaroychowdhury.blogspot.in, (January 13, 2015).

Indian Media, Netaji Subhas Chandra Bose and the INA: A Case Study

Sandhya Jain

On August 18, 1945, one of India's most charismatic freedom fighters, Netaji Subhas Chandra Bose walked out of history into a shroud of mystery. For decades thereafter, Netaji became the undying hero of the freedom struggle, a man spotted but never caught in various Asian cities, until it began to be accepted that even if he had not perished in the air crash at Formosa (Taiwan) as alleged, he was unlikely to be alive anymore. The goal has now shifted to finding out the truth about what happened to Netaji at the end of the Second World War.

It bears mentioning at the outset that the Congress Party or the then Congress-dominated governments, such as that of Prime Minister P.V. Narasimha Rao, were less than enthusiastic about pursuing the quest for Netaji. India's otherwise raucous media, barring some stray news items here and there, and some excellent legwork by the then *Hindustan Times* journalist Anuj Dhar, has tended to regard Netaji with stoic silence. It may be premature to call this a conspiracy, but it defies rational explanation.

The official stand of the British Government in 1946, and of the successive Congress governments, that Bose had died in an air crash in Taiwan, received a jolt in February 2005 when the BBC reported that the External Affairs Ministry of Taiwan had informed Justice M.K. Mukherjee that Subhas Chandra Bose could not have died in a plane crash in their country, as there was no plane crash at the old Matsuyama Airport, Taipei, between August 14 and September 20, 1945 – a span of five weeks.

The one-man Mukherjee Commission was appointed by the Atal Bihari Vajpayee government in 1999, after the persistent pressure from many quarters, including MP Samar Guha. So, persistent was the quest for truth about Netaji that in 1978, N.G. Goray, the former MP, wrote to Lord Mountbatten who replied that there was never any official record of Bose's death, but that as he never surfaced, he could be presumed dead.

Previously, journalist Anuj Dhar had elicited the information regarding the missing air crash *via* e-mail from Taipei Mayor and Minister of Transportation and Communication, Lin Ling-San. The only plane crash thereafter was of a USC-47 Transporter plane carrying 26 persons, mostly former American prisoners-of-war released from camps in The Philippines. It crashed between September 20 and 23, on Mount Trident in Taitung, roughly 200 nautical miles away from Taipei.

The official story about Netaji's death was now officially debunked. Interestingly, one eminent person who showed keen interest in the fate of Netaji was the then President R. Venkataraman. He raised the issue with Prime Minister V.P. Singh in 1991, renewed his quest with the next Prime Minister Chandrashekhar even though his government was propped up by the Congress party, and pursued it with Prime Minister P.V. Narasimha Rao before he retired.

What is certain is that from August 18, 1945, Netaji, then just 48 years old, was never seen again. The circumstances of his disappearance are confusing and contradictory. The little that has come to light in these intervening years has discredited the Nehruvian-Leftist historians, who actively collaborated to cover up the fate of this unconventional thinking warrior.

In a public life, spanning two-and-a-half decades, Netaji moved seamlessly from a successful Indian Civil Service candidate to a freedom fighter, and was twice president of the Indian National Congress (1938, 1939), to which he officially belonged from 1921 to 1940. In the last year of this association, after falling out with Mahatma Gandhi and being forced to step down from the presidentship of the party, he founded the Forward Block faction within the INC (1939-40). The name derived from the newspaper, *Foreword*, founded by his mentor Chittaranjan Das.

When the Second World War broke out, Bose suggested a mass movement to wrest freedom from the British. Jawaharlal Nehru was opposed to the Nazis and accordingly, the Congress Working Committee condemned the invasion of Poland and opted for non-cooperation in the War effort until the promise of freedom was made explicit.

The British arrested Netaji, but when he went on hunger strike in jail in November 1940, put him under house arrest so that he did not die in prison. This enabled him to plan his dramatic escape to Peshawar in the North West Frontier Province on January 17, 1941, from where he surfaced in Kabul two weeks later. The complete details of this journey have still to be unveiled, but some gaps have been filled in by Dr. Purabi Roy (of Jadavpur University), who visited Moscow in 1994 and 1995 under an agreement between the Asiatic Society of Calcutta and the Institute of Oriental Studies of the Academy of Sciences, Moscow, to compile the archival materials available in the Russian archives pertaining to Indo-Russia relations from 1947.

Briefly, the materials unearthed in this short span showed that Netaji had contacts with many Soviet leaders prior to Independence, as did others who had hopes from the Soviet Union, most notably Virendranath Chattopadhyaya who worked for the League against Imperialism and for freedom in Berlin, law student A.C.N. Nambiar, M.N. Roy, and V.K. Krishna Menon. When Bose had visited Berlin in 1933, Nambiar had helped to connect him with TASS representatives. This helps explain why Netaji decided to visit Russia after the defeat of Germany and Japan in the Second World War.

Those who helped Netaji escape to Afghanistan include Nirjan Talib, the editor of *Desh Darpan*, Sardar Baldev Singh (the first defence minister in 1947), and Achar Singh Cheema of the former Ghadar Party, whose members were known as the Kirti Communist Group. Achar Singh, codenamed Larkin by the Soviets, worked out the details with Ajoy Ghosh of the Communist Party of India. A critical role was played by Bhagat Ram Talwar who accompanied Netaji to Kabul and made contacts with the Soviet and German emissaries there.

As the Soviets could not decide how to respond to the overtures, Bose proceeded to Germany with an Italian passport in the name of Orlando Mazzatto, issued by the Soviet embassy in Kabul with the help of G. Dimitrov of the Comintern. The details of Bose's travel through Soviet territory from March 23 to 31, 1941 are still not public. Talwar remained in Afghanistan as a German agent, though in reality he was a committed communist who reported everything to the Soviet embassy in Kabul.

Netaji arrived in Berlin on April 2, 1941, a time when Germany had dominated much of Europe, from the Arctic to the Pyrenees, the Atlantic to the Black Sea. Soon it won impressive victories in Yugoslavia, Greece and North Africa.

Bose tried to persuade Germany, Italy and Japan to promise freedom to India and the Arab world, and agree to a military liberation of India. He mooted a Free India Government and proposed intensive propaganda and subversion in Afghanistan and the tribal North West Frontier, adding that the pro-British government in Afghanistan should be overthrown and military aid given to Iraq to resist Britain. Arguing that if the British held India, they could regroup and challenge the Nazis, he suggested that Japan advance in Southeast Asia, defeat the British Army and destroy its Singapore base.

Hitler's foreign minister, Joachim von Ribbentrop, had similar ideas *vis-à-vis* the Arabs but was doubtful about sending troops to India. However, he provided a clandestine radio to broadcast to the Indian people. Though Hitler asserted that the Arab freedom movement was a "natural ally" of Germany, he only promised but never made a statement on India's freedom, because he hoped till the very end of the War that London would negotiate with him. In May, Ribbentrop met Italian leader Benito Mussolini, who agreed that Italy and Germany should stand up for the liberation of all people under British oppression, but the explicit statement never came.

Pragmatic, Bose dropped the idea of a Free India Government and created the Free India Centre in Berlin as the "brain of Indian revolution", and broadcast every night from the Free India Radio. Germany gave the Free India Centre the status of a diplomatic mission; it was headed by A.C.N. Nambiar. The Free India Legion, crafted out of some 3000-odd Indian soldiers captured by General Erwin Rommel's Afrika Korps, trained for freedom as Bose continued to hope for German help in a land invasion of India. He later used the same model to revive the moribund Indian National Army of Rash Behari Bose when he moved into Japanese-controlled territory in Southeast Asia.

The Allied powers were shocked that Bose had established a rapport with the German leadership and won some support from them. But when Hitler invaded Russia in June 1941 (Operation Barbarossa), Bose lost hope of German assistance for India's liberation. By this time, moreover, the tide was turning against Germany; the Iraq resistance had failed and Britain had regained control and marched into Vichy Syria. Both Italy and Germany concurred that a statement on India would be premature.

In May 1942, Bose met German Chancellor Adolf Hitler and requested his help in moving to Tokyo as the Japanese were on the ascendant in Southeast Asia. In February 1943, Bose made a perilous submarine journey to the South Africa coast, from where he boarded a Japanese submarine in mid-ocean, to Japanese-held Sumatra. He reached Tokyo in May 1943, and met Prime Minister Hideki Tojo in June. Tojo gave unconditional support to the Indian struggle. On June 16, Bose was a special guest in the Imperial Diet, where Prime Minister Tojo said that Japan would do "everything possible" to help India attain freedom.

In July 1943, Rash Behari Bose and Subhas Chandra Bose moved to Singapore, where Netaji took over and revived the defunct INA with the Indian soldiers of the British Indian Amy who had been captured by the Japanese in the Battle of Singapore, and also the civilian volunteers of Indian-origin from Malaya (mainly toddy tappers) and Singapore. Tojo himself took the salute at the INA parade on July 6, 1943.

The expatriate Indians also responded financially to Netaji's call for sacrifice for the cause of freedom. As in Berlin, Netaji abolished the caste/religion-based Regimental model of the British and launched an all-India model that included all groups and was officered entirely by Indian officers, something the British had never permitted. In pre-independence India, this was truly revolutionary. The INA had a separate women's unit, the Rani of Jhansi Regiment, headed by Capt. Lakshmi Swaminathan, the first of its kind in Asia.

The INA joined the Japanese thrust towards India's eastern frontiers of Manipur and Nagaland, alongwith the Burmese National Army led by Ba Maw and Aung San. The Japanese took possession of Andaman & Nicobar Islands in 1942 and on October 21, 1943, Bose formed the Provisional Government of Free India here and renamed the islands as *Shaheed* and *Swarajya*; Lt. Col. A.D. Loganathan was appointed the Governor General.

Three days later, Netaji declared war on the United Kingdom and the United States, as a message to the Axis Powers that he stood with them against their most formidable foes. The Azad Hind Government issued its own currency, postage stamps, court and civil code, and was recognised by Germany, Japan, Italy, and their allies. In October 1943 itself, Bose made attempts to contact the Soviet authorities, through the aegis of the Soviet ambassador in Tokyo, Jacob Malik. Later, he set up headquarters in Rangoon. The Japanese helped establish a radio link between India and Burma.

In the brief period that he was head of the Provisional Government of Free India (1943-45), Netaji inspired millions with the dream of an India freed from the shackles of colonialism by dint of her own valour. At an INA rally in Burma in July 1944, he gave his clarion cry, "Give me blood, and I shall give you freedom!"

As is well known, Japan was defeated at the battles of Kohima and Imphal. The retreating INA fought in key battles against the British Indian Army in its Burma campaign, notably in Meiktilla, Mandalay, Pegu, Nyangyu and Mount Popa. But with the fall of Rangoon, Bose's government ceased to be an effective political entity. The bulk of the INA troops surrendered under Lt. Col. Loganathan in Rangoon and the remaining retreated towards Malaya and Thailand. The INA prisoners were repatriated to India and some were tried for treason.

Netaji was in Penang (Malaya) on August 11, when he learnt of the Japanese surrender. A prescient student of international affairs, Bose anticipated that the Anglo-Americans would fallout with the Soviet Union after the War. Having long tried to cultivate the Russians, he decided to escape to Soviet-held Manchuria and seek Stalin's help in his quest for freedom. Foreseeing the rift was truly perceptive as it was only in March 1946, that the British Prime Minister Winston Churchill gave his famous 'Iron Curtain' speech that signaled that the Allies would have problems with Russia. As the War wound to a close, the victorious Allies raced to capture as much liberated territory as possible and triggered the Cold War.

Even before Japan's surrender, however, Netaji had discerned its impending defeat, just as he had foreseen that of Germany, and again tried to contact the Soviet authorities *via* Jacob Malik, in November 1944. In a speech at Bangkok in May 1945, he spoke about Soviet support for India. Throughout June-July 1945, he concentrated on his press statements and broadcasts and often visited Singapore. In one speech, he noted the growing differences between the war aims of Soviet Russia and the Anglo-American powers and their escalating competition in the Far East. He now hoped for Soviet help for Indian Independence.

In July 1945, Japan was in dire straits and Bose sought permission to enter the USSR *via* Manchuria, though advised to proceed to Tokyo, he said on August 16, that he would go alone if he had to. Thereafter, on August 24, news reached India about his death in an air crash at Taipei on August 18, 1945.

As Japan had already surrendered, the British immediately began scrutinising all records left by the Japanese agency Hikari-Kikan in its offices in the East Asian Centres. Since, all documents had been destroyed, they felt that the few that remained in Bangkok were a decoy to mislead them. According to the documents found, on September 20, 1945, the Hikari-Kikan reportedly received a message from the Chief of

Staff, Southern Army, reporting the death of Chandra Bose and Lt. Gen. Shidei at Formosa while on their way to Tokyo, around midnight, after serious injuries; the body was flown to Tokyo by the Formosan Army. On August 24,, a message said that the Indian communities should be informed about Bose's death.

On recovering such information in September 1945, the British found it difficult to conclude that Bose was actually dead. They also noted that from Rangoon, Bose carried four iron boxes of gold (either 50 or 200 lbs. in weight) and had stated at Bangkok (August 17) that he was unlikely to return to that part of the world. This suggests he was preparing to go underground and that the Japanese were protecting him.

We know that on August 16, 1945, Netaji left Singapore for Manchuria *via* Bangkok and Saigon. At Saigon, Bose was asked to switch planes and most likely did not take the boxes with him as there was only room for two Indian passengers despite the use of turret accommodation for two Japanese officers. (Most likely the boxes were left in Singapore, though there are some hints that some of his wealth surfaced in Tokyo). His next destination is a mystery. We know there was no plane crash at Taihoku, but we don't know if Taiwan was part of his onward journey.

Looking at the bare bones of the story, we are told that the chief pilot, co-pilot and Lieutenant-General Tsunamasa Shidei, the Vice Chief of Staff of the Japanese Kwantung Army, who was to have negotiated for Bose with the Soviet army in Manchuria, were instantly killed. Bose's colleague Habibur Rahman was unhurt but lost consciousness briefly, and Bose, though conscious, was soaked in gasoline. When Rahman recovered consciousness, he and Bose tried to leave by the rear door, which was blocked by luggage, so they had to run through the flames and exit from the front. Rahman received superficial burns, but Bose was seriously burnt and died of his injuries after a few hours.

The official account states that a truck which served as ambulance rushed Bose and the other passengers to the Nanmon Military Hospital, south of Taihoku. The airport personnel called Dr. Tanioshi Yoshimi, surgeon-in-charge at the hospital at around 3 p.m. Bose was conscious and mostly coherent when they reached the hospital, and for some time thereafter. He was naked, except for a blanket wrapped around him, and Dr. Yoshimi saw third-degree burns on many parts of his body, especially the chest. He treated Bose assisted by Dr. Tsuruta.

The account continues that Bose was cremated in the main Taihoku crematorium on August 20, 1945. But it was only on August 23, 1945, that the Japanese news agency, *Do Trzei*, announced the death of Bose and Lt. Gen. Shidei. [We may note in passing that this account already contradicts the Hikari-Kikan documents of September 20, 1945, which state that Bose's body was flown to Tokyo by the Formosan Army; similar contradicts abound at each stage of the story].

To continue the old thread, on September 7, Lt. Tatsuo Hayashida carried Bose's ashes to Tokyo and handed them over to the president of the Tokyo Indian Independence League, Ramamurti. On September 14, a memorial service was held for Bose in Tokyo and a few days later the ashes were given to the priest of the Renkoji Temple of Nichiren Buddhism in Tokyo, where they rest to this day.

But Netaji's shadow continued to loom large. On December 31, 1945, the *National Herald*, Delhi, reported that Bose was in Russia. On June 4, 1946, *Blitz*, Bombay, published an article by Russi Karanjia saying that Bose was in Russia and was a guest of honour according to some sources and a badly treated prisoner-of-war by others.

In March 1946, the Viceroy, Lord Louis Mountbatten, sent Jawaharlal Nehru to South East Asia to investigate stories of the huge INA treasure/funds reported to have been left by Netaji and his Azad Hind Government. On May 2, 1946, the Director of Intelligence Branch (DIB) requested the Indian Political Intelligence for a final report on Bose. It stated that Bose was alive in Russia. This prompted the British to abruptly release a final death report in 1946.

Clearly, all reports were contradictory and confusing. A letter from W. Mck Wright to Major Young, both intelligence officers (February 19, 1946), notes that the list of passengers and crew reported by Capt. Habibur Rahman matched that given by Capt. Yoshida of the JAF staff in a report dated October 7, 1945. The passengers were S.C. Bose, Capt. Habibur Rahman, Lt. Gen. Shidei, Lt. Gen. Sakai, Nonogaki, Major Kawano, Takahashi, Takazawa, Lt Arai.

The Japanese reports indicate Lt Gen Shidei and two others died instantaneously inside the plane, whereas Bose died later. Rahman however, said five persons, not four, died. He said Lt Col Sakamaki (Sakai?) was unhurt and they both travelled to Fukuoka in the same aircraft on September 4, 1945. Sakamaki, who held Bose's ashes, travelled by train from Fukuoka to Tokyo. Two Japanese officials removed Bose's ashes after the funeral on August 23.

Even in 1946, there seem to be two death reports prepared by two different doctors at two different times, *viz.*, in July and October 1946. The first report was prepared by the military adviser attached to the UK Liaison Mission in Japan, drafted by Lt Col J.G. Figgess on July 25, 1946. It stated that Sub-Lt (Medical) Tsuruta Toyoshi who treated Bose at Taihoku Medical Hospital, issued a certificate indicating "death due to heart failure resulting from multiple burns and shock… S.C. Bose died in Taihoku Military Hospital (Nanmon Ward) sometime between 19 hours and 20 hours local time on 18th August 1945".

However, Dr. Yoshimi Tanioshi, medical officer of Japanese Imperial Army, claimed Bose was treated under his supervision. This statement was received originally from the war crimes liaison officer, Hong Kong, where Yoshimi was interned at the Stanley Goal in Hong Kong. He signed his statement in Goal on October 19, 1946 before A.R. Turner, War Crime Liaison Section, Formosa. Yoshimi said Bose died at 23 hours (11p.m.), a discrepancy of four hours. Around this time, the KGB dossier from Tokyo said "Subhas Chandra Bose, who was in Japan, died." For Indians, the news was fishy from the word go.

Netaji's elder brothers, Suresh Bose and Sarat Bose, refused to believe in the story of his death, throughout their respective lifetimes. His close associate Lt. Col. Habibur Rehman (who left for Pakistan after the Partition) and Bose's widow, Emilie Schenkl, refused, to the end of their respective lives, to assent to repeated requests by the Government of India that he had died in an air crash. However, Sarat's son, Sisir Bose and his son, Sugata Bose, embraced the theory in return for generous patronage for their Netaji Research Bureau.

In April 2015, declassified files from the Indian Government revealed that Bose's immediate family members were intensively surveilled by the Indian Government from 1948 until the early 1970s, and that this information was shared with British Intelligence. This was the first official confirmation that neither the British nor the Nehru Government believed that Bose had died in the air crash and expected him to get in touch with his brothers, while they were alive.

We are left to glean what we can from the reports of the fact-finding bodies appointed by the Jawaharlal Nehru, Indira Gandhi and Atal Bihari Vajpayee Governments, respectively. Some documents have been declassified by the Indian and British governments and by the erstwhile Soviet Union, but a wealth of information is still hidden in the archives of the German, Japanese, British, American and highly sensitive Russian archives. In India, Prime Minister Narendra Modi acceded to the demand of the Bose family (minus the section that believed in the official story) to make all archival documents available to scholars by January 31, 2017. These documents will be studied by scholars in due course. However, the critical documents that will unveil the truth are believed to be in the possession of the Governments of the UK, USA, Japan, and the Russian Federation.

The Shah Nawaz Committee (1956), Khosla Commission (1972) and Mukherjee Commission (1999) all failed to acquire clinching evidence regarding his fate. Shah Nawaz, a Netaji aide, was appointed one man Committee after remitting office as a Deputy Minister in the Nehru Government. After he submitted his report, he was repeatedly made a minister, this time with full Cabinet rank, and held other ministerial-level posts in successive Congress governments. Many of Netaji's erstwhile colleagues made peace with the Indian Government.

The Shah Nawaz Committee included Suresh Chandra Bose, eldest living brother of Netaji, and an official of the West Bengal government. The Committee was undermined from the start as it was not allowed to visit Taihoku for an on-the-spot investigation of the accident site, but nevertheless, concluded that Bose had died in the crash. Suresh Bose refused to accept the findings or to sign the report.

As the controversy persisted, Prime Minister Indira Gandhi was forced to appoint a one-man Commission of Inquiry headed by Justice G.D. Khosla, the former Chief Justice of the Punjab High Court, in July

1970. Khosla visited Japan, Burma, Thailand, Singapore, Malaysia, South Vietnam and Taiwan, examined 224 witnesses, including 100 abroad, and submitted his report on June 30, 1974.

The Commission courted controversy by ignoring all inconvenient facts, particularly photographs that discredited the plane crash theory, but the report was adopted during the Emergency without any discussion in Parliament as most opposition leaders were in jail. Both the Shah Nawaz Committee and Khosla Commission were widely perceived as cover-up jobs, and need not detain us.

Justice M.K. Mukherjee went to England but was denied access to records. The Commission requested Lord Peter Archer, member, House of Lords, for help to get the requisite permission from the Lord Chancellor, but in vain. Archer suggested the matter be taken up at government-to-government level. The Commission's suggestion that a DNA test of the ashes at the Renkoji temple could resolve a part of the mystery has not yet been taken up.

In Tokyo, the Commission met Dr Yoshimi Tanioshi, the only surviving witness of Netaji's alleged death in a military hospital in Taihoku, who claimed that time had dimmed the details of the event in his mind. But tangible success was in Taipei, where it learnt that there was no air crash in Formosa. But it came nowhere close to unravelling the truth. Though it concluded that Netaji did not die in an airplane crash in Taihoku, the UPA government, while tabling the report in Parliament on May 17, 2006, disagreed "with the findings that Netaji did not die in the plane crash and the ashes in Renkoji Temple were not of Netaji".

The Indian media covered the news that there was no air crash at Taihoku as a news item, with no attempt at follow-up investigations into the fate of one of the most daring freedom fighters. When the Congress-led UPA came to power, it swallowed its verdict about Netaji and the Renkoji Temple ashes without demur.

As previously mentioned, Dr. Purabi Roy visited Moscow in 1994 and 1995, and came across some archival evidence about Netaji in Moscow. She also learnt from Russian scholars that much material lay in different archives, which only Government-to-Government cooperation would unearth.

According to news reports, archival evidence hints that Netaji was in Russia long after the alleged plane crash. A Document No. 22, purported to be a statement by the then Soviet envoy to Teheran, states that the ambassador had delivered a letter from Nehru to Stalin in October 1946, wherein Nehru mentions Netaji's stay in the USSR at that time. Another document records a meeting at Moscow in October 1946 between Stalin, Soviet Foreign Minister Molotov and other high officials, wherein Netaji is refered to "in the present tense," and as present in the USSR at that time (*The Hindustan Times, 23 December 2000*).

In her book, *The Search for Netaji: New Findings* (2011), Roy notes that at the end of his Southeast Asia visit, Nehru had tried to contact the Soviet leadership *via* V.K. Krishna Menon, but in vain. A Soviet agent, V. Sayadiyants, who lived in Bombay, delivered a secret letter from Nehru to Stalin – the contents of which remain unknown to this day. Despite this, Roy notes, Nehru visited the Soviet Union as Prime Minister only in 1955 (Stalin died in 1953). Stalin had refused to meet the first Indian ambassador to Moscow, Mrs. Vijaylakshmi Pandit, sister of Nehru; he met the second envoy, Dr. S. Radhakrishnan only once, and the great India-Russia friendship began only after his death.

Most people, following the Netaji saga, accept that he was *en route* to the Soviet Union *via* Manchuria after Japan lost the war. In his quest for Indian Independence, he had collaborated with both the Germans and the Japanese, the losers of the War, and the Soviet Union had fought the War on the side of Britain and America. In the circumstances, it is difficult to imagine that Stalin saw him in favourable light, especially given the tremendous sacrifices made by the Russians during the Second World War, where atleast 22 million gave their lives to beat back the Axis powers. Possibly the gracious reception he received in Germany and Japan convinced Netaji that he would be similarly well received in Moscow.

In April 2015, journalist Madhav Nalapat, writing for the *Sunday Guardian*, claimed that Russia-based sources have revealed that Bose's "aircraft landed safely in a Manchurian airbase" and that he was "taken custody of by Soviet troops and security personnel" and "flown to

Moscow". He was first interned in a security prison in Moscow for 17 months and then sent to a gulag where he passed away 11 years later.

It is believed that Stalin was asked by the UK Foreign Secretary Ernest Bevin through Foreign Minister Vyacheslav Molotov to "ensure that Bose never returned to India and was never heard from again". As he attracted the loyalty of Hindus and Muslims and had created a secular army with patriots from all communities who shared a common kitchen, there was a strong possibility that should he have returned, Netaji would have challenged British plans for the partition of India.

At the time of the Mukherjee Commission, news reports stated that an Indian envoy to the USSR, Sarvepalli Radhakrishnan, saw Subhas Chandra Bose in a prison near Moscow soon after taking charge at the embassy in 1949. He subsequently became the Vice President and then President of India (1962). [This was personally conveyed to me by Rai Singh Yadav, a former intelligence officer and one of the witnesses before the Mukherjee Commission, who died sometime thereafter].

Netaji may have been incarcerated in a Soviet Gulag (Camp no 48 in Lezhnevesky district, 50 km from Suzdal in Siberia; others say he was in the Lubyanka in Moscow). We do not know if the Soviets handed him over to the British as a war criminal or dealt with him by themselves. However, in December 1941 and March 1944, there were two secret agreements between the NKVD (USSR) and MI-6 (Great Britain) regarding intelligence sharing and cooperation in covert operations. Many Indians suspect that the Nehru Government connived with Netaji's captors and perpetuated the falsehood that he had died in an air crash. The story of Bose living as a reclusive Gumnami Baba in Faizabad, UP, debunked by the Mukherjee Commission, is too puerile to merit serious discussion.

Under President Mikhail Gorbachev's doctrines of *glasnost* and *perestroika*, things began to change. A Russian India expert, T.F. Devyatkina, wrote in her article, *Social and Political Views of S.C. Bose* (1989), that "There is reason to doubt the theory that he died in 1945".

All indicators point to a Russian hand in the disappearance. After the collapse of the Soviet Union, only a handful of archives have been opened to scholars. Prof. Alexander Kolesnikov, Russian Academy of

Natural Sciences, has said that Netaji's Provisional Government of Free India was recognised by the Soviet Union and that Bose had reached the Soviet Union at the end of the War. He claimed to have seen a file that referred to a meeting between Stalin, Molotov, Vischenskii and Malik, in which the subject of "Chandra Bose" was discussed.

In 1997, *The Mainstream*, Delhi, (Vol. 35, no 32, 19 July 1997) reprinted Kolesnikov's article from the Russian weekly *Patriot*, which spoke of the arrival of Kato Kochu, Netaji's representative, in Omsk, and hints that Bose possibly reached the Soviet Union at the end of the War; he underlined the inconsistencies in the attempts to establish Bose's "death". Some articles published in Russian in 1995 mentioned Bose's presence in the KGB's famous Lubyanka prison in Moscow.

Kolesnikov dodged the Mukherjee Commission with Moscow stating that his whereabouts were unknown, though he was posted as a diplomat in Turkey. However, many Russian journalists began to receive some primary materials from different Russian archives that hinted at Bose's presence in their country.

Dr Purabi Roy learnt that there are a plethora of archives in the erstwhile Soviet Union, each a potentially rich source of information on Netaji, and that only a miniscule number of documents - from the Russian State Archive of Socio-Political History (RGASPI) pertaining to *Bose and the Communist Party of Soviet Union* - have been released.

In the early 1990s, Russian scholars and journalists unearthed many documents from the Archive of the Foreign Policy of the Russian Federation (AVPRF) and the Archive of the Foreign Security Service (FSB). The Soviet news agency, TASS, reported Bose's movements in Afghanistan, Germany and other countries and its reports are available in the State Archive of Russian Federation (GARF). But even this information failed to excite the curiosity of the Indian media.

However, the richest and as yet inaccessible sources include the Archive of the Ministry of Foreign Affairs (MID); the Archive of the Chief Intelligence Directorate of the Russian General Staff (GRU) and, most importantly, the Archive of the President of the Russian Federation (APRF). The President's archives contain material related to the Comintern, Stalin and Bukharin, and can only be accessed by Government-to-Government cooperation.

One reason why commissions investigating Netaji's death failed is because they focused solely on one man. Had they tried to investigate each of the alleged victims of the crash – Habibur Rahman said there were five victims and not four as stated by the Japanese – they might have uncovered some interesting leads.

Since the plane crash never happened, it follows that the Japanese victims too did not die. Yet they seem to have escaped arrest by the American occupation forces. Of particular interest is Lt Gen Shidei, who was to have negotiated Netaji's transfer to the Soviet authorities in Manchuria. Where did he go after the War? The Japanese authorities should be urged to reveal where these men hid in the post-War era, and if they left behind any personal records, which might be with the authorities. Above all, to which destination did they transfer Netaji on August 18, 1945? This can be done by a simple government-to-government request.

New Delhi should engage with Japan and Russia on the fate of Netaji, at the highest levels. Both are friendly nations, and there are no dramatis personae alive to be hurt by any revelations. Besides, the time for any more subterfuge is long gone. Bose's disappearance and death has troubled India's soul for over seven decades. Both Netaji and his country deserve peace.

References

1. Srinath Raghavan, India's War, *The Making of Modern South Asia 1939-45*, Allen Lane, Delhi, 2016.
2. Purabi Roy, *The Search for Netaji: New Findings,* Purple Peacock Books & Arts Pvt. Ltd., Kolkata, 2011, 2nd ed. 2012 .
3. G.D. Bakshi, *Bose*: *An Indian Samurai. Netaji and the INA*: *A Military Assessment*, Knowledge World, 2016.
4. Anuj Dhar, *What Happened to Netaji*, Vitasta Publishing Pvt Ltd., 2016.
5. Anuj Dhar, India's Biggest Cover Up, Vitasta Publishing Pvt Ltd., 2012, 20th impression, 2016.
6. Sandhya Jain, *Netaji:* 'The Remains of History', *The Pioneer*, 16 January 2001.

Taiwan rejects Bose crash theory, BBC, 4 February 2005 http://news.bbc.co.uk/2/hi/south_asia/4236189.stm

8. Sandhya Jain, 'Re-evaluating Netaji's Legacy', in *The Pioneer*, 24 January 2017 http://www.dailypioneer.com/columnists/edit/re-evaluating-netajis-legacy-contribution.html
9. Stalin 'dealt with' Netaji on London's request, Madhav Nalapat, *Sunday Guardian*, 11 April 2015 http://www.sunday-guardian.com/news/stalin-dealt-with-netaji-on-londons-request

Subhas Chandra Bose's Views on Foreign Policy Dominance of Realism

Raj Kumar Sharma

Introduction

Idealism and realism are two of the earliest theories in the field of international relations. As the name suggests, idealists stood for high ideals and moral principles while conducting a country's foreign policy. The genesis of idealism could be traced to Stoicism that originated in Athens in the 3rd century B.C. which emphasiszed on values like ethics and self-control. Idealists think that human beings are good natured and assisted by proper direction, education and international structures; they can help in building a cooperative and peaceful international order.[1] If every individual (or State in international relations) tries to improve his standards of purity and morality, conflict is unlikely to arise.[2] Idealists attach importance to global governance structures like the United Nations and profess that reason and discussion can eliminate crude power from international relations. That is why the; arms manufacturers and suppliers have been often criticized by idealists.[3] They focus on common problems like poverty and inequality which would create cooperative mechanisms between states, negating use of force and violence in international relations. In essence, it could be said that focus of idealism remains on 'what should be'. Its main proponents include Woodrow Wilson, J. M. Keynes, J. A. Hobson, A. Toynbee and Mahatma Gandhi.

Realism emerged in sharp reaction to idealism and its supporters include E. H. Carr, Hans Morgenthau and Kenneth Waltz. They have been influenced by the earlier thinkers like Thomas Hobbes, Kautilya and Niccolo Machiavelli. Realists see human beings as selfish who like to further their own interests. They argue that in foreign policy, national interest comes ahead of global interest. Driven by their urge to maximize their national interest, nations seek to accumulate power which becomes central principle of international relations. Instead of global cooperation, realism hints at conflict which is 'ever present' and a state needs to work for 'self preservation' by enhancing its military power in order to deter its adversaries. Realists see international relations in terms of 'what is' rather than 'what should be'. Two World Wars and the death of League of Nations in the first half of the 20th century dealt a serious blow to idealism, which contributed a great deal towards popularity of realism.

The 'realism-idealism' debate dominated the international affairs during the inter War period (1919-1939). This debate was pursued in India as well during the late 1930s and 1940s, when the Indian freedom struggle was at its peak. Subhas Chandra Bose had curious interest in the world politics and his views on India's foreign policy are discussed in succeeding paragraphs.

Bose's Views on Indian Foreign Policy

Subhas Chandra Bose saw himself as a realist in the foreign policy matters. The supporters of realism were in minority during the late 1930s in the Congress, as the majority was shaped by idealism as professed by Nehru and Gandhi. He confessed that:

"Foreign Policy is a realistic affair to be determined largely from the point of view of a nation's self-interest. Take Soviet Russia for instance. With all her Communism in her internal politics, she never

allows sentiments to dominate her foreign policy. Frothy sentiments and pious platitudes do not make foreign policy."[4]

His belief in realist thought was the main driving force behind his attempts to seek support from the Axis powers, Germany and Japan, for securing Indian's Independence from the British. By the time War broke out in 1939, there emerged two strands in the Congress. One was led by Gandhi and Nehru which supported the Allies, while Bose and his followers supported the Axis powers. They wanted to use the international situation to India's advantage. Bose was of the view that alliances could be stitched with the powers which were 'morally abhorrent', as he believed in *Kautilya's Mandala Theory* which states that '*enemy's enemy is a friend*'. He believed India should not be influenced by internal politics of a country or form of its State and should try to find people who will sympathize with Indian cause irrespective of their own political views.[5]

Bose believed that external help was necessary to liberate India, as "*...history did not furnish a single instance where freedom had been won without help of some sort from abroad.*"[6] Seeking help from Germany and Japan was a *tactical decision* in his overall strategy of direct action which would have allowed India to use the international situation to its advantage. Bose felt more so as India was not direct military target of the Axis powers.[7] In foreign policy terms, it is external balancing behaviour that a state resorts to while tackling a direct threat by befriending enemy of one's own enemy. Bose was a '*calculating rationalist*' in the field of foreign policy. He had no sympathy for Japanese imperialism but he held back open criticism of Japan since Tokyo seemed to be a potential partner against the British.[8] Bose also emphasized on the military component because it was necessary if a country wanted to be taken seriously by its friends and foes. Speaking in July 1943 in Singapore, while reviewing the Indian National Army, Bose said, "...though India is otherwise ripe for independence in every way, she has lacked one thing, namely, an army of liberation."[9]

In contemporary times, states widely use soft power and mass media to create favourable public opinion in other countries. Bose understood the power of mass media and information campaign and wanted to use it for creating awareness about India's struggle in other countries as there was 'colossal ignorance' about Indian cause in the outside world. He said, "*we should aim at developing a nucleus of men and women in every country who would feel sympathetic towards India...through the foreign press, through Indian made films, through art exhibitions...*"[10] Bose was impressed by the Chinese who had made themselves popular in Europe through their art exhibitions. He did not like the word 'propaganda' as it had an air of falsity about it.[11] He was aware of the British propaganda against India and termed BBC as '*Bluff and Bluster Cooperation*' and All India Radio as '*Anti-India Radio*'[12], which were used to justify British rule over India in the name of 'civilizing' the Indians. That is why, Bose and his supporters started radio broadcasts like *National Congress Radio, Azad Hind Radio and Azad Muslim Radio.*[13]

The Indian diaspora too figured prominently in Bose's strategy and he mobilized Indians living in Southeast Asia for his Indian National Army. He continues to be fondly remembered by the people of Singapore, Malaysia, Japan and other countries.

Differences with Nehru

Jawaharlal Nehru emerged as a leading voice in Congress in the late 1930s on matters of foreign policy and his approach was different from that of Bose. In one of his private correspondences, Nehru observed, "*One of Subhas's grievances against me, which is coming out more definitely in his correspondences, is his objection to foreign policy I have sponsored. In a recent letter to me he talks about the folly of my espousing lost causes and of always condemning Germany and Italy. He calls himself a realist in foreign as well as internal politics. This realism of his leads entirely to different conclusions.*"[14]

Bose saw Nehru's views on foreign policy as rigid, due to his perennial opposition to Germany and Italy. He believed that foreign policy should be flexible in order to increase space for diplomatic manoeuvring and seek external assistance in India's freedom struggle. Nehru believed that high principles trumped the use of force in conduct of Indian foreign policy. However, these views were in contrast to those of Subhas Chandra Bose who believed in the use of force as an instrument of politics. That is why, he turned to seek support from the Germans and Japanese for raising the Indian National Army to fight the British.[15] Nehru and Gandhi believed in non-violent methods against the British and opined that the Indian freedom struggle should be framed in larger international situation where the Allies were fighting 'amoral' forces of Germany and Japan.

Nehru's Foreign Policy in Independent India

Jawaharlal Nehru's impact on Independent India's foreign policy was immense and sometimes, his foreign policy is described as 'idealist'. However, a closer look at some of his decisions shows that realism was very much a component of his foreign policy. Nehru's world view was shaped by idealism and he wanted to achieve the idea of 'One World'.[16] One could also add his emphasis on Non-Alignment as the basis of Indian foreign policy which sought to achieve idealist targets like disarmament and a vision to stay away from bloc-politics. Nehru's foreign policy turned realist when it came to the Indian neighbourhood as he sought Indian primacy in South Asia. Nehru's treaties with Nepal, Bhutan and Sikkim were an extension of British policy in South Asia which gave primacy to India. This was also a decision influenced by balance of power politics, as China had annexed Tibet and India needed states which could act as buffers between China.[17] Nehru's decision to liberate Goa from Portuguese control in 1961 was also a realist decision influenced by India's security concerns.

Nehru suffered criticism over his policy of Non-Alignment which could not guarantee Indian security against the Chinese in 1962. The principle of staying non-aligned backfired on India, as only two countries from the NAM group – Cyprus and Ethiopia supported India against China. In 1962, Nehru accepted that India was getting out of touch with reality, living in an artificial atmosphere of our own creation. In December 1962, Nehru confessed that there was no non-alignment as far as China was concerned as one cannot be non-aligned towards a threat to his nation.[18] Nehru accepted military assistance from the US after the China war in 1962. In a way, he chose the lesser evil (the US) against bigger evil of openly aligning with any of the superpowers of the day. It is evident that the Nehruvian idealism of the 1930s on foreign policy had started to wane when he became the Prime Minister of Independent India. The Cold War had reached South Asia in the 1950s as Pakistan became member of the South East Asia Treaty Organization (SEATO) and Central Treaty Organization (CENTO). India faced twin threats from Pakistan and China and had to inject realism in its foreign policy formulation which started with Nehru.

Conclusion

Subhas Chandra Bose was influenced by the great power politics and formulated his foreign policy views in realist terms. Inspired by *Kautilya' smandala theory*, he favoured seeking help from Axis powers against the British as '*enemy's enemy is a friend*'. He was convinced that until India has something to offer to others, no one will help in Indian freedom struggle. He also laid emphasis on military power, as a state would not be taken seriously without an Army. He exhibited farsightedness as he was aware of information warfare raised by the British to justify their rule over India in the name of civilizing the Indians. Bose wanted to combine soft power and mass media to fight British propaganda. He also mobilized the Indian diaspora in the Southeast Asian countries to fight for India's freedom. Bose comes across as a tactician and strategist, who would have proven effective in foreign policy matters. In contrast, Nehru and Gandhi had idealist position and did not wish to exploit weakness of the British during the Second World War by aligning with the Axis powers. Ironically, after Nehru became the Prime Minister of Independent India, his foreign policy could not stick to the idealist credentials alone and realism formed its important part. Nehru had to seek military help from the West whom he criticized in the name of imperialism. Bose and Nehru were two opposite spectrums on foreign policy, and India continues to have a curious mix of idealism and realism in its foreign policy in the contemporary times

References

1. Wold, Irina (2001), J.J. Rousseau, I. Kant and the Theories of International Relations, URL: http://www.grin.com/en/e-book/130066/j-j-rousseau-i-kant-and-the-theories-of-international-relations.
2. The Rt. Hon. the Earl of Birkenhead (1923), Idealism in International Politics, URL: http://www.gla.ac.uk/media/media_191058_en.pdf.
3. Wilson, Peter (2011), Idealism in International Relations, URL: http://eprints.lse.ac.uk/41929/1/Idealism%20in%20international%20 relations%20(LSERO).pdf.
4. Bose in his letter to Nehru, 28th March, 1939, A Bunch of Old Letters, p. 334, quoted in Bhave, Y. G. (1995), *The First Prime Minister of India*, New Delhi, Northern Book Centre. p. 59.
5. Subhas Chandra, Bose (2010), *Words of Freedom: Ideas of a Nation*, New Delhi: Penguin Books, p. 57.
6. S. C. Bose to Mahatma Gandhi, The Oracle, Vol. xvi, No. 1 (January 1994), p. 3, cited in Abul Kalam (1997), *Subhash Chandra Bose: Strategic Concepts and Diplomatic Thought*, New Delhi: Manohar Publishers & Distributors, p 73.
7. Abul Kalam , *Subhash Chandra Bose: Strategic Concepts and Diplomatic Thought*, New Delhi: Manohar Publishers & Distributors, 1997, p. 78.
8. Pelinka, A (2003), "*Democracy Indian Style: Subhash Chandra Bose and the Creation of India's Political Culture*", Translated by Renee Schell, New Jersey, Transaction Publishers.
9. Devare, Sudhir (2006), "*India & South East Asia – Towards Security Convergence*", Singapore, *ISEAS* Publications, p. 174.
10. Zaidi, A.M. *et.al.* (1980, eds), "The Encyclopaedia of Indian National Congress", New Delhi, S. Chand & Co., p. 420, quoted in Jivanta choettli (2011), *Vision and Strategy in Indian Politics: Jawaharlal Nehru's Policy Choices and the Designing of Political Institutions*, Oxford and New York: Routledge. p. 81.
11. Bose, Subhas Chandra (2010), *op. cit.* p. 59.
12. Chatterjee, Reva (2000), *Netaji Subhash Chandra Bose: Bengal Revolution and Independence*, New Delhi: Ocean Books, p. 186.
13. Abul Kalam (1997), *op.cit.* p. 96.
14. Nehru to V. K. Krishna Menon, April 4, 1939 in *SWJN*, Vol. 9, p. 550 quoted in William F. Kuracina (2008), *Toward a Congress Raj: Indian*

Nationalism and the Pursuit of a Potential Nation-State, Michigan: Pro Quest LLC. p. 198.

15. Cohen, S.P and Dasgupta, S (2010), *Arming without Aiming: India's Military Modernization*, Washington, The Brookings Institution. p. 3.
16. Mohan, C. Raja (2015), "India's Foreign Policy: Nehru's Enduring Legacy", URL: http://blog.oup.com/2015/10/india-foreign-policy-nehru-legacy/.
17. *Ibid.*
18. Srinivasan, K. (2015), "Nehru & Non-Alignment", URL: http://www.thestatesman.com/opinion/nehru-amp-non-alignment-103710.html

The Indian Independence League, Indian Legion and the Azad Hind Radio under Subhas Chandra Bose

Md. Naushad Ali

Introduction

This article aims to delve into Subhas Chandra Bose's foremost role in the Indian Independence League's activities after his arrival in Germany in April 1941 and subsequently, the creation of Indian Legion and the foundation of Azad Hind Radio under his fervent leadership. The study will also focus on the role of the Indian revolutionaries and the civilians living in Europe who went hand in hand with Bose in his efforts of uniting the Indian soldiers (captured by the German army on European fronts) and establishing the Indian Legions to fight the British forces, and also the setting up Azad Hind Radio to propagate the cause of Indian liberation.

Undoubtedly, Subhas Chandra Bose was one of the frontline leader, a great patriot and a valiant fighter who devoted his entire life for the freedom of his country. This paper aims to highlight Bose's endeavours for the liberation of India from outside with special reference to Germany from where he, perhaps, for the first time, tried-out his strategies and tactics of military struggle against the British from outside India which were to be proved vital in the coming days of struggle, *i.e.*, in his campaign from South Asia.

I

Subhas Chandra Bose, in an interview to the *Nippon Times* on 4 July 1943, revealed three reasons behind his decision to leave India in early days of 1941: (i) to find out the correct war situation, general international conditions and to ponder about the results of the war; (ii) to get into the contact with the Axis Powers and to see their attitude regarding India and the possibility of co-operating with them against the common enemy, the British; and (iii) to make contacts with Indians abroad in order to organize them, so that they would become a force in the freedom struggle.[1]

This contemplation perhaps started with his resignation as President of the Congress in 1939 on the ground of widening difference with other frontline leaders of it. Consequent upon, he was marginalized in the Congress. In the emerging scenario, Bose had to reinvent himself politically. [2] Anticipating Germany's win in the ongoing Second World War, Bose thought, it was ideal situation to develop a more aggressive and militant alternative from outside India.[3] Gandhiji's slogan of *Karo ya Maro* during the Quit India Movement perhaps a testimony of Bose's believe that time of pacifism had gone. To fulfil his audacious desire, he undertook a sudden revolutionary escape on the night of 16 January 1941 from his Elgin Road residence[4] from his house arrest and proceeded incognito to the North-West Frontier Province, from where a local Forward Bloc activist smuggled him to Afghanistan. And from Afghanistan, he landed in Berlin on 2nd April in 1941 *via* Moscow under assumed Italian name Orlando Mazzotta.[5]

Now, the question arises why did Bose move towards Germany and allied with the Axis Powers? May be because, he looked at problems very realistically. It appeared to him to be important that he needed to seek asylum in the country of greater military importance among the Axis Powers. On the other hand, it is also a fact that he would have even gone to Moscow if he was allowed by the Soviet authorities when he contacted them in Kabul in February 1941.[6] In the end, it appears that he adopted the concept of 'enemy's enemy is your friend'.

II

As soon as Bose reached in Berlin, he met the higher officials of the Foreign Department Germany and expressed his desire to form an 'Indian Government in Exile' and expected it's immediate diplomatic recognition from the Axis Powers. Bose's main thrust was to persuade the German Government to adopt a '*Declaration of India*' which he hoped to be signed also by the Italy and Japan. It contained a commitment of the Axis Powers to India's Independence after the expected victory over Great Britain.[7] This figured prominently in Bose's talk with representative of the German Government, including Ribbentrop, the German Foreign Minister, Heinrich Himmler, the Commander of the SS of Auschwitz Concentration Camp, and eventually with Hitler. His desire in this regard remained to be fulfilled as Romain Hayes quotes from the official Minutes; Hitler finally rejected this citing it as premature. Consequently, Bose's meeting with the Chancellor of Germany on 29 May, 1942, a year after his arrival in Germany, was not up to his expectations though the Chancellor assured him all possible help, including military training for Indians. But at the same time Bose was in realization that his telephone called were on surveillance and his belongings were under search time to time that he told to one of his Indian friend.

Within few days of his arrival in Berlin, Bose, on 9 April, 1941 submitted a memorandum to the German Government on the possibilities of co-operation between Germany and India, *i.e.*, 'Indian Government in Exile'. In this draft, Bose proposed for the establishment of Free India Centre, the creation of Indian Legion in Germany and close cooperation between the high Commands of the Wehrmacht. The Indian Legion aim was to create disturbance and sabotage against the British Army in the tribal areas between Afghanistan and India[8] to launch an offensive against the British in India *via* Russia and Afghanistan[9] which did not happen at all. Understanding the need of radio broadcast, Bose, via this memorandum, requested the German Government for directing broadcast towards the India in order to make Indian people more and more cautions against the brutal nature of the British administration in

India.[10] The same memorandum was put forward to Italy Government as well.[11] The draft itself shows Bose's incisiveness in planning his strategy.

In response to his memorandum, Netaji's activities were guaranteed in principle by the German Government and subsequently a 'Special India Division' was instituted with office and facilities at the Foreign Office in Berlin. Adam von Trott was made it's head and Alexander Wreth his deputy.[12] Wilhelm Keppler State Secretary was made Liaison Officer to the German Foreign Minister and Chancellor.[13]

Due to untiring efforts of Netaji, the Free India Centre (FIC) started with only a handful of Indian workers including Habibur Rahman, M.G. Ganguley, N. G. Swamy and Vayas under aegis of the Special India Division. Very interestingly, Bose's efforts inspired two veteran communists, ACN Nambiar, a journalist and GK Mukharji from Paris to join him on 25 January, 1942. The number of the active workers increased to 35 by the summer of 1942 and they were mostly Indian students. It is Bose's persona that the workers of the FIC were given diplomatic privileges.

The students were entrusted up the work of editing of all the broadcast of Azad Hind Radio, National Congress Radio and Azad Muslim Radio directed towards sub-continent. They were also engaged in editing of *Azad Hind*, a periodical having more than 5000 copies in circulation. Another important work assigned to them by Netaji was to look after the entire community in Germany.[14]

III

Following the Creation of FIC, Netaji's long cherished desire of having National Army of modern standard posing discipline training and equipment had to be at his disposal in order to fight for freedom and to defend it after it was won. [15] For that purpose, he met Dr. Seifriz, who had great respect for Indian philosophy helped out Bose to fulfil the pursuit of having an Army to launch armed struggle against the British.[16] Later, Harbich together with his 2 civilian aids, N.G. Swami and Abid Hasan alongwith numerous trained Indian soldiers, holding different ranks, constituted the framework for a future Indian Legion. [17]

In September 1941, the recruitment for Indian Legion started and Netaji undertook visits to the Camps of Prisoners of Wars (PoW) and demanded a clear allegiance towards a Free India as well as an absolute readiness to undergo sacrifices for this purpose which did not fail to impress a great numbers of soldiers.[18] Indian Prisoners of War captured in North Africa by field Marshal Erwin Rommel's Afrika Korps were released into Netaji's custody and went on to form the Indian Legion that fought against the allied forces at the western front.[19]

After a year of hard work, the Legion strength reached between 3000 and 4000 comprising of four battalions in December 1942. Subsequently, the first military exercise with three battalions was held on 28 January, 1943 attended by Netaji and his friend Colonel Yamamoto, the Military attaché of Japan in Berlin. One the same day, the soldiers under the command of Colonel Krappe were sworn in to their flag which was the same as the Congress Tricolour but showing a 'Leaping Tiger' instead of conventional spinning wheel. The leaping tiger was adopted by Netaji, his friends and colleagues as the symbol of the struggle for Indian's freedom, the official greeting was '*Jai Hind*' and '*Jana Gana Mana*' was declared as the National Anthem.[20]

In the light of Bose's memorandum, to sensitize Indian masses back in India and the members of Indian Independence League and other Indian living in different parts of the world, Azad Hind Radio was started with its first transmission in October 1941 with 20 Indians and some German typists and technicians.[21] It transmitted the programme in seven languages that were English, Hindustani, Bengali, Persian, Tamil, Telugu and Pushtu. The daily broadcast in these 7 languages took 3 hours and 50 minutes and they were transmitted over shortwave. [22] It is almost unbelievable that these programs had at no time to pass any kind of pre or post censorship. It is quite interesting to note that in order to attract the listeners in India, music recorded from the Indian programme of the BBC was partly used in the daily broadcasts. There is only one instance in its transmission history when the broadcast was cancelled due to Joseph Goebbls (propaganda chief of Hitler)'s reply on radio to President Roosevelt's speech. [23] Bose's voices on radio transmitted towards India and South Asia had greatly enthused the Indian masses to fight against the colonial masters. Azad Hind Radio while serving met an unfortunate incident during an air raid in Dresden in 1943 in which one of its officials, Dr. Majumdar lost his life.[24]

Hitler sudden attack on Russia halted Bose's plan and strategy and, despite all his hard work, he could not created an Indian Army as he desired. The emerging scenario in Europe compelled Bose to look towards other options. Simultaneously, the Japanese success in South Asia prompted him to take over the leadership of INA on the invitation of Rash Behari Bose.

For his final struggle, Bose left Germany on 8 February, 1943 alongwith his trusted aid Abid Hasan. He took a voyage by a German Submarine, handing over the charge of the leadership of the FIC to his deputy, ACN Nambiar.

The colourful and vigorous personality of Netaji has perhaps been removed for all time from our minds, but his sprit dwells in the heart of every Indian and will continue to burn as pure flamer for centuries to come.

Refrences

1. *Nippon Times,* 4 July 1943 cf. T R Sareen, *Indian National Army*, A Document Study, V-II, pp. 123-27.
2. Romain Hayes, *Bose in Nazi Germany*, London, 2011, p. 23.
3. *Ibid.*
4. Sisir K. Bose and Sugata Bose (eds.), *Netaji Collected Work*, Vol.11, Calcutta, 2002, p. 1.
5. Sisir Kumar Bose and others (eds.), *A Bacon Across Asia*, New Delhi, 1973, p. 16.
6. *Ibid.*, p. 119.
7. Anand Singh Bawa, *Netaji Subhash Chandra Bose and Germany*, New Delhi, p. 175.
8. Sisir K. Bose & Others, *op cit.*, p. 121.
9. Purabi Roy, *The Search for Netaji: New Findings*, Kolkata, 2012, p. 21.
10. Sisir, *op cit.*, p. 121.
11. Subhas Chandra Bose, *The Indian Struggle,* 1920-42, compiled by Netaji Research Bureau, Calcutta, 1964, pp. 425-18.

12. Alexander Werth and Walter Harbich, *Netaji in Germany*, Netaji Research Bureau, Kolkata, p. 23.
13. *Ibid.*, p. 20.
14. *Ibid.*
15. Sisir Kumar Bose and others (eds.), *A Bacon Across Asia*, New Delhi, 1973, p. 129.
16. *Ibid.*, p. 31.
17. *Ibid.*
18. *Ibid.*, p. 32.
19. *Ibid.,* p. 34.
20. Confd./8(1) declassified F No. Secret/58/93.
21. *Ibid.*, p. 35.
22. *Ibid*, p. 28; Ganpuley, *op cit.*, p.55.
23. *Ibid.*, p. 29.
24. *Ibid.*, p. 25.
25. Besides above references the following readings also enriched the information on the subject and helped in drafting the text: Arun (compl. & ed.), *Testament of Subhash Chandra Bose*, Delhi, 1946; Netaji Research Bureau (compl.) *Crossroads*, 1938-1940, 1962; P.D. Saggi & Others (ed.), *A Nation's Homage, Life and Work of Netaji Subhash Chandra Bose*, Bombay, n.d.; Netaji Subhash Chandra Bose, *Impression in Life,* Lahore, 1947; Durlab Singh & Others (ed.), *Formation and Growth of the Indian National Army*, Lahore, 1946; S.K. Bose, *Netaji Collected Works*, Vol. 2, NRB, n.d.; Rudolf Hartog, *The Sign of the Tiger: Subhash Chandra Bose and His Indian Legion in Germany, 1941-45*, New Delhi, 2001.

Subhas Bose - The Eternal Legend

Abhijit Bhattacharyya

"Subhas Chandra Bose"! What do the three-worded name denote to common Indian? And also to a student of world and Indian history? Simply put: the name Subhas Chandra Bose has been an inspiration, an icon, to every freedom-aspiring, English-hating Indians of 1930s and 1940s and beyond. To contemporary times. And yet, ironically this very inspiration has an uncanny resemblance to that of a rabid India-hater and racist former British Prime Minister Churchill, who too was an inspiration to his English-speaking countrymen in 1940s, at the height of a real-possibility of imminent and inevitable defeat at the hands of Hitler's Germany.

Regretfully, however, Bose, unlike Churchill, evoked different (and more often than not, supremely indifferent) reactions from his own political peers and purported nationalist colleagues. Thus, even a part, one-third, utterance of (only) the surname "Bose" triggered shivers down the spine and created envy, in the heart and head of some of his contemporaries who subsequently "mattered" in the polity of nascent Indian democracy. Why? Because the very existence of Bose was perceived a potential existential threat to his peers; whose intense (human) jealousy-cum-rivalry was born out of their collective inability and failure to match the unmatched brilliance and merit of one individual. Bose. It virtually became a tug of war between individual brilliance and institutional mediocrity. As it so often happens in the life of humans.

Understandably, therefore, Bose had to be the target of an orchestrated canard and calumny of/by the white British (mis)rulers of subjugated India; and post-1947 independence, (even much after he ceased to operate across the sanctum-sanctorum of the Indian democracy), he became an object of visceral dislike by a section of self-trumpeting "neo-liberal" and "socialist, secular, democratic" elite of new India some of whose myopic political actions constituted monumental blunders thereby resulting in unforgettable adverse side effects in the polity of new India. In this scenario, when the unwritten edict of the new Indian state tried to silently (with an unwritten and unspoken code) ban him or banish him, the name Bose, dead or alive, nevertheless came back to haunt all who loved to hate, or hated to love him.

For millions of common, non-VIP Indians, Bose continued, and continues, to be legend. An unrivalled icon. Forever, to eternity. Bose could not be banned or banished by any edict or ordinance, fatwa or 'firman'. He survived; nay thrived; and flourished without any fanfare, in spite of being dubbed as "also-ran" and snubbed through the footnoted lines, "mention-in-despatches" history syllabus of Indian school, college and university! His flame could not be extinguished by "small mortals" of new India. By those who created, re-created and destroyed the basic features, fabric and structure of history of India. Why? Because of destiny of the man; the un-destroyed child of destiny smoothly and gloriously placed himself as a live sample of Bhagvad Gita's Chapter 3, "Karma Yoga", thereby emerging as the eternal and indestructible "Karma Yogi"; the epitome of ethical, metaphysical, moral, spiritual and ethereal warrior.

Carrying Bhagvad Gita in his pocket all times, in the thick of jungle battle field of Burma to "twenty thousand leagues under the sea" or while flying twenty thousand feet above the sea. Which "senior" political mentor or competitor would stomach such superior sentinel of spiritual disposition? Who was admired, nay worshipped, across country for his boundless love for his bonded motherland, and whose presence could not be predicted, whose movement remained undetected, whose actions unanticipated and yet from nowhere who popped up here, there, somewhere and everywhere to remain a magnet to, and for, Indians across globe?

Nevertheless, Bose too was mortal. He must have had fault lines in his character. He must have had committed follies. He also must have had fair share of failures. Frustrations. What were those? Why is he being ceaselessly eulogised and glorified, and seldom criticised, by his admirers, thereby giving an impression of being a band of blind, irrational, supporters and devotees? Surely Bose must have had committed mistakes. And there were several. Yet, in overall arch of things, those follies and failures, appear virtually pardonable and invisible owing more to his peer and competitors' attempt to paint Bose in poor light and whitewash from the pages of history book, than the actual poor performance, if any, of Bose. That is the genesis of Bose. More the suppression, more it blossomed. Hence Bose lived, and still lives, in the psyche of India. It, therefore, is time to revisit Bose from an Indian's perspective and assess his place in history of the geography of South Asia at least.

To understand the psyche and eternal legend of Bose, one has to at least cursorily, have a stark look and, glance through the 40 year history of Hindu Bengalis (in pan-India perspective) between 1857 and 1897, the year Bose was born. Let us face it and see the reality. Till 1857, Hindu Bengalis hardly (should one say never!) existed, in any position, anywhere, in any official capacity, big or small, important or unimportant, in Delhi Durbar of the Mughals. Why? To this author, the main reason possibly was the inherent inability, or unwillingness, of Hindu Bengalis to follow the fabled, prostrating-courtiers of the capital citadel of Delhi, and to master the lingua franca of, and for, the court-craft; the Persian language. Most of the Hindu Bengalis, till date, (even the most successful and prominent) usually are not known to be well-versed with any of the languages like Persian, Arabic, or for that matter even Urdu or Hindi. There appears to be an invisible psychological barrier. Understandably, this inability to master the Mughal Durbar's lingua franca deprived the Hindu Bengalis of any position, clout, influence and authority for hundreds of years. Hence, Hindu Bengalis were conspicuous by their absence in Delhi Durbar's legendary power and political hierarchy and, therefore, hardly had anything to do with the power-play thereof; and across the vast political geography of Mughal India. They were isolated, ostracised and aloof; constricted to/in the riverine eastern fringe of Mughal empire.

Surprisingly, however, post-1857 Sepoy Mutiny, when English education was introduced in India's first university, set up 1857 in Calcutta, which by now had transformed from the centre of English East India Company to the capital city of the (Her or His Majesty's) Crown Empire in the east of Suez, the same Hindu Bengalis not only became pioneers amongst the English knowing and English educated Indians, but their stunning performance and presence across India had undergone a bewildering, astonishing, and electrifying change. Their unmatched excellence in all things-English simply had no peers. Just as fish takes to water, Hindu Bengalis took to English-medium education. Overnight, from doctors, engineers, professors, civil servants, chartered accountants, factory managers, bankers, traders, industrialists to political leaders they spread from Calcutta to Delhi, Peshawar to Patna; Baroda and Bilaspur to Bombay; Gwalior to Gorakhpur; Srinagar and Sibsagar to Singapore; Ranigunge and Raipur to Rangoon.

Thus, the former Persian-trained elite Muslim ruling class and its ilk were pushed out from all important social and economic spectrum by a "non-existing and nobody" Hindu Bengalis who took to English like their long-lost and separated-at-birth English language. The brilliance of Subhas Bose has to be seen in this light and background. Thus when Subhas did exceptionally well in (English medium) school and college and made into ICS in 1921, it had its roots in the collective rise of Hindu Bengalis and the psyche and tradition they developed for strong English education over more than four decades.

It was an easy formula. Hindu Bengalis learnt English. Through English language, they became aware of Liberty, Equality, Fraternity. And through this process itself they challenged the ruling Englishmen as to why are they not putting into practice what they are professing and preaching from the roof top? Why this brazen double-standard? They asked and challenged constantly.

Thus when Subhas Bose allegedly took part in the "slapping" of his Englishman teacher in Presidency College it was the manifestation of Newton's third law of "equal and opposite reaction" as Bose had experienced around the Central districts of Calcutta wherein the "black" native Indians were not allowed to travel along with "white" Englishman without facing discrimination and humiliation in the same tram car. Application of force and fighting physically (if need be) on behalf of his "black" native Indian countrymen against injustice, unlike the later-day political peers, came naturally and spontaneously to Bose's character. After all Subhash, unlike Gandhi, faced discrimination in his own motherland instead of in a distant alien soil of South Africa! Understandably, therefore, was sown the seeds of discord and difference between the "junior" and "violent" Bose and the "senior" passive, "non-violent" Indian leaders, led by Gandhi, who had an "abiding faith" in, and respect for, the justice, equity, fair play and sanctity of British. One suspects to protect the interests of those moneyed men who otherwise would have had suffered owing to British backlash to contain physical force of the "native black" Indians. Bose, on other hand, had hardly any moneyed men to back his single minded crusade to evict the British by force.

Coming next, should one see Bose through the philosophy, ideology and eyes of Bose himself to re-evaluate and re-assess his place in history? Will it be impossible to do so? Not quite, this author feels. Going purely by indisputable and recorded facts, one may see the merit or demerit of his actions.

Let the tone, tenor, language of Bose speak his mind and psyche, who from his own writing appears articulate, precocious, sensitive, spiritual, selfless, bold, brave, wise. One wonders as to how did a young boy even before reading or understanding the essence of the Bhagvad Gita appear to be a part thereof? Else, how did he write to his mother about "character" at the age of 15? "Revered mother, what is the object of education? If an educated man has no character, shall I call him a Pundit? Never".

"But if an uneducated person is conscientious, believes in, and loves God, I am prepared to accept him as a Maha-Pundit. I worship the man whose heart is overflowing with love of God" (AN INDIAN PILGRIM:- AN UNFINISHED AUTOBIOGRAPHY AND COLLECTED LETTERS 1897-1921, PAGE 117-118). A bare teen aged speaks about education, character, belief in, and love for, God! How many of his contemporaries are recorded to have spoken at the age of 15 like this? Giving clear glimpse of selflessness, love for character and defining as well distinguishing between an educated and the uneducated?

A streak of renunciation and the pleasure of pain appeared to run through the veins of Bose at an early stage as he was in search for a Guru. Though he found none, yet his companionship with a "young ascetic on the bank of the Ganges" greatly impressed Bose, the seeker for divinity and truth. Hailing from the Punjab, the sadhu's "complete renunciation of worldly desires, his utter indifference to heat, cold etc., his mental purity and loving temperament", had great impact on Bose for his future actions as he recorded about the man:- "The sky the roof, the grass the bed; And food what chance may bring" (AN INDIAN PILGRIM PAGE 59-60).

Again the mind of Bose was revealed, even before he attained adulthood in letter to his elder brother:- "I have been realising....that I have got a definite mission in my life and for that I am bearing my body and I am not to drift in the current of popular opinion. People will speak well or ill- this is the way of the world- but my deepest consciousness consists in this that I am not moved by it.......When I left school, I had by then made certain definite decisions for myself I was not going to follow the beaten track, come, what may; I was going to lead a life to my spiritual welfare and uplift of humanity........I was not going in for a worldly career. This was the outlook with which I faced a new chapter in my life.... Standing on the threshold of my college career, I felt convinced that life had a meaning and a purpose" (AN INDIAN PILGRIM PAGE-49). How many of India's later day political leaders, or peers of Bose, could match the deep understanding of the profound philosophy of life by a young precocious mind of a chained country under white foreign rulers? Undoubtedly, the young Bose had displayed all the ingredients to be an adorable leader for his transparent commitment to service to the people and renunciation of pleasure. Simply put: dedicate one's life to/for the bonded nation. To free India from brute forces of foreigners.

The soldier in Subhas too came to fore during his college days when he joined the University Training Corps (UTC), equivalent to National Cadet Corps (NCC) of independent India. Jubilant Bose in soldier's attire was ecstatic in expressing:- "What a change it was from sitting at the feet of anchorites to obtain knowledge about God to standing with a rifle in my shoulders."(AN INDIAN PILGRIM PAGE 80)

At age 24 again, the ascetic Bose came back to his "renunciation best". Having stood fourth in ICS merit list, it was time to introspect. "To be or not to be"! Wrote Subhas to his elder brother Sarat:- "You will readily understand my mental condition as I stand on threshold of what the man-on-the-street would call a promising career. There is much to be said in favour of such a service. It solves once and for all what is the paramount problem for each of us- the problem of bread and butter. One has not to face life with risk or any uncertainty as to success or failure. But for a man of my temperament who has been feeding on ideas which might be called eccentric- the line of least resistance is not the best line to follow. Life loses half of interest if there is no struggle, if there are no risks to be taken. The uncertainties of life are appalling to one who has not, at heart, worldly ambitions……I am at a cross-ways and no compromise is possible…….I have written to father and mother to permit me to take the vow of poverty and service….Personally, I am not afraid of suffering- in fact I would rather welcome it than shrink from it". (AN INDIAN PILGRIM PAGE 95-98).

Just see what is being spoken by a young, rare enlightened mind of a subjugated country? He virtually calls his ideas "eccentric" knowing full well that avoiding the line of least resistance is going to make him face problems in life and yet the warrior in Bose unfolds, who is bent on blossoming with all its glory and beauty. In midst of adversity. He is game for the fight. Fight to finish. There is no full stop till the man himself stops, or is stopped. Stopped by either the nature or the God Almighty. The God Almighty alone!

And who is God? How does man deal with God? Bose explanation is logical, simple yet profound. My attitude to this question is one of "benevolent agnosticism"- if I may coin this expression. "On the one hand, I am not prepared to take anything on trust....On the other hand, I cannot just rule out as sheer moonshine what so many individuals claim to have experienced in the past". The logical, rational, tolerant and accommodating mind of Bose speaking once again! How profound an analysis?

Aside God, Bose rejection of life of bed-of-roses, unlike modern human samples of unfulfilled promise, had of no use per se. "Life loses half its interest if there is no struggle, if there are no risks to be taken. The uncertainties of life are not appalling to one who has not, at heart, worldly ambitions". Emphatic indeed. Bose ambition and aim was service for the state before self. And there clearly lay the deep divide, the unbridgeable fault line, between an individual legend and the conglomeration consisting of the motley crowd of a few mediocre mettle.

However, when Bose met Gandhi in Bombay (now Mumbai) on latter's return from UK after refusing ICS 1921 he was far from satisfied. Why? One could not get an authentic answer to the meeting of two men; Gandhi a 52 year old former Barrister and 24 year old Bose (who refused-to-join) ICS. It is possible, according to this author, that the 28 year age difference between a distant, South Africa-returned Non-resident Indian (NRI), Barrister and a brilliant son-of-the-soil mind of a successful civil service examinee from India had different perspectives to look at the situation in India thereby resulting in non-meeting of their mind, thoughts, belief, ideology and conviction!

That Subhas being a born fighter and a person who targetted the British with single-minded determination, having made it his lifetime mission, it did not come as a surprise when he was subsequently hounded by an Indian political brigade of his own party in 1939. Freedom attainment definitely did not have a common-road approach and objective for the political leaders of the country. Indeed, 1939 Tripuri Congress session was the high (should I say low, unscrupulous and unethical) watermark of the senior political leadership of India who, instead of going all out against the English rulers, preferred to show their infinite and inexhaustible capability and expertise to resort to civil war type fighting with their brilliant colleague, Bose. To pin him down. The way Mahabharata epic's Arjun son Abhimanyu was obliterated by a gang of monsters! Tripuri Congress nevertheless clearly showed that Subhas was the only top leader of India who had to face two front war:- first, the civil war waged by his own countrymen against him and the second, his incessant and relentless war against foreign lords of London. No wonder Bose has been wiped out from history books of Indian education system by those who emerged victorious through wiping out their own colleague thereby proving the old proverb:- "History is always written by the ("vicious and venomous") victor and not the vanquished".

The question is, how did Bose deal with such situation? Fire, coming from friends instead of foreign foes? The answer can be found in a startling revelation of his fighting philosophy as expressed to his childhood friend Dilip Roy:- "Having lived beside a river in Cuttack, I have seen that the tides recede only to surge back again, especially in the rains, with mounting force. Day after day I would watch on in curiosity. They strike the solid banks for sometimes at flood-tide but, it seems, only to troop away- shamed faced, defeated. After a time they appear again and hurtle with a stronger impetus. This play of rising and subsiding is repeated, the assaulting continues, and the banks, their enemies, get weaker and weaker, imperceptibly- till the fateful day when chunks of them fall plop into the swirling, eddying tides and the battle is won…" (AN INDIAN PILGRIM).

Little wonder Bose transcended all barriers; expanding his Arjun's Lakshya Bheda type determination to oust the foreign rulers whom he had singled out as the sole enemy of India. Unfortunately for India, the senior political stalwarts who were trying to outpace and outrun Bose as rival, vacillated between goodness and badness, benevolence and malevolence of the British rulers. In the process, perhaps a common focus turned into a multi-front target in which the biggest losers were the Indian leaders themselves. Between Bose, the recalcitrant Muslim League leadership and the cunning British rulers, things were frittered away by the leading lights of Indian freedom movement. Fractious political leaders could not hold on, in front of foreign rulers whose ability to exploit the division in the ranks of Indian leadership was too conspicuous to be missed. Though fortuitously not for long as Second World War ultimately destroyed the grand calculation of the mighty British.

Before concluding the legend of Bose, one may like to ask a few politically incorrect questions to our countrymen. Did the post-independence Indian ruling class try to tamper with the professed objective writing of Indian history to suppress or eliminate the "unwanted" chapters thereof? Like that of the role of Bose, INA and the armed forces revolt on the eve of independence, in the freedom movement in India? Perhaps something definitely did happen to compel this author ask this question. Especially after reading words from preface to the first edition of the magnum opus "HISTORY OF THE FREEDOM MOVEMENT OF INDIA VOLUME- I" written by one of one of the greatest scholar-extraordinary historians of India, Dr. Ramesh Chandra Majumdar!

Thus wrote Dr. Ramesh Chandra Majumdar: "It may appear somewhat strange that having devoted myself for more than forty years exclusively to the study of ancient Indian history, I should have undertaken, at the fag-end of my life, to write the history of the freedom movement in India....I gave a brief account of it in the Preface to my book, 'The Sepoy Mutiny and the Revolt of 1857', published 1957. Since then the Government of India have published the first volume of the 'History of the Freedom Movement in India', written by Dr. Tara Chand, which gives an altogether different version. In his Preface Dr. Tara Chand says that the idea of writing a history of the freedom movement 'emanated from the late Maulana Abul Kalam Azad', Minister of Education, Government of India, and when 'he asked me to take up the work I gladly accepted the offer'. In the Foreword to this book Humayun Kabir, Minister for Scientific Research and Cultural Affairs, however contradicts Dr.Tara Chand when he says that 'at the very first meeting of the Indian Historical Records Commission held after India became free, a resolution was passed for preparing an authentic and comprehensive history of the different phases of the Indian struggle for independence. This recommendation found an immediate response from the late Maulana Abul Kalam Azd who directed that steps should forthwith be taken to give effect to it'. He then briefly describes the various steps taken by the Government over a period of four years before a Board of Editors was finally entrusted with the task in 1953. But even Humayun Kabir's account, though a great improvement upon the cryptic statement of Dr. Tara Chand, is very sketchy, inaccurate and misleading" (HISTORY OF THE FREEDOM MOVEMENT IN INDIA VOLUME-I. PREFACE TO THE FIRST EDITION. PAGE XI).

The confusion and chaos seem to have been deliberately created by the Government of a nascent nation to keep the best and most competent historians away, lest they write an objective, scholastic and 'true' history of the freedom movement in India. The likes of Maulana Azad and Humayun Kabir either were playing into game plan of some hidden hand or were too naive to comprehend the seriousness of writing a correct history of the new India. Either way, therefore, it is the history of India which fell victim to the political machination of the state. No wonder whereas a few individuals appear to have emerged as the monopoly stakeholders of India's freedom movement, some of the real heroes like Bose have been given a short shrift and hit with a hidden stick to prove as if they never existed.

Thus lambasts Dr. R.C. Majumdar: "all the relevant facts on this subject I took in compiling a history of the freedom movement in India, and all my labours were lost by the unceremonious rejection of my draft, not by the Board, an autonomous body, for which and under which I alone worked, but by the Government of India which dissolved the Board with effect from January 1, 1956, and took upon itself the task of writing the history" (PAGE XI & XII IBID).

The woes of Dr. R.C. Majumdar, the indisputable leading light amongst all contemporary Indian historian, were yet to end. He lamented: "I expected that the Government of India would soon make some new arrangements to complete the work left unfinished by the Board. But we had to wait long before it was announced that Dr. Tara Chand had been commissioned to write the history of the freedom movement in India. I was under no illusion as to the nature of the history that would be written by him. As everyone has now a full opportunity of judging for himself the quality of Dr. Tara Chand's work from the first volume already published by him. I need not comment on it" (PAGE XII IBID).

Majumdar clarified further: "But being convinced that his plan of the history was radically different from mine, I decided to write a history in my own way, so far as I could do it within the limited resources at my command. But as an offset to this I had one great advantage. I have written with complete freedom, un-trammelled by the vacillations and varying moods of the Board. I have approached the subject from a strictly historical point of view. It is an ominous sign of the time that Indian history is being viewed in official circles in the perspective of recent politics".

"The official history of the freedom movement starts with the premises that India lost independence only in the eighteenth century and had thus an experience of subjection to a foreign power for only two centuries. Real history, on the other hand, teaches us that the major part of India lost independence about five centuries before, and merely changed masters in the eighteenth century" (PAGE XIII IBID).

How precise, pointed, poignant and pungent are Dr. R.C. Majumdar's statement? Can anyone doubt, dispute or debate? Just impossible. Now we know what sort of history has been written and by what type of historians? Courtier historian or panegyrist perhaps would be a better and more suitable an epithet to be used for the post-independence writers of Indian history. One had heard the term "yes-men" civil servants through an English TV serial "Yes Minister". Is it time to use the word "Yes-men-Yes-Sir-historians" of Indian history!

Indeed, one is amazed at the passive, rather pacifist (so-called) liberal lobby's recurring whitewashing of the greats of India who fought with single-minded determination, dedication and devotion to oust the foreigners and evict their forced rule of/in India. In fact even a short list of some names who are conspicuous by their absence in the history syllabus of India makes one sad.

In this connection the name of political stalwart Maulana Abul Kalam Azad crosses one's mind. After the 1939 Tirupati Congress session Gandhi-led forced resignation of Bose, Rajendra Prasad succeeded as interim President of the party. Nevertheless Maulana Azad soon came thereafter as the Party President. And co-incidentally when the Pakistan Resolution was passed in Lahore by the Muslim League on March 23, 1940, Maulana Azad was the President of Congress. Again, co-incidentally Azad continued in that position for a record 6 years from 1940 to 1946, the year when the Muslim League unleashed its Direct Action Day (Friday, August 16, 1946) which resulted in the death of more than 5000 non-Muslims known as the Great Calcutta killings. Understandably, as an indisputable patriot to the core, Maulana Azad became the first Education Minister of India; a position which he held for a record 10 year, 5 months and 7 days, from August 15, 1947 to January 22, 1958. Should it not have been his duty and responsibility to look into proper writing and reconstruction of history of India? Why deny the jewels of India the proper place to which they legitimately belong? Is it too late?

For that matter, can successive Education Ministers of India be perceived to have missed their opportunity to make a sincere attempt to write fair and objective history of the freedom movement in India as was pointed out by one of the greatest 20th century historians of India, Dr. R.C.Majumdar? Now can we go through the list of Indian Education Ministers, who missed the opportunity to take corrective actions in the first thirty years of new India; from 1947 to 1977?

EDUCATION MINISTERS OF INDIA 1947-1977

1. Maulana Azad. August 15, 1947 to January 22, 1958. (10 year, 5 month, 7 days).
2. K.L.Shrimali. January 22, 1958 to August 31, 1963. (5 year, 7 month, 9 days).
3. Humayun Kabir. September 1, 1963 to November 21, 1963. (2 month, 20 days).
4. M.C.Chagla. November 21, 1963 to November 13, 1966. (2 year, 11 month, 23 days).
5. Fakhruddin Ali Ahmed. November 14, 1966 to March 13, 1967. (4 months).
6. Triguna Sen. March 16, 1967 to February 14, 1969. (1 year, 10 month, 29 days).

7. K.V.R.Rao. February 14, 1969 to March 18, 1971. (2 year, 1 month, 4 days).
8. S.S. Ray. March 18, 1971 to March 20, 1972. (1 year, 2 days).
9. Nurul Hassan. March 24, 1972 to March 24, 1977 (5 years).

At the end, one is neither shocked nor surprised at the treatment meted out to Bose and innumerable heroes of Indian history by the successive ruling class of India. Bose hurt their ego. The single-minded determination of Bose to oust the British by force hit their pride. It made them look small, in their own esteem. Bose emerges victorious in defeat as he continues to be adored and admired by millions despite permanent blackout. He is a loser. Long lost. Yet, the lost and the loser is the living legend who is more powerful than those alive to take over the reins of the state. To date, Bose overshadows all those who outlasted him.

Indeed, the old adage once again comes back as a reality that history written by victors and vanquished can be respected or vilified, presented or deleted, in accordance with the wishes and orders of the victors. The famous lines of late E.H.Carr too comes alive: "History is the moving procession" and that the angle of vision of the historian determines the study and course of history. However, one must study the historian before studying the history written by him. This by itself once again makes real that old saying: "whereas usually heroes make history, it is also equally true that history, written by historians, also makes heroes". Classic example is there for all to see. Objective change is an anathema. Subjective history constitutes, and continues, as the system. Despite all this, comes back the legend Bose to prove the profound verdict of the scientist: "And yet it" (Bose!) "moves"!

List of Contributors

Major General (Dr.) GD Bakshi, SM, VSM (retired) is a combat veteran of many skirmishes. He is a prolific writer on matters military and non-military and has published 25 books and over 130 papers in many prestigious research journals. Dr. Bakshi holds a Masters degree in Defense Science and an M.Phil in Strategic Studies from the University of Madras. He completed his PhD on 'Limited Wars in South Asia'. Dr. Bakshi is an Associate member of I.D.S.A. and a distinguished fellow at Centre for Air Power Studies. He is editor of *Defence and Security Alert*. His important publications are: *Afghanistan – the First Fault Line War*; *War in the 21st Century; The Indian Art Of War*; *The Paradox of Pakistan; The Rise of Indian Military Power: Evolution of an Indian Strategic Culture* and most recently *Bose: The Indian Samurai Netaji and the INA, a Military Assessment.*

Professor Sumit Mukerji is presently Director, Centre for Studies on Bengali Diaspora, University of Kalyani. He was awarded his Ph.D. degree from Jadavpur University for his thesis entitled *Political Thought and Principles of Netaji Subhas Chandra Bose, 1921-41* which was subsequently published as a book named *Subhas Chandra Bose, The Making of a Warrior Philosopher 1921-41.* Apart from this, other books authored by him include *Gorkhaland, the Dormant Volcano, The Rebels of Kamrup, A Search for identity among Ahoms and Rajbanshis and Subhas Chandrer Jibane Rabindranather Probhab.* He has written a number of research papers on the life and thought of Netaji Subhas Chandra Bose. His major areas of interest include Netaji Studies, Indian Freedom Movement, Political Thought, Terrorism, and Ethnic and Sub national movements.

Dr. Kaushik Roy is Guru Nanak Chair Professor, Department of History, Jadavpur University, Kolkata, and Global Fellow, Peace Research Institute Oslo (PRIO), Norway.

P.K. Chakravorty is an alumnus of National Defence Academy, the officer retired in 2010. He has served as the Defence Attaché to Vietnam and is a prolific writer on strategic subjects. Post retirement he was appointed as an advisor to Brahmos Aerospace and is currently pursuing a Ph.D from Hindustan Institute of Technology and Science. He has written several books, articles and projects for IDSA, USI, CLAWS, and VIF. His areas of interest are Strategy, Firepower, Defence Procurement, Net Assessment, South and South East Asia, Indo Pacific and Left Wing Extremism.

M. Jugindro Singh is a columnist, writer, counsellor, active member of INA Memorial complex in Manipur, a dedicated member of youth and women employment, social worker and reformer and educationist.

Dr. Er. Vekho Swuro is a civil engineer by profession who is an ambassador of Peace and Unity and a strong proponent of "dignity of Labour" especially for the youths. He is a recipient of Governor's award for his contribution towards society. He also published several books which are widely used as practical books by the youths in Nagaland. He has been awarded an Honorary Doctorate for Historical research and Youth Development specialising on the life of Netaji Subhas Chandra Bose.

Dr. Vijay Kumar Vashishtha retired as Professor and Head of History Department in Maharshi Dayanand Saraswati University, Ajmer (1990-2000). He has worked as UGC Award post of Research Scientist B, been Fellow at the Indian Institute of Advanced Study, Shimla and Senior Fellow of Indian Council of Historical Research. His major publications are: *Rajputana Agency 1832-1858*; *Bhagat Movement : Study of Cultural*

Transformation of the Bhils of the Southern Rajasthan; *1857; Revolt in the Princely State of Jaipur*; and *Role of Gandhi's Ideas in Mobilization of Adivasis of Southern Rajputana Princely States (1921-1948).* The Maharana Mewar Foundation, Udaipur bestowed on him the prestigious Maharana Kumbha Award (1993) for his contribution to the history and culture of Rajasthan.

Professor Abhijit Choudhury taught History at St. Edmund's College, Shillong, Meghalaya, for thirty years (1981-2011), retiring as Head of Department. He has contributed three entries on prominent historians—Marc Bloch, E.P. Thompson and Eric Hobsbawm to the Axomiya Biswakosh, vols.8 & 9 (Assamese Encyclopaedia), published by the Axom Xahitya Xabha (2005). He has also co-edited a book titled *The Making of the Union* (2007), on the merger of the princely states end excluded areas in the Indian Union. His areas of special interests are Prehistory and Palaeo-anthropology, Tribal Studies, Khasi and Jaintia Folklore, History of China and Political theory. He has published articles and research papers on Rabindra Nath Tagore, Mohandas Karamchand Gandhi and Subhas Chandra Bose in Bengali and English.

Dr.Tapan Chattopadhyay, Ph.D. and D.Litt. in history, is the author of pioneering research works such as *The Story of Lalbazar – Its Origin and Growth* (Kolkata, 1982), *Lepchas and Their Heritage* (New Delhi, 1990), *The INA's Secret Service in Southeast Asia – Its Background, Infrastructure, Resources and Activities During World War II* (Kolkata, 2011), and *Kolkata and Its Police – A History of City Police from Charnock's to Present Day* (Kolkata, 2013). He received the Michael Madhusudan Award and Gold Medal for his literary work in 2005. He is now engaged in research and writing, as also teaching at different institutes.

Colonel Gautam Das (retired) did his M.A. in Defence Studies. He has been writing on military history as well as politico-military subjects. Six books have been written by him and a new book is under publication. He is presently working with the History Division, Ministry of Defence, Government of India, for an official publication on the 'Indian Armed

Forces in the First World War'. The INA is one of his military history and political science interests.

Saradindu Mukherji (Ph.D. Delhi) has written on peasants' movements, freedom struggle, forced migration, foreign relations, cultural nationalism, historiography and various "controversial" issues. Currently, a Member of the Indian Council of Historical Research, he has taught Modern History at Hansraj College, Delhi University, and for some time, at Delhi University's (P.G.) North and South Campus. A Post Doctoral Research Scholar at the Department of History, Birkbeck College, University of London, a Charles wallace Visiting Fellow at the Centre for Indian Studies, Department of Politics, University of Hull, he has been a Member of the Indian Council of Social Science Research and various academic bodies in Allahabad, Hyderabad and Kolkata.

Professor Nirmala Joshi is a former Professor at the Centre for Russian and Central Asian Studies of the School of International Studies, Jawaharlal Nehru University, New Delhi. She is currently Director of think tank India-Central Asia Foundation. She was also Research Advisor at the United Service Institution of India from September 2012 to October 2014. She was also the Director of the University Grants Commission's Programme on Russia and Central Asia, and a Member of the Indian Council for Social Science Research's Indo Russian Joint Commission for Cooperation in Social Sciences. She was a Member of the University Grants Commission Standing Committee on Area Studies in 2002, and a Nominated Member of the Executive Council of the Indian Council in 2001. In 2014 she was awarded the Magtymguly Pyragy Medal by the Government of Turkmenistan. She has contributed several chapters to books and published articles in international and national research journals.

Monmayee Basu has distinguished herself in the study of certain critical topics on contemporary historical and social issues, in particular gender issues, events arising out of, and connected to the partition of India, and the study of leading social and political leaders of India who influenced these developments. She has several publication to her credit. Her book *Hindu Women and Marriage Law*, published by Oxford University

Press, and later developed by them into an omnibus, *Women and Law*, is an authoritative study of the influuence of legislative measures in addressing women's issues in India. She has also co-authored textbooks in Bengali, which has been the standard history text for West Bengal School Board. Her treatise *Comprehensive History of Modern Europe* is soon to be published by Orient black Swan. Dr. Basu studied in Presidency College and is a gold-medalist from the University of Calcutta. Currently she is Associate Professor, Department of History, Hansraj College, University of Delhi.

Dr. Roshan Khanijo is a Senior Research Fellow and Research Co-coordinator at the Centre for Strategic Studies and Simulation, United Service Institution of India (USI), New Delhi. She specializes in Nuclear issues, and her other principal areas of interest are China and Pakistan. She writes on Nuclear Energy, Nuclear Disarmament and Arms Control and Nuclear Weapons Programme of China and Pakistan. She has written a book titled *Complexities and Challenges of Nuclear India* and a Monograph on "Iran: Nuclear Conundrum".

Kingshuk Nag retired recently from *The Times of India* after serving for 24 years. His last position was Resident Editor of the newspaper's Hyderabad edition. An M.A. in Economics from the Delhi School of Economics, Nag started his career with The Tata Economic Consultancy Services but after a few years shifted to journalism. He is the author of six best -selling books of which the latest is *Netaji: Living Dangerously*.

Sandhya Jain is an author and independent researcher, and writes a fortnightly column on political and contemporary affairs for *The Pioneer*, New Delhi. Jain is a post graduate in Political Science from Delhi University, Delhi, and has had over three decades of experience as a professional journalist in leading newspapers such as ***The Hindustan Times, The Telegraph,*** and ***Sunday Mail*** (weekly). She briefly worked with the Indian Institute of Mass Communication (IIMC), New Delhi.

Her published works include *Adi Deo Arya Devata. A Panoramic View of Tribal-Hindu Cultural Interface*, Rupa, 2004; Contributed a chapters in: *Sacred Rights*, (ed.) Dan Maguire, Oxford University Press, New York, 2003; *Evangelical Intrusions. Tripura: A Case Study,* Rupa, 2009.

Dr. Raj Kumar Sharma holds a doctorate from School of International Studies, Jawaharlal Nehru University. He is a Research Fellow at the United Service Institution of India (USI), New Delhi. He has contributed to different projects on Indian security and foreign policy for the Ministry of Defence. He is a contributing writer for the Nikkei Asian Review (Japan) and has taught Political Science at the University of Delhi.

Dr. Md. Naushad Ali, currently working as Deputy Director (Publication) in the ICHR. Completed Doctorate in Modern Indian History on the topic, 'Changes in Indian Agriculture in the Late Colonial Era, *c.* 1888-1947'.Worked as Research Assistant on the project "Minerals, Mining and Metal Working Crafts in Medieval India c. 1600-1750" funded by INSA, New Delhi in 2009 and 2010. As Research and Editorial Assistant at ICHR, he contributed in the publications of the Dictionary of Martyrs: India's Freedom Struggle (1857-1947), Volumes 1-5.

Abhijit Bhattacharyya is a practising Advocate in the Supreme Court, he previously taught at many colleges of Delhi University. He writes on various subjects on contemporary history of India. Till date, he has published over 600 articles, and is a visiting speaker to several defence/ security establishments.